Praise for *All* C

"A brilliant, gripping narrative ... I urge that everyone read [*All Our Relations*] ... which describes the ravages of corporations and government activity on the reservations of our first natives. This is a beautifully written book.... As Winona LaDuke describes, in moving and often beautiful prose, [these] misdeeds are not distant history but are ongoing degradation of the cherished lands of Native Americans."
—Ralph Nader

"As Winona LaDuke's *All Our Relations* shows, a vital Native American environmentalism is linking indigenous peoples throughout North America and Hawaii in the fight to protect and restore their health, culture, and the ecosystems on their lands. LaDuke herself is a member of the Anishinaabeg nation and was Ralph Nader's Green Party running mate in 1996. These Native American activists take inspiration from their forebears' responsible treatment of natural systems, based on a reverence for the interconnectedness of all life forms."
—*The Nation*

"In this thoroughly researched and convincingly written analysis of Native American culture ... LaDuke demonstrates the manners in which native peoples face a constant barrage of attacks that threaten their very existence."
—*Choice*

"[LaDuke presents] strong voices of old, old cultures bravely trying to make sense of an Earth in chaos."
—*Whole Earth*

"With a good ear and sharp eye, LaDuke introduces us to Native activists and records gross environmental abuse and creative resistence. By placing people in the center of the industrial soup, LaDuke tells a story that has not been told before in this way."
—*Radcliffe Quarterly*

"A rare perspective on Native history and culture."
—*Sister to Sister*

All Our Relations

Native Struggles for Land and Life

By Winona LaDuke

Haymarket Books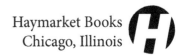
Chicago, Illinois

© 1999 Winona LaDuke
First published 1999 by South End Press, Cambridge, Massachusetts.

Cover art, "The Turtle," by Ojibwa artist Joe Geshick
Maps by Zoltan Grossman of the Midwest Treaty Network in Madison,
Wisconsin. www.treaty.indigenousnative.org.

This edition published in 2015 by
Haymarket Books
P.O. Box 180165
Chicago, IL 60618
773-583-7884
www.haymarketbooks.org
info@haymarketbooks.org

ISBN: 978-1-60846-629-0

Trade distribution:
In the US, Consortium Book Sales and Distribution, www.cbsd.com
In Canada, Publishers Group Canada, www.pgcbooks.ca
In the UK, Turnaround Publisher Services, www.turnaround-uk.com
All other countries, Publishers Group Worldwide, www.pgw.com

This book was published with the generous support of Lannan Foundation
and Wallace Action Fund.

About the Cover Art:
"The Turtle" was created to honor the Earth: Turtle Island. The turtle is a geat
healer and teacher on our spiritual journey. Its pace reminds us to slow down and
pay attention as we interact with the world.

The turtle shows us everything we need is always within us. The spiritual
journey results when our inner life connects with out outer surroundings. Our goal
is to find the balance and live with the tension between social turbulence (the red
rocks) and serenity (the open sky).

—Joe Geshick

Library of Congress Cataloging-in-Publication data is available.

Contents

Acknowledgements

In my life, I have had the honor of meeting and working with a great number of courageous, visionary, and good hearted people. Their struggles to preserve that which they value, to live in dignity, and to ensure that a good way of life is passed to their descendants have been a constant source of inspiration. Some of these people I attempt to honor with my words in this book. I hope I do so with some integrity.

Others remain constant fires in their homelands, in our memories, and in our hearts. Some include: Phillip Deere, Bill Wapepah, Arlene Logan; Janet McCloud, my parents, Betty and Peter LaDuke Westigard, Helen Bernstein, Vincent LaDuke, Terri LaDuke, Anne Dunn, Priscilla Settee, Agnes Williams, Cecilia Rodriguez, Cynthia Perez, Lorna Hanes, Lisa Jackson, Sharon Asetoyer, Mililani Trask, Luana Busby, Paul Bogart, and others who love me and support me with unwavering patience. For their spiritual guidance to our community, Tommy Stillday and Eddie Benton Benai.

Special thanks to Jose Barriero who first published my writings, Jimmie Durham, John Redhouse, Mark Tilsen, Ward Churchill, Paul DeMain, Sluggo, Rory O'Connor, and others who urged me to continue writing. To Carrie Dann, Roberta Blackgoat, Suzanna Santos, Margaret Flint Knife Saluskin, Ted Strong, Tom Goldtooth, Louise Erdrich, Ralph Nader, and many others for their tenacity and the light that shines through us all. And especially Faye Brown, Kevin Gasco, Nilak Butler, Lori Pourier, Amy Ray, Emily Saliers, and my WELRP staff: Donna Cahill, Florence Goodman, Ronnie Chilton, Pat Wichern, Juanita Lindsay, Robynne Carter, and Joanne Mulbah, and my children, for all their work, love, and beauty. This book is theirs too.

Finally, deep appreciation to Idelisse Malve and the Tides Foundation for their generous support, which allowed Honor the Earth to co-publish this book. And *miigwech* to Sonia Shah at South End Press for her patience, good eye, and commitment, and to Allison Garber, the footnote queen.

Dedicated to three fine friends who now live in the spirit world.

Ingrid Washinawatok-El Issa,
who resonated the sun in her warmth and love;
Walt Bresette, who like the North Star, showed a clear path; and
Marsha Gomez, whose hands were the Earth.

And to those yet unborn.

Introduction

We are a part of everything that is beneath us, above us, and around us. Our past is our present, our present is our future, and our future is seven generations past and present.

—Haudenosaunee teaching

The last 150 years have seen a great holocaust. There have been more species lost in the past 150 years than since the Ice Age. During the same time, Indigenous peoples have been disappearing from the face of the earth. Over 2,000 nations of Indigenous peoples have gone extinct in the western hemisphere, and one nation disappears from the Amazon rainforest every year.

There is a direct relationship between the loss of cultural diversity and the loss of biodiversity. Wherever Indigenous peoples still remain, there is also a corresponding enclave of biodiversity. Trickles of rivers still running in the Northwest are home to the salmon still being sung back by Native people. The last few Florida panthers remain in the presence of traditional Seminoles, hidden away in the great cypress swamps of the Everglades. Some of the largest patches of remaining prairie grasses sway on reservation lands. One half of all reservation lands in the United States is still forested, much of it old-growth. Remnant pristine forest ecosystems, from the northern boreal forests to the Everglades, largely overlap with Native territories.

In the Northwest, virtually every river is home to a people, each as distinct as a species of salmon. The Tillamook, Siletz, Yaquina, Alsea, Siuslaw, Umpqua, Hanis, Miluk, Colville, Tututni, Shasta, Costa, and Chetco are all peoples living at the mouths of salmon rivers. One hundred and seven stocks of salmon have already become extinct in the Pacific Northwest, and 89 are endangered. "Salmon were put here by the Creator, and it is our responsibility to harvest and protect the salmon so that the cycle of life continues," explains Pierson Mitchell of the Columbia River Intertribal Fishing Commission.[1] "Whenever we have a funeral, we mourn our loved one, yes, but we are also reminded of the loss of our salmon and other traditional foods," laments Bill Yallup Sr., the Yakama tribal chairman.[2]

The stories of the fish and the people are not so different. Environmental destruction threatens the existence of both. The Tygh band of the Lower Deschutes River in Oregon includes a scant five families, struggling to maintain their traditional way of life and relationship to the salmon. "I wanted to dance the salmon, know the salmon, say goodbye to the salmon," says Susana Santos, a Tygh artist, fisherwoman, and community organizer. "Now I am looking at the completion of destruction, from the Exxon Valdez to...those dams.... Seventeen fish came down the river last year. None this year. The people are the salmon, and the salmon are the people. How do you quantify that?"[3]

Native American teachings describe the relations all around—animals, fish, trees, and rocks—as our brothers, sisters, uncles, and grandpas. Our relations to each other, our prayers whispered across generations to our relatives, are what bind our cultures together. The protection, teachings, and gifts of our relatives have for generations preserved our families. These relations are honored in ceremony, song, story, and life that keep relations close—to buffalo, sturgeon, salmon, turtles, bears, wolves, and panthers. These are our older relatives—the ones who came before and taught us how to live. Their obliteration by dams, guns, and bounties is an immense loss to Native families and cultures. Their absence may mean that a people sing to a barren river, a caged bear, or buffalo far away. It is the struggle to preserve that which remains and the struggle to recover that characterizes much of Native environmentalism. It is these relationships that industrialism seeks to disrupt. Native communities will resist with great determination.

> Salmon was presented to me and my family through our religion as our brother. The same with the deer. And our sisters are the roots and berries. And you would treat them as such. Their life to you is just as valuable as another person's would be.
>
> —Margaret Saluskin, Yakama[4]

The Toxic Invasion of Native America

There are over 700 Native nations on the North American continent. Today, in the United States, Native America covers 4 percent of the land, with over 500 federally recognized tribes. Over 1,200 Native American reserves dot Canada. The Inuit homeland, Nunavut, formerly one-half of the Northwest Territories, is an area of land and water, including Baffin Island, five times the size of Texas, or the size of the entire Indian subcontinent. Eighty-five percent of the population is Native.

While Native peoples have been massacred and fought, cheated, and robbed of their historical lands, today their lands are subject to some of the most invasive industrial interventions imaginable. According to the Worldwatch Institute, 317 reservations in the United States are threatened by environmental hazards, ranging from toxic wastes to clearcuts.

Reservations have been targeted as sites for 16 proposed nuclear waste dumps. Over 100 proposals have been floated in recent years to dump toxic waste in Indian communities.[5] Seventy-seven sacred sites have been disturbed or desecrated through resource extraction and development activities.[6] The federal government is proposing to use Yucca Mountain, sacred to the Shoshone, as a dumpsite for the nation's high-level nuclear waste. Over the last 45 years, there have been 1,000 atomic explosions on Western Shoshone land in Nevada, making the Western Shoshone the most bombed nation on earth.

Over 1,000 slag piles and tailings from abandoned uranium mines sit on Diné land, leaking radioactivity into the air and water. Nearby is the largest coal strip mine in the world, and some groups of Diné teenagers have a cancer rate 17 times the national average. According to Tom Goldtooth, executive director of the Indigenous Environmental Network,

> Most Indigenous governments are over 22 years behind the states in environmental infrastructure development. The EPA has consistently failed to fund tribes on an equitable basis compared with the states. The EPA has a statutory responsibility to allocate financial resources that will provide an equitable allocation between tribal governments and states.[7]

The Descendants of Little Thunder

In our communities, Native environmentalists sing centuries-old songs to renew life, to give thanks for the strawberries, to call home fish, and to thank Mother Earth for her blessings. We are the descendants of Little Thunder, who witnessed the massacre that cleared out the Great Plains to make way for the cowboys, cattle, and industrial farms. We have seen the great trees felled, the wolves taken for bounty, and the fish stacked rotting like cordwood. Those memories compel us, and the return of the descendants of these predators provoke us to stand again, stronger, and hopefully with more allies. We are the ones who stand up to the land eaters, the tree eaters, the destroyers and culture eaters.

We live off the beaten track, out of the mainstream in small villages, on a vast expanse of prairie, on dry desert lands, or in the forests. We often drive old cars, live in old houses and mobile homes. There are usually small children and relatives around, the kids careening underfoot. We seldom carry briefcases, and we rarely wear suits. You are more likely to find us meeting in a local community center, outside camping, or in someone's house than at a convention center or at a $1,000-per-plate fundraiser.

We organize in small groups, close to 200 of them in North America, with names like Native Americans for a Clean Environment, Diné CARE (Citizens Against Ruining Our Environment), Anishinaabe Niijii, and the

Gwichin Steering Committee. We are underfunded at best, and more often not funded at all, working out of our homes with a few families or five to ten volunteers. We coalesce in national or continental organizations such as Indigenous Environmental Network, a network of 200-plus members, which through a diverse agenda of providing technical and political support to grassroots groups seeking to protect their land, preserve biodiversity, and sustain communities, seeks ultimately to secure environmental justice. Other such groups include the Southwest Network for Environmental and Economic Justice, Honor the Earth, Indigenous Women's Network, Seventh Generation Fund, and others. In addition are the regional organizations and those based on a shared ecosystem or cultural practice, such as the California Indian Basketweavers Association, Great Lakes Basketmakers, or Council of Elders.

Despite our meager resources, we are winning many hard-fought victories on the local level. We have faced down huge waste dumps and multinational mining, lumber, and oil companies. And throughout the Native nations, people continue to fight to protect Mother Earth for future generations. Some of the victories described in this book include a moratorium on mining in the sacred hills of Northern Cheyenne, Blackfeet, and Crow territory; an international campaign that stopped the building of mega-dams in northern Canada; the restoration of thousands of acres of White Earth land in Minnesota; and the rebuilding of a nation in Hawai'i.

Grassroots and land-based struggles characterize most of Native environmentalism. We are nations of people with distinct land areas, and our leadership and direction emerge from the land up. Our commitment and tenacity spring from our deep connection to the land. This relationship to land and water is continuously reaffirmed through prayer, deed, and our way of being—*minobimaatisiiwin,* the "good life." It is perhaps best remembered in phrases like: *This is where my grandmother's and children's umbilical cords are buried.... That is where the great giant lay down to sleep... These are the four sacred Mountains between which the Creator instructed us to live.... That is the last place our people stopped in our migration here to this village.*

White Earth

I live on an Anishinaabeg reservation called White Earth in northern Minnesota, where I work on land, culture, and environmental issues locally through an organization called the White Earth Land Recovery Project and nationally through a Native foundation called Honor the Earth. We, the Anishinaabeg, are a forest culture. Our creation stories, culture, and way of life are entirely based on the forest, source of our medicinal plants and food, forest animals, and birch-bark baskets.

Virtually my entire reservation was clearcut at the turn of the century. In 1874, Anishinaabe leader Wabunoquod said, "I cried and prayed that our trees would not be taken from us, for they are as much ours as is this reservation."[8] Our trees provided the foundation for major lumber companies, including Weyerhauser, and their destruction continued for ten decades.

In 1889 and 1890 Minnesota led the country in lumber production, and the state's northwest region was the leading source of timber. Two decades later, 90 percent of White Earth land was controlled by non-Indians, and our people were riddled with diseases. Many became refugees in nearby cities. Today, three-fourths of all tribal members live off the reservation. Ninety percent of our land is still controlled by non-Indians.

There is a direct link in our community between the loss of biodiversity—the loss of animal and plant life—and the loss of the material and cultural wealth of the White Earth people. But we have resisted and are restoring. Today, we are in litigation against logging expansion, and the White Earth Land Recovery Project works to restore the forests, recover the land, and restore our traditional forest culture. Our experience of survival and resistance is shared with many others. But it is not only about Native people.

In the final analysis, the survival of Native America is fundamentally about the collective survival of all human beings. The question of who gets to determine the destiny of the land, and of the people who live on it—those with the money or those who pray on the land—is a question that is alive throughout society. The question is posed eloquently by Lil'wat grandmother Loretta Pascal:

> This is my reason for standing up. To protect all around us, to continue our way of life, our culture. I ask them, "Where did you get your right to destroy these forests? How does your right supercede my rights?" These are our forests, these are our ancestors.[9]

These are the questions posed in the chapters ahead. Through the voices and actions featured here, there are some answers as well. Along with the best of my prayers is a recognition of the depth of spirit and commitment to all our relations, and the work to protect and recover them. As Columbia River Tribes activist Ted Strong tells us,

> If this nation has a long way to go before all of our people are truly created equally without regard to race, religion, or national origin, it

has even farther to go before achieving anything that remotely re-sembles equal treatment for other creatures who called this land home before humans ever set foot upon it.... While the species themselves—fish, fowl, game, and the habitat they live in—have given us unparalleled wealth, they live crippled in their ability to persist and in conditions of captive squalor.... This enslavement and impoverishment of nature is no more tolerable or sensible than en-slavement and impoverishment of other human beings.... Perhaps it is because we are the messengers that not only our sovereignty as [Native] governments but our right to identify with a deity and a his-tory, our right to hold to a set of natural laws as practiced for thou-sands of years is under assault. Now more than ever, tribal people must hold onto their timeless and priceless customs and practices.[10]

"The ceremony will continue," Strong says. "This is a testament to the faith of the Indian people. No matter how badly the salmon have been mis-treated, no matter how serious the decline. It has only made Native people deeper in their resolve. It has doubled their commitment. It has rekindled the hope that today is beginning to grow in many young people."[11]

Katsi Cook. Photo © Susan Alzner.

A k w e s a s n e

Mohawk Mothers' Milk and PCBs

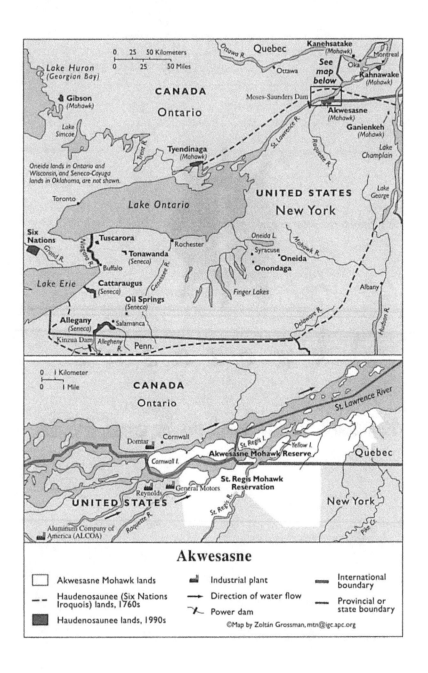

Akwesasne

Map by Zoltán Grossman, mtn@igc.apc.org

In the heart of the Mohawk nation is Akwesasne, or "Land Where the Partridge Drums." A 25-square-mile reservation that spans the St. Lawrence River and the international border between northern New York and Canada, Akwesasne is home to about 8,000 Mohawks.

I'm riding the Akwesasne reservation roads with Katsi Cook, Mohawk midwife turned environmental justice activist. It is two o'clock in the morning, and Katsi is singing traditional Mohawk songs. Loud, so strong, is her voice. We are driving between Katsi's meetings, planes, and birth practice. The birthing chair she uses is wedged in her trunk between our suitcases. Her stamina is almost daunting. That may be the gift of a life-bringer, a midwife—all that power of birth and rebirth, which stays in your presence month after month. (Or, perhaps, it is just that she is a Mohawk. And, as Katsi jokes, *if you want something done, get a Mohawk to do it.*) My head droops to the side as we careen down the country roads of upstate New York, and my attention rivets back to her words, her company. Katsi is alternating between singing and explaining to me the process of bioaccumulation of polychlorinated biphenyls (PCBs) in breast milk. A combination of Mother Theresa and Carl Sagan.

She comes from a family whose tradition feeds her political work, and from a community with a long history of political resistance. "My father, mother, and grandparents of past generations distinguished themselves as political and cultural activists, who upheld community service as one of their highest standards," she explains. "My grandmother Elizabeth Kanatines [She Leads the Village] Cook, a traditional midwife, delivered me and many of the babies in my generation at the Mohawk territory at Akwesasne. My father, William Rasenne Cook, organized a cooperative at Akwesasne among the farmers and consumers. He also organized the peaceful ousting of New York State enforcement jurisdiction on our lands in 1948."[1]

Well, some things change, and some things do not. The Mohawks and Katsi Cook can tell you that. She is cut of the same cloth.

So it is that a culture and identity that are traditionally matrilineal will come into conflict with institutions that are historically focused upon their eradication. Katsi Cook, Wolf Clan mother and an individual who strives to uphold those traditions, finds that she must confront some large adversaries. Besides "catching babies," as she calls it, and raising her family of four children (the oldest of whom, Howie, bore her first grandchild in the Winter of 1998), Katsi finds herself in a stand-off against her adversary, one of the largest corporations in the world: General Motors (GM). At its Massena, New York, power train plant, General Motors has left a Superfund site—one with approximately 823,000 cubic yards of PCB-contaminated materials. GM has tainted the land, water, and ultimately the bodies of the Mohawk people, their babies included. Katsi's work is precedent-setting environmental justice work that links the intricate culture of the Mohawk people to the water, the turtles, the animal relatives, and ultimately the destruction of the industrialized General Motors Superfund site. "Why is it we must change our lives, our way of life, to accommodate the corporations, and they are allowed to continue without changing any of their behavior?" she asks.

The Mohawk Legacy

Mohawk legend says that at one time the earth was one, never-ending ocean. One day, a pregnant woman fell from the sky. A flock of swans carried her down to earth, gently placing her on the back of a large sea turtle. Some beavers then swam to the bottom of the ocean and picked up some soil and brought it back to this woman so she could have some dry ground on which to walk. She then walked in an ever-widening circle on the top of the turtle's back, spreading the soil around. On this giant turtle's back the earth became whole. As a result, North America is known today by the name *Turtle Island.*

As in the creation legend, the turtle remains the bedrock of many ecosystems. But snapping turtles found at so-called Contaminant Cove on the Akwesasne reservation contained some 3,067 parts per million (ppm) of PCB contamination; others were found with 2,000 ppm PCB contamination. (According to EPA guidelines, 50 ppm PCBs in soil is considered to be "contaminated.") The story of how that turtle became contaminated in many ways mirrors the story of the Mohawk people of Akwesasne.[2]

> The Haudenosaunee, or Six Nations Iroquois Confederacy, is among the most ancient continuously operating governments in the world. Long before the arrival of the European peoples in North America, our people met in council to enact the principles of peaceful coexistence among nations and in recognition of the right of peoples to a continued and uninterrupted existence. European people left our council fires and journeyed forth in the world to spread principles of justice and democracy which they learned from us and have had profound effects upon the evolution of the Modern World.
>
> —Haudenosaunee Statement to the World, April 17, 1979[3]

The Mohawk people, like other Haudenosaunee, or Six Nations peoples, have lived in the eastern region of the continent for many generations. The Mohawks themselves are referred to as the Keepers of the Eastern Door of the Haudenosaunee Confederacy—the People of the Flint. It is said that the Six Nations peoples were once virtual slaves to the neighboring Algonkin peoples. Amidst their agricultural economy, they'd labored long and hard to pay the heavy tolls imposed upon them by the Algonkin.

But as the story goes, between miracles and sheer determination, the Six Nations peoples came to prosper in the region. As the generations passed, the differences grew between the peoples, and they divided into the Mohawk, Oneida, Onondaga, Cayuga, Seneca, and Tuscarora—the Six Nations. Early in their history, the great prophet Aiionwatha created the Haudenosaunee Confederacy, one of the most prominent and far-reaching forms of government ever created on the face of the earth. From this form of government came the concepts of constitutional government and representative democracy, the very foundation of the principles of the new American state. This form of government remains today in the Haudenosaunee Confederacy.

The Mohawk Nation expanded under the principles of the Great Law, established by Aiionwatha's teacher, the Great Huron Peacemaker. That law, *Kaienarakowa* (the Great Law of Peace and the Good Mind), upholds principles of kinship, women's leadership, and the value of the widest possible community consensus. Through these teachings and many others, the Mohawks eventually established communities scattered over 14 million acres of land that straddle what would become the U.S.-Canada border. These lands would come to be home for seven major communities—Kahnawake, Kanehsatake, Akwesasne, Ganienkeh, Tyeninaga, Ohsweken, and Wahta.

While new American leaders such as George Washington, Patrick Henry, and Benjamin Franklin studied the Haudenosaunee government, they also engaged in land speculation over territory held by these peoples, and Mohawk lands were ceded through force, coercion, and deceit until fewer than 14,600 acres remained in New York State. By 1889, 80 percent of all Haudenosaunee land in New York State was under lease to non-Indian interests and individuals.[4]

For the Mohawks, words were not enough to defend their land. During the 1900s, additional land and jurisdiction grabs continued in Mohawk communities, along with Mohawk resistance to them. Whether through Katsi's father or the armed take-overs and struggles in the Mohawk communities of Ganienkeh (1974), Kahnawake (1988), or Kanehsatake (1990), the Mohawks have been vigilant in their commitment to their land, way of life, and economy.

Faced with heavy impacts on their traditional economy, the Mohawks adapted economically. First, as legendary high-steel workers, they built much of the infrastructure for eastern cities. Then, in more recent years, they have creatively used their strategic position on the national border to tap into the controversial "export-import" business, traversing colonial borders that separate the various Mohawk communities.

The Mohawks are also adept at both maintaining and recovering their culture and way of life. The Akwesasne Freedom School is foundational to that process. An independent elementary school run by the Mohawk Nation, the school was founded in 1979 by Mohawk parents concerned that their language and culture would slowly die out. In 1985, Mohawk-language immersion began. The Mohawk "Thanksgiving Address," which teaches gratitude to the earth and everything upon it, is used as the base of the curriculum. The students study the Mohawk ceremonial cycle, as well as reading, writing, math, science, and history, combining solid academics with Mohawk culture. "The prophecies say that the time will come when the grandchildren will speak to the whole world. The reason for the Akwesasne Freedom School is so that the grandchildren will have something significant to say," explains Sakokwenionkwas, or Tom Porter, a Mohawk chief.[5] (Porter is also known for his recovery of traditional land. Leading some Mohawks into a different part of their traditional territory, Porter has successfully purchased some land and, with a number of traditional families, is in the process of restoring their village, in their own terms, and in their own way.)

Environmental struggles have also been a part of Mohawk history. In the 1950s, while Indian people nationally were mired in efforts to oppose termination, 130 acres of Akwesasne were flooded by the St. Lawrence Seaway project, and in 1967, 9,000 acres were flooded by the notorious Kinzua Dam project in upstate New York, which affected Seneca communities. In 1958, the New York State Power Authority attempted to seize half of the Tuscarora reservation; when the Tuscaroras physically blocked access to the site, "a 'compromise' was then implemented in which the state flooded 'only' 560 acres, or about one-eighth of the remaining Tuscarora land."[6]

Industry Takes Over

There is, through all of this, very little land left for the Mohawks and the Haudenosaunee. The St. Lawrence River, called *Kaniatarowaneneh*, which means "Majestic River" in Mohawk, has been the wellspring for much of Mohawk life. It has also been the target for much of the industrialism in the region.

In 1903, the Aluminum Company of America (ALCOA) established a factory a few miles west of Akwesasne. Less than 30 years later, a biological survey noted serious local pollution problems. That was just the beginning. In 1949, the St. Lawrence Seaway and Moses-Sanders Power Dam were built and hailed as the eighth wonder of the world. Dams and locks allowed huge ships to enter the Great Lakes from the Atlantic Ocean and produced cheap hydro-electric power that lured giant corporations to the St. Lawrence. In the late 1950s, General Motors, Reynolds, and Domtar (in Canada) became the Mohawks' neighbors, and the majestic river became a toxic cesspool.

In 1959, Reynolds established an aluminum plant one mile southwest of Akwesasne, and within a decade the facility was emitting fluorides into the atmosphere at a rate of 400 pounds per hour. In 1973, pollution control devices reduced this level of emissions to 75 pounds per hour, but the cost of the pollution was high.[7]

According to Dr. Lennart Krook and Dr. George Maylin, two veterinarians from Cornell University, Mohawk farmers suffered severe stock losses of their dairy herds in the mid-1970s due to poor reproductive functions and fluorosis, a brittling and breakage of teeth and bones, which they found were linked to the fluoride emissions.[8] Additional studies have shown that area vegetation suffered as well. The impact on area wildlife is still unknown.[9]

Today, an estimated 25 percent of all North American industry is located on or near the Great Lakes, all of which are drained by the St. Lawrence River.[10] That puts the Akwesasne reservation downstream from some of the most lethal and extensive pollution on the continent.

Canada has singled out the Akwesasne Mohawk reservation from 63 Native communities in the Great Lakes basin as the most contaminated—a dubious honor. On the American side of the border, things aren't much better. Until the mid-1980s, five saturated lagoons and a number of PCB-filled sludge pits dotted GM's 258-acre property, adjacent to the reservation.[11]

Until 1978, when PCBs were banned, all of these companies used PCBs. Virtually all of those PCBs ended up in the surrounding water, soil, or air. Many of them have ended up in the fish, plants, and people of the Mohawk territory. An insidious chemical known to cause liver, brain, nerve, and skin disorders in humans, shrinking testicles in alligators, and cancer and reproductive disorders in laboratory animals, PCBs are one of the most lethal poisons of industrialized society.

Studies of PCB contamination of alligators in the Everglades indicate a problem called emasculization—shrinking testicles in subsequent generations. A study of boys in Taiwan born to mothers exposed to PCBs found that they also had smaller penises. Studies of polar bears in the Arctic indicate dropping reproduction rates associated with PCB contamination, a concern in animals that are already threatened with extinction.[12] It will take a while for most Americans to consume levels of PCBs capable of causing such damage. But what happens if a segment of the population does become affected? Most of the information regarding the effects of PCBs and dibenzofurans on human health is based on accidental poisonings.

In Japan in 1968 and in Taiwan in 1979, thousands of people accidentally ingested PCB-contaminated rice oil, which contained PCB concentrations as high as 3,000 ppm. In Taiwan, 12 of 24 people died from liver diseases and cancers. Following both incidents, many people suffered from a severely disfiguring skin acne. Other problems included the suppression of the immune system, making individuals more susceptible to many diseases. Thirty-seven babies born to PCB-poisoned Taiwanese women suffered from hyperpigmentation, facial swelling, abnormal calcification of the skull, low birth weight, and overall growth retardation. Eight of the infants died from pneumonia, bronchitis, or general weakness.[13]

Similarly, recent studies of malignant breast tumors indicate that PCBs may be linked to breast cancer. Researchers in Hartford, Connecticut, found that malignant breast tumors contained more than 50 percent as many PCBs as were found in the breast fat of women the same age and weight who did not have cancer.[14] Wayne State University's Joseph and Sandra Jacobson's study of 212 children reported worrisome data showing learning deficits in children who had the highest, although still modest, exposures to PCBs in the womb. Those children were reported to have scored about six points lower on IQ tests and also lagged behind on achievement tests that rely on short-term memory, planning ability, and sustained attention. Their word comprehension fell six months behind that of their less exposed 11-year-old peers. Of the 212 children that were studied, 167 had been born to women who had eaten a modest amount of fish—at least 11.8 kilograms of Lake Michigan salmon or lake trout during the six years preceding their children's births.[15]

PCB Contamination at Akwesasne

In 1979, the Haudenosaunee called for thoughtful ways of living and issued the following statement to the world:

> Brothers and Sisters: Our ancient homeland is spotted today with an array of chemical dumps. Along the Niagara River, dioxin, a particularly

deadly substance, threatens the remaining life there and in the waters which flow from there. Forestry departments spray the surviving forests with powerful insecticides to encourage tourism by people seeking a few days or weeks away from the cities where the air hangs heavy with sulphur and carbon oxides. The insecticides kill the black flies, but also destroy much of the food chain for the bird, fish, and animal life which also inhabit those regions.

The fish of the Great Lakes are laced with mercury from industrial plants, and fluoride from aluminum plants poisons the land and the people. Sewage from the population centers is mixed with PCBs and PBS in the watershed of the great lakes and the Finger Lakes, and the water is virtually nowhere safe for any living creature.[16]

In 1981, the New York State Department of Environmental Conservation blew the whistle on General Motors' dumping of PCB-contaminated materials, reporting that there was "widespread contamination of local groundwater" by PCBs and heavy metals such as lead, chromium, mercury, cadmium, and antimony. Several Mohawks lived less than 100 yards from the General Motors facility. At least 45 Mohawk families drew their water from area wells, while over 200 families relied on water from an intake on the St. Lawrence River, which was only a half-mile from the GM plant.[17]

In October of 1983, after 25 years of dumping toxics, General Motors was fined $507,000 by the EPA for unlawful disposal of PCBs—in total, 21 violations of the Toxic Substances Control Act, or TSCA. Among the charges, General Motors was cited for ten counts of unlawful disposal of PCBs and 11 counts of unlawfully using PCB-laden oil in a pumphouse with no warning sign. At that time, GM received what was the highest EPA fine levied against a U.S. company for violations of the TSCA. The EPA placed the GM site on the National Priority List of Superfund sites that urgently need cleanup.[18]

But the EPA's early resolve quickly eroded. The latest battle with General Motors has been over regulatory gymnastics and some interesting redesignations of what the EPA admits is a very dangerous site. The EPA estimated that it could cost $138 million to clean up the GM site, but during the mid-1990s has balked and backed down, redesignated and allowed for new proposals, proposals which would save General Motors a considerable amount of money. In August of 1990, the EPA suggested that "containment" rather than "treatment" can be appropriate for industrial sites contaminated with PCBs between 10 and 500 ppm. The redesignation by EPA meant that GM would have to dredge and/or treat only 54,000 cubic yards of contaminated soils, in contrast to the 171,00 cubic yards it currently has on-site or in nearby rivers and creeks. This redesignation of the numbers has saved General Motors over $15 million dollars in cleanup costs.[19]

"In one core sample of the river bottom at the GM site we tested, we found over 6,000 ppm of PCBs," says Dave Arquette, an environmental specialist with the tribe. "GM put sand and gravel over those areas and considers that to be a permanent cap," he adds.[20] Today, the GM dump site is landscaped and covered with grass. But absent a liner under the waste, the GM contaminants still leach into the majestic river. The GM landfill "frustrates Tribal environmental standards applicable within the same ecosystem only a few feet away," according to the Akwesasne Task Force on the Environment.[21] "Capping is to cover up, not a cleanup," says an exasperated Jim Ransom of the Task Force.[22] The tribe's position is that the Mohawk PCB standard of 0.1 parts per million be applied to the entire cleanup, not just Mohawk land.

"This is a classic environmental justice site," says Ken Jock, a director of the Akwesasne Environment Program. A slight man, with soft eyes and a quiet manner, he spends much of his time arguing with agencies about implementation of the law. His huge office is full of reports and photos documenting the extent of the contamination. The reports, photos, and sheer size of the Akwesasne Environment Program dwarf the infrastructure of most Indian nations in the country. Yet it seems that even with reams of paper, the action taken by federal agencies is minimal. "This all used to be a fishing village. That's all gone now. There's only one family that still fishes," Jock says. "We can't farm here because of all of those air emissions. Industry has pretty much taken the entire traditional lifestyle away from the community here."[23]

Today, 65 percent of the Mohawks on Akwesasne reservation have diabetes, says Jock. Henry Lickers, director of the environmental health branch of the Mohawk Council of Akwesasne echoes Jock: "Our traditional lifestyle has been completely disrupted, and we have been forced to make choices to protect our future generations," says Lickers. "Many of the families used to eat 20–25 fish meals a month. It's now said that the traditional Mohawk diet is spaghetti."[24]

The Mothers' Milk Project

"The fact is that women are the first environment," says Katsi. "We accumulate toxic chemicals like PCBs, DDT, Mirex, HCBs, etc., dumped into the waters by various industries. They are stored in our body fat and are excreted primarily through breast milk. What that means is that through our own breast milk, our sacred natural link to our babies, they stand the chance of getting concentrated dosages." When the Mohawks found this out in the early 1980s, Katsi explains, "We were flabbergasted."[25]

Katsi Cook and other Mohawk women wanted to know the extent of their risk. In the Fall of 1984, Katsi went to the office of Ward Stone, a wildlife pathologist. Stone's work documented toxicity in animals in the St. Lawrence/Mohawk/GM ecosystem and has been very influential internationally in the study and cleanup of the Great Lakes region. Stone showed that beluga whales of the St. Lawrence River carry some of the highest body burdens of toxic chemicals in the world and suffer from a host of problems, including rare cancers and pronounced disease and mortality among young whales. These whales have a reproductive success rate one-third that of belugas in the Arctic Ocean.[26] Katsi also went to the office of Brian Bush, a chemist at the Wadsworth Center for Laboratories and Research at the New York State Department of Health in Albany. She explained the concerns of the Mohawk women.

In 1985, Katsi helped create the Akwesasne Mothers' Milk Project in an effort to "understand and characterize how toxic contaminants have moved through the local food chain, including mothers' milk," as Katsi wrote. "You're not going to find a lot of women that went away to the universities and then came back to the community with degrees in environmental engineering," Katsi says. "It's hard to get the women involved although they are so impacted by all of this.... Now [with the Mothers' Milk Project] the women are learning to apply science in their everyday lives."

Katsi's persistence, along with the work of Henry Lickers and Jim Ransom, former director of the St. Regis Mohawk Tribes Environmental Office, evolved into a bioaccumulative analysis of the entire food chain at Akwesasne, from fish to wildlife to breast milk. The collaborative epidemiological research project that ultimately resulted from Katsi's work was one of a scant 11 Superfund studies funded by the U.S. Congress, and the only one focused on human health.

Under Katsi's supervision, the research project studied 50 new mothers over several years and documented a 200 percent greater concentration of PCBs in the breast milk of those mothers who ate fish from the St. Lawrence River as opposed to the general population. "But their PCB levels came down after they stopped eating fish," Katsi explained. "I've got myself 0.108 parts per billion of mirex [a flame retardant], 22 parts per billion PCBs, 0.013 parts per billion HCBs, and 13.947 parts per billion DDC [a pesticide related to DDT] in my breast milk," Katsi said in an early 1990s interview, acknowledging the personal nature of the concern.[27] Related studies of fetal umbilical cord samples showed similar results. Subsequent studies indicated a decline generally, a result of the mothers reducing the consumption of natural foods.[28]

The Mohawk officials reassured the community to continue breast feeding their infants in spite of high levels of toxic contamination in the local fish and wildlife. But this advice was only viable because of the drastic reduction in the amount of fish consumed in the community.

Mohawk mothers voiced their anger at the contamination and the impact on their way of life. "Our traditional lifestyle has been completely disrupted, and we have been forced to protect our future generations. We feel anger at not being able to eat the fish. Although we are relieved that our responsible choices at the present protect our babies, this does not preclude the corporate responsibility of General Motors and other local industries to clean up the site," Katsi charges.

"The beauty of the response of the mothers," Katsi says, "is that they saw everything in a bigger picture. Many of us bless the seeds, pray to corn, and continue a one-on-one relationship with the earth." That process of remembering and restoring the relationship between people and the earth is a crucial part of healing the community from the violations of the industry in their way of life.

But "GM has been fighting us every step of the way," she says. In 1997, General Motors sat at the top of the U.S. Fortune 500 list. It also sat on top of the world's Fortune 500 list. Not bad. So it's not like they couldn't spring some money for cleanup. But instead, they have fought the Mohawks' water, air, and soil quality, and pushed for more lenient cleanup.

Part of the Mohawks' challenge is navigating the many jurisdictions and global corporations that have a stake in the region, as a bizarre result of colonialism. Akwesasne contends with two federal governments—Canada and the United States. Then there are two other governments—the province of Quebec and New York State. Then there are several separate Mohawk jurisdictions, those recognized by the U.S. and Canadian federal governments, and the traditional Mohawk government. It seems that between them, no one can really make any progress. "New York State doesn't care, because as far as they're concerned, we're not part of New York State, we might as well be in Canada," says Ken Jock.[29] Canada views the problem as originating on the other side of the border, and among all of them, there seems to be limited application of the law. Except, that is, the law according to GM.

GM Goes Global

The Mohawk relations with GM, however, are not unique. In 1994, GM was hailed by *Multinational Monitor* as one of the ten worst corporations in the world and profiled in the illustrious Corporate Hall of Shame. GM was called on the carpet for the infamous exploding gas tanks, this time not on a Ford Pinto, but on a GM pickup. Two years before, the Council on Economic Priorities listed General Motors as a bad boy as well, mostly because of toxic releases.[30] In its annual rankings in the Campaign for Cleaner Corporations, the council and a jury of investors, academics, religious institutions, and activists determine the largest culprits in relation to the environment. GM came in number two, after Cargill. In 1988 and 1989, for instance, GM released nearly three times as much toxic material into the environment as Ford Motor Company, its principal competitor. The company is also potentially responsible for about 200 Superfund sites.[31]

And the Mohawks' problems with GM are no longer just local problems for Mohawks; they are of urgent international concern. The national movement to stem the impact of PCBs and other toxic contamination, now often called "POPs," or persistent organic pollutants, is increasingly turning to international forums. POPs are airborne, ranging from the Arctic to the Antarctic, and are present in every segment of our environment. Theo Colburn, chief scientist to the World Wildlife Fund and author of *Our Stolen Future,* illuminates the scope of the problem in some remarks given at the State of the World Forum in 1996.

> Every one of you sitting here today is carrying at least 500 measurable chemicals in your body that were never in anyone's body before the 1920s.... We have dusted the globe with man-made chemicals that can undermine the development of the brain and behavior, and the endocrine, immune and reproductive systems, vital systems that assure perpetuity.... Everyone is exposed. You are not exposed to one chemical at a time, but a complex mixture of chemicals that changes day by day, hour by hour, depending on where you are and the environment you are in.... In the United States alone it is estimated that over 72,000 different chemicals are used regularly. Two thousand five hundred new chemicals are introduced annually—and of these, only 15 are partially tested for their safety. Not one of the chemicals in use today has been adequately tested for these intergenerational effects that are initiated in the womb.[32]

International discussions on POPs are now part of the United Nations, which in 1995 directed several international agencies to begin evaluating POPs, starting with the 12 most hazardous known substances (dubbed the "dirty dozen") and under a cooperative effort with more than 100 countries.[33] It is hoped that an international protocol will stem their production and distribution. It will require much, particularly when one considers that the cleanup of a single site has met with so much red tape and foot dragging.

The Great Law of Peace and Good Mind

> When you are out there on that river, you can think, you're at peace
> with yourself. You can talk to your Maker.
>
> —Francis Jock, Mohawk fisherman[34]

Meanwhile, back at Akwesasne, Ken Jock and others are working on ecologically and culturally appropriate solutions. A new aquaculture project is underway. The fish farm consists of cages suspended off the bottom of the river, away from contaminated sediments. The fish are raised in the cages and fed on a diet of nutrient-rich, contaminant-free food. So far, the project shows promise and is expanding.

"The real question," Katsi says about all of this environmental justice work, is, "How are we going to recreate a society where the women are going to be healthy?" That first environment, from Katsi's perspective, is the starting place for it all, and the best indicator. The first environment is about a baby, a woman, and family. Katsi's approach, not unlike that of her grandmother, the noted midwife from half a century ago, is that everything the mother feels, eats, and sees affects the baby. That is a part of the Mohawk belief system. That is why, whether it is GM contamination or the mental health of the mother, all must be cared for if the baby is to be healthy. And that is Katsi's work, holistic midwifery. "One home birth will impact 30 people," she tells me and acknowledges it as a form of strengthening the social bonds of the community. She has deliveries coming up almost every month, but keeps her midwifery practice small so that she can attend to the holistic nature of bringing life into the world.

"The midwifery work is what keeps it all from being so damn depressing," she explains. "It's one thing to look at a statistic, it's another to look at and feel a baby," she continues. Katsi hopes one day to see a midwifery center and an exemption for aboriginal midwives to support their practices. "That is small remediation for the loss of self-esteem as a result of the breast milk contamination," she says.

In mid-September of 1997, Katsi Cook had her first face-to-face meeting with Carol Browner, the director of the Environmental Protection Agency. A decade after her first interactions with the federal agency, this would be the first time Cook would speak with Browner. She spoke mother to mother, explaining that the Mohawk mothers needed the EPA mother to help them. The Mohawks are hoping that the Great White Mother, the Environmental Protection Agency, will do her job. That she will protect the water, the air, the soil, and the unborn Mohawks. As of this writing, the Great White Mother has done little, but GM has budged slightly, because of all the community pressure. In 1998-99, some cleanup began. GM dredged some of the contaminants out of the bottom of the St. Lawrence and shipped them off to some unlucky community in Utah. According to Ransom, GM plans to "identify...hot spots inside the dump. Then, based on what they find, they may consider more remediation, or go back to...capping."[35]

According to the Mohawks, industry, along with government officials and policy makers worldwide, must heed the warnings that contaminated wildlife are sending before it is too late. The creation is unraveling, and the welfare of the entire planet is at stake. As the Mohawks would say, when the turtle dies, the world unravels. Instead of letting that happen, the Mohawks are determining their history. They are facing down General Motors, the Environmental Protection Agency, and the big industries. They are demanding a change and making stronger their community. Rebirthing their nation, from the first environment of the womb to the community and future generations, they are carrying on the principles of *Kaienarakowa*, the Great Law of Peace and the Good Mind.

Danny Billie, surrounded by supporters from several tribes,
stands on a hill overlooking his land in Immokalee, FL.
Photo by Mary Annette Pember, Red Cliff Ojibwe.

Seminoles

At the Heart of the Everglades

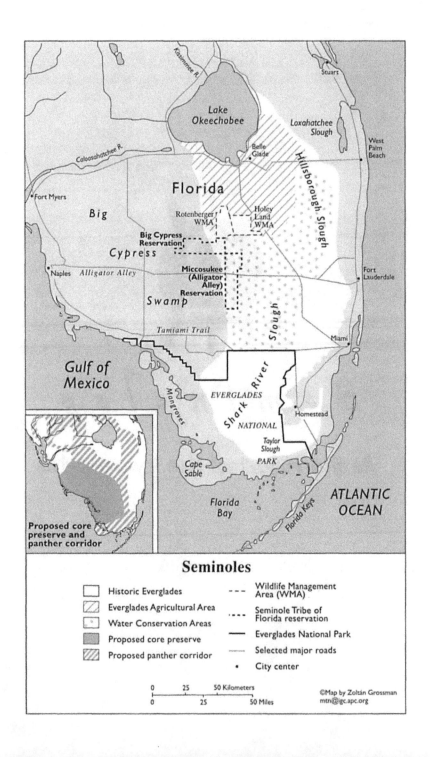

Kissimmee R.

Stuart

Lake
Okeechobee

Loxahatchee
Slough

Belle
Glade

Hillsborough Slough

West
Palm
Beach

Caloosahatchee R.

Florida

Fort Myers

Big

Rotenberger
WMA

Holey
Land
WMA

**Big Cypress
Reservation**

Cypress

Naples   *Alligator Alley*

**Miccosukee
(Alligator
Alley)
Reservation**

Fort
Lauderdale

Swamp

Slough

Tamiami Trail

Miami

**Gulf of
Mexico**

Mangroves

EVERGLADES

Shark River

NATIONAL

Homestead

Taylor
Slough

Cape
Sable

PARK

**ATLANTIC
OCEAN**

*Florida
Bay*

Florida Keys

Proposed core
preserve and
panther corridor

Seminoles

☐ Historic Everglades	- - - Wildlife Management Area (WMA)
▨ Everglades Agricultural Area	····· Seminole Tribe of Florida reservation
▦ Water Conservation Areas	—— Everglades National Park
▨ Proposed core preserve	—— Selected major roads
▨ Proposed panther corridor	• City center

0   25   50 Kilometers

0   25   50 Miles

©Map by Zoltán Grossman
mtn@igc.apc.org

W here the natural world ends and the human world begins, there you will find the Seminoles. There is no distinction between the two worlds—the Creator's Law governs all. It has always been like that, since the beginning.

"The Creator made our people and gave us the laws on how we're supposed to conduct ourselves," explains Danny Billie, spokesperson for the Independent Traditional Seminole nation, which consists of about 300 people in the midst of the Florida Everglades. He is trying to keep that law: the Creator's Law, the Breathmaker's Law.[1]

The Independent Traditional Seminole nation of Florida steadfastly keeps its traditions—language, culture, housing, ceremony, and way of life—against the forces of colonialism, assimilation, globalization, and all that eats cultures. The presence of these traditions in the Native community provides a yardstick against which to measure your own values, your own way of life, and your choices. That is the lesson these traditions will teach without speaking. And that is a great gift.

In the center of their chickee (traditional house) Seminoles keep a fire—always, it seems. It is the fire of culture, the fire of life. I am not so different. I tend my fire, that one in the woodstove, which keeps my northern house warm. Watch the fire, nurture it, and it will feed your soul and warm your body. Leave the fire, and it may get away from you. That lesson is worth remembering.

The Panther Clan of the Seminole nation consider the Florida panther their closest animal relative. There are only about 50 of these panthers left.[2] Both the panther and the Seminole have fought for their land, and they intend to remain there. But industrialization and the drive for profit are squeezing the life-blood out of the Everglades, and it's not possible for the Seminole and panther alone to change that.

Two hundred years ago, the Seminoles and the animals had most of the Everglades to themselves. Blooming flowers of every shape and color were intertwined with the textured green of shrubs, grasses, and trees. Small hills rose among the great waterways, in whose fertile soils the Seminoles planted small gardens. In their massive dugout canoes, they traveled as far as Cuba and the Bahamas.[3] At home, they prayed for and feasted on fish and animals, and made their shelter from the great cypress swamps and palm trees. From other plants they made their medicines, and each day they gave thanks to the Creator for their way of life. To the Seminole, like other Indigenous people, the way of life is a ceremony in itself, and they acknowledge it historically and today through a language called *Hitchiti.*

The Seminoles, it is said, had once been closely affiliated with the Creeks. Their name, *Seminoles,* came from a Creek word meaning "runaway," or "wild," or alternatively, "people of the distant fire." When they decided to keep to themselves, they started an independent, village-based system of governance. But their land was coveted. First by the Spaniards, who imagined a Fountain of Youth amidst the sea of grass, pink flamingos, blue herons, and brilliantly colored birds, and then by the Americans, who, as time would tell, coveted all.[4]

The Seminole Wars

> You have guns, and so have we. You have powder and lead, and so have we. Your men will fight, and so will ours—until the last drop of Seminole blood has moistened the dust of his last hunting ground.
>
> —Osceola, Seminole leader

In 1817 (according to the laws of colonialism), Florida became a Spanish possession. And the United States was in an expansionist mood. (Each subsequent colonizer has sought to attain that which they could not—the heart of the Everglades and the souls of the Seminoles.) What was worse to Eurocentric eyes was that the Seminoles had taken in runaway Black slaves. That was a sore point with southern slaveholders. Most of those escaped slaves became members of the community. Even those who lived separately had their own villages, ran their own affairs, and grew their own crops. The Africans were sometimes adopted as members of a Seminole family, and the freeing of Blacks was common practice. Mixed-bloods and Blacks became chiefs and sub-chiefs in the regular Seminole settlements.[5] In fact, to this day, there are still, primarily in Oklahoma, Black Seminole families, or Seminole Freedmen, who remain as a bridge between two cultures and histories.

All of this was infuriating to the southern slaveowners and provided a large part of the impetus for the First Seminole War, fought under the command of one General Andrew Jackson, who was later made military governor of the new territory. Thus provoked, in 1816, the military sent a detachment into Florida to pursue runaway slaves. Under the command of General Andrew Jackson, a year later they attacked a Seminole village in northwest Florida. So began the Seminole Wars, which lasted from 1817 to 1855. The First Seminole War technically began in 1817 and came to a close two years later when the Spanish ceded Florida to the United States. The Second Seminole War was a military disaster. It required 50,000 soldiers and, between the daunting natural tangle that is the Everglades and the fierce resistance of the Seminoles, the United States suffered an expensive and humiliating defeat. The Second Seminole War, which was waged between 1835 and 1842, took the lives of almost 1,500 American soldiers with a federal government price tag of at least $40 million.

In 1830, Andrew Jackson signed the Indian Removal Act, giving him the power to remove all eastern Indians from their land to "Indian territory"—government-established areas west of the Mississippi. The Florida Seminoles were to be relocated to Oklahoma, for, among other things, their villages had impeded white settlement of what the local Florida Legislative Council deemed the "fairest part of Florida." In the various dubious treaties and agreements signed over the next years, Jackson tried to force the Seminoles to leave Florida, but, as reporter Catherine Caufield notes,

> One young warrior, Osceola, resisted and inspired others to follow him.... As the deadline for the move to Oklahoma approached they went on the offensive against the troops who had been sent to organize the exodus. A series of surprise attacks in the last days of 1835, in which a handful of Indians killed more than a hundred soldiers, launched the Second Seminole war, which continued for nearly eight years and was one of the bloodiest, costliest and least successful wars in American history.[6]

In 1837, 33 Seminole leaders, including Osceola, were captured while negotiating under a flag of truce. Osceola later died in captivity, succumbing to complications from malaria. The U.S. Army imported bloodhounds from Cuba in an unsuccessful attempt to track the remaining Seminoles. Even without the dogs, the odds were heavily against the Seminoles. Fifty thousand federal soldiers served in the Second Seminole War, and there were never fewer than 3,800 soldiers in the field at any one time. The Seminoles, by contrast, had no more than 1,500 warriors total.

By 1842, almost 4,000 Seminoles had been shipped west to Oklahoma Indian Territory, and at the close of the war in 1855, fewer than 500 Seminoles remained in the Everglades and Big Cypress Swamp, north of the Everglades.

In the ten years following the end of the Second Seminole War, Florida's non-Indian population almost doubled, and the newcomers wanted the Indians out of the way. With bribes, bounty hunters, and armed troops, the United States managed by 1861 to move 200 more Seminoles to Oklahoma. Finally, the looming Civil War and the western Indian wars forced the U.S. government to end its war against the Seminoles. Three hundred Seminoles remained in the Florida swamps.[7]

The Land

The Everglades begin at Lake Okeechobee, one of the largest freshwater lakes in the continental United States. The Everglades originally sloped 200 miles south in a natural drain system of rivers, lakes, and wetlands. This rich ecosystem of water, grasses, cypress, meadows, marshes, and waterways provides a haven for a wealth of life. Rare birds such as wood storks, whooping cranes, and American peregrine falcons, along with crocodiles and Florida panthers, all find a refuge there.

Wetlands are often called the kidneys of the earth, recharging or cleansing water that enters the system through flooding or rainfall. The wetlands remove sediment, pollutants, minerals, and other materials from waters washed in from upland areas. The water is then either stored in the vast root and vegetation systems or released through evaporation. Although the Everglades and other wetlands are an important source of many medicines and biological diversity and are crucial in the ecosystem, for the past hundred years, the U.S. government, Anita Bryant, and all those citrus and sugar growers, along with some big-time development money, have been messing with them.

As a result, America has lost half of its wetlands.[8] It is estimated that 458,000 acres of U.S. wetlands were lost annually between 1954 and 1974—87 percent due to agricultural conversion. The state of Florida contains 20 percent of the nation's wetlands and lost over eight million acres between 1850 and 1984. From 1960 to 1984 alone, south Florida permanently lost one-fourth of its wetlands.[9]

The Seminoles, like many other Native people, will tell the great engineers who move the rivers and drain the wetlands that man should not do the Creator's work. Or, perhaps, as the Cree said, in reference to the mega-dams of northern Quebec: "Beavers are the only ones allowed to make dams in our areas."

Over the past 50 years, half of the Everglades—1.5 million acres—has been drained by 1,400 miles of canals, cutting a five-mile straight channel and roads through the heart of the ecosystem. Pollution has vanquished wading bird populations, which have plummeted to less than a fifth of their 1930s levels. The ivory-billed woodpecker, once common in Big Cypress Swamp, is now extinct. About one-third of the plants and animals on the federal endangered species list can be found in the Florida wetlands.[11] Adding insult to injury, a nuclear power plant was built on the freshwater diversion created by the St. Lucie canal.

Through the years, the canals have been enlarged and interconnected into a vast network, and even the once-meandering beauty of the Kissimmee and Caloosahatchee Rivers has been lost to dredges and straight-line engineering. Today, the movement of water through the Everglades is entirely unnatural, and the Everglades are considered one of the most endangered ecosystems on the planet.[12]

As 106-year-old Marjorie Stoneman Douglas, longtime Everglades advocate explains,

> The lake's entire southern rim was diked by a high levee, so that the only outlets were the canals, all fitted with gates to control the waters in an effort to put man, not nature, in charge of the Everglades. All this provided an enormous area upon which agriculture, mostly sugarcane, developed to the south and southeast of the lake.[13]

Since the mid-1970s, Florida wetlands have been converted less for agriculture and more for development. According to the *National Real Estate Investor,* two of the top-ten growth cities in the United States are in Florida.[14] All of which means that the wetlands are getting more and more squeezed.

The Animals

The steep decline of the Florida panther population was initially brought on by widespread hunting. Next it was the cars driving down the highways cut through the swampland that killed the big cats. Today, pollution in the ecosystem has moved up the food chain to endanger big cats and humans.

Because the Everglades function like kidneys, most of the toxins that are in the larger ecosystem end up in the Everglades eventually. More pollution and less Everglades means less filtering, and the system becomes a toxic sink. In 1989, federal and state scientists discovered that freshwater fish in the Everglades had high levels of mercury, largely, they surmised, from the post-harvest burning of the cane fields. Raccoons, alligators, and panthers in the area are also contaminated with large amounts of mercury.[15]

High up on the food chain, the big cats and the big crocodiles are the first to go from pollution. In mid-1989, a Florida panther was found dead in the Everglades. Liver samples from the cat found 110 ppm of mercury, indicating that mercury poisoning may have been the cause of death. This particular panther frequented the Shark River Slough, where deer were scarce, but likely was living on raccoons and alligators, which are even higher up on the food chain. In 1991, the last two female panthers living in the Everglades National Park died. Their mercury levels were lower than that of the dead panther found in 1989, but heavy metal poisoning was considered a contributing factor in their deaths.[16] The mercury, along with the other pollutants found in the Everglades, also makes the animals sick. One of the most frightening and foreboding problems faced by the panthers today is their declining ability to reproduce: scientists estimate that 90 percent of today's male panthers have testicles that have not descended from their scrotums. Two females are known to have benign vaginal tumors and haven't bred in nearly seven years, despite being around the males.[17]

Danny Billie and Bobby Billie, the spiritual leader of the Traditional Seminole, took a walk with reporter Catherine Caufield and remembered the Fakahatchee Strand, a small remnant of cypress forest that is now a state park.

> [Bobby] remembered that thirty years ago, "We used to go to Marco Island to hunt gophers and pick mangos," he said. "Now it's full of big old hotels and condominiums." We walked a bit farther, and then Danny said, "Only about twenty years ago, you could go [down the Everglades] and see all kinds of birds. The water would stand all year round, but now you'll be lucky if there's a swamp pond that stands year round."

Another day, Caufield reports, she was taken to see a place at Collier-Seminole State Park that locals use as a garbage dump.

> As we stared in silence at piles of construction rubble and household rubbish, Bobby whispered, "Let me lie down and cry."[18]

The Reservation and the Village

At each intersection on the path of life, there is a choice to be made, and it is weighed against the values, the history, the present circumstances, and the futures of generations of people. These decisions are not taken lightly in most Indigenous societies, but are carefully deliberated, in the best of circumstances.

In the worst of circumstances, these decisions are made behind closed doors by a select few—all too often, those few selected in some fashion by the federal government or some other vested interest. These decisions, however, in the case of most peoples, will affect the entire social and political fabric as well as the next set of decisions, the next forks in the road, whether on an individual level, a family level, or a community level.

The choices made over the past decades by the various Seminole leaders and their people on the reservation and in the Independent Traditional Seminole nation have led to distinctly different ways of living today. While they are all the same people, they are living in almost different worlds.

In this century, two major events pushed the Seminoles apart: the creation of the Everglades National Park in 1947 and further subsequent development, and a 1976 Indian Claims Commission (ICC) settlement offer. The former left hundreds of families homeless and pushed some onto the federally created reservations. Some traditional Seminoles feared this move would further change Seminole culture.

The ICC settlement, like others across the country, also increased divisions. In 1976, the claims commission recognized Seminole title to 30 million acres of Florida and offered to buy it for $16 million (or a little more than 50 cents an acre). The pressure to accept meager settlements was and is immense in Native communities. But others feel, as traditional Seminoles' Buffalo Tiger says, "It's like accepting a couple of dollars for selling a piece of your mother."[19] For similar reasons, the Lakota nation and Shoshone nation have thus far resisted their ICC settlements. For the Seminoles, the internal debate over whether to accept the offer delayed the final judgement for 14 years.

By 1990, the settlement, including interest, amounted to $47 million, and some Seminoles accepted the money. Those Seminoles came to be known as the Seminole Tribe of Florida.

The Seminole Tribe of Florida, Inc.

On August 21, 1997, the Seminole Tribe of Florida celebrated the 40th anniversary of the creation of its single governmental unit, the Seminole Tribal Council, and their business managers, the Board of Directors of the Seminole Tribe of Florida. Under the leadership of a series of charismatic leaders, the Seminole Tribe of Florida has since the 1950s survived and flourished, using the economics of the white man, matched with the unique location and savvy of the Seminoles.[20] In 1957, the Seminole Tribe of Florida received its charter from the secretary of the interior. Each person who signed up received 25 bucks and became eligible for various federal benefits. Today, there are about 2,000 members and five reservations totaling 78,000 acres.[21]

Patricia Wickman, director of anthropology for the Seminole Tribe of Florida, describes the predicament that faces many Native nations—the struggle of dealing with immense poverty and its related social implications:

The economic battle for survival was so fierce that the late 20th century might be termed the Fourth Seminole War.... Throughout the 1970s, federal dollars from the Great Society programs and the War on Poverty...supported the rapid expansion of Seminole social service programs...clinics, Head Start, education, and housing programs were established.... Cattle, land leases, citrus, and federal loans provided an economic base for the Seminoles through the 1970s. The smokeshop business was a shot in the arm also, but bingo had the greatest potential.[22]

The Seminole Tribe found its cash cow in the late 1970s, when it opened up the country's first high-stakes bingo hall in Hollywood in 1979. Subsequent court decisions (such as *Butterworth v. Seminole Tribe of Florida)* determined that Indian tribes could conduct bingo enterprises without state regulation, and their operation quickly became one of the most successful gaming ventures in Indian country.[23] That gaming enterprise has been the foundation of new tribal development and a great source of pride for each subsequent administration. In their public relations literature, the Seminole Tribe notes,

The economic impact of Seminole gaming reaches far beyond the reservations and contributes significantly to the economy of the State of Florida. Seminole gaming establishments employ 2,200 Floridians, 95% of whom are non-Indian. With a payroll of almost $25 million, Seminole gaming activities generate more than $3.5 million a year in payroll taxes and unemployment insurance payments. Seminole gaming establishments purchase more than $24 million in goods and services from more than 850 Florida vendors each year, as well. These dollars go to education, health care, infrastructure development, fire and emergency management services, economic development activities, and delivery of other basic government services to tribal members.[24]

The Florida Seminoles have also dealt with the desire of many Americans to see "real Indians." Hoping to divert traffic through their own communities, they created the Billie Swamp Safari, which opens 2,000 acres of the Big Cypress Reservation to the tourist market. How all this came to be was explained by Chief James Billie, chairman of the Seminole Tribe of Florida. "The idea of presenting a safari experience here on the reservation was developed as many people traveled through our reservation looking for native village chickees and Indian culture.... However, they couldn't find it. So we planned Billie Swamp Safari and opened it up to visitors from around the world."[25]

The federal government and the state of Florida are likely somewhat pleased with all the economic contributions made by this branch of the Seminole people and their leadership. (The state, however, in typical style of states with any Native population, did challenge in court the Seminole Tribe's rights to have virtually any enterprises.) To others, the spreading enterprises of the *Bingo Seminoles* may rankle their sensibilities. There is an internal discussion on cultural transformation within the Seminoles.

"They broke away from us," Danny Billie explains about the decision of some Seminoles to change their path. James Billie, the tribal chairman, offers a similar explanation when asked about the differences between the traditional Seminoles and the Seminole Tribe. "We are the same people. They have their way of doing things, and we have ours.... Those different ways are pretty distinct."

But the Seminole Tribe makes no apologies. Tribal attorney Jim Shore explains that "the fact that Indians are not sitting around by the railroad station selling their moccasins and beads, and are instead traveling in three-piece suits in Lear jets to New York doesn't mean the culture is dead."[26] The Florida tribe also takes a different eye to the environment and what can be done to preserve the remaining ecosystem. When asked by reporter Jordan Levin about the tribe's concern for the ecosystem of the Everglades, Shore continues, with somewhat defeatist nonchalance, "I'm not sure the Everglades can be saved.... If there's any plan out there we can all agree with that can save the Everglades, we're in favor of it. But we're not taking any lead to save the whole of South Florida. After all...no one ever listened to us before, so why get into it now?"[27]

Shore's beleaguered defeatism is echoed by tribal chairman James Billie. (Note there are lots of Billies, Tigers, and Osceolas down there in the Seminoles. In some deep sense they are all related, but don't make the mistake of generalizing them in any other sense.) James Billie's comments to Levin resonate with phrases and terms used at times by other Indian Reorganization Act Native leaders nationally when trying to come to terms with a bad deal and, quite often, their own eventual or coerced complicity in it.

> How can we be worried? We're already sitting in the cesspool. The Seminole Indian didn't exactly create this problem. See, we were confined to the reservation. We were animals in cages, being looked at, ridiculed, laughed at. Stab at 'em a little bit, throw a peanut at 'em. Let's experiment on him to see if he acts like a white man. Then one day, when they need to use us as a stepping stone, they say the Indians are supposed to be the earth keepers. What a bunch of jack-asses. The thing I like about

this race that condemns the others is that they never accept their own failures. They just want to throw it on somebody else.[28]

The Independent Traditional Seminole Nation

The Creator didn't mention reservations. Where does it say we have to live on a reservation to live the way we want?

—Bobby Billie[29]

Danny and Bobby Billie's people, the Independent Traditional Seminoles, made sure they stayed out of the mud-wrestling over federal money from the ICC and for tribal programs. They have pretty much stayed out of everything. Their villages could be 300 years old, except for the pickup trucks and the big van. A group of thatched-roof houses, a central cooking tent with their fire, gardens, and a few scraggly chickens. Near the fire is what I called the Sewing Machine Shrine, the head of an old Singer sewing machine planted in a mound and surrounded by flowers. That machine had undoubtedly seen a lot of fabric, an immense amount of that stunning Seminole patchwork, before they retired it. Bands of young children and toddlers play in the middle, scooped up by hovering mothers and aunties in long, willowy Seminole skirts. There is a different feel here. Like a different world, not America. It is a world these Seminoles made and kept. This is their path. They speak their own language, live in their own traditional chickees, conduct their own form of governance and ceremonies, and teach their children their own way. They are strict.

The traditional Seminoles and their attorneys at the Indian Law Resource Center, went to Congress to get an amendment added to the distribution bill to insure that the settlement money would not be forced on them. It began, however, almost 30 years earlier when, on March 1, 1954, George Osceola, Jimmie Billie, and Buffalo Tiger, representing the Seminole General Council, climbed the steps of the Capitol, carrying a large buckskin scroll. The Buckskin Declaration was a formal petition to the president of the United States from the General Council of the traditional Seminoles. It said, in part:

> We have, and have had for centuries, our own culture, our own customs, our own government, our own language, and our own way of life, which is different from the government, the culture, the customs, the language, and the way of life of the White Man.... We are not White Men, but Indians who do not wish to become White Men but wish to remain Indians and have an outlook on all of these things dif-

ferent from the outlook of the White Man. We do not wish to own lands because our land is for all of us. We have failed to have your Indian Agent or your Secretary of Interior or your other government officials understand our outlook.[30]

According to Tim Coulter of the Indian Law Resource Center,

Even among Indians, these people were known to be particularly adamant about their refusal to become involved in the outside world.... And the cost of keeping to their principles was high—they had no land of their own, no reservation, they were ignored when the government made decisions that affected them, and there they were fighting like hell against having this compensation money forced on them. I was impressed, I think anyone would be impressed, with their determination and their success at actually maintaining their way of life in the face of an overwhelming culture, a culture that has practically dominated the entire world.[31]

"I have a lot of respect and admiration for the Billie family," says Lori Pourier of the Indigenous Women's Network, who among others has visited the traditional Seminoles and worked with them on projects ranging from grassroots gatherings to United Nations meetings in Geneva, Switzerland. "They stand strong, true to their traditional way of life, despite the dominant world that surrounds their community. They never did lose sight of their original instructions from the Creator. That is something we can all learn from as we strengthen and restore our nations," Pourier says.[32]

Even today, when the traditional Seminoles arrive at a meeting, it is an event. The Billies show up in what I call the Billie-mobile, a 12-passenger van full of Seminole shirts, skirts, and Seminole babies. They all pack into that van and drive from Florida to Haida Gwaii (northern British Columbia) if they think it's important, then they talk and converse among themselves in a group. Amidst giggles and teasing, their *Hitchiti* transcends the din and is both urgently whispered and a source of laughs. Those of us meeting with them always smile knowingly: that's the best strategy, we figure. They are not people to decide quickly. Each decision is made by the collective, their different representatives, and is then communicated to us, those who are meeting with them, through their spokesperson, usually Danny Billie.

The traditional Seminoles are clear that they do not want to go to the reservation. They have never wanted to. "What's wrong with a reservation," Bobby Billie explains to me,

I can tell you from what my elders told me, when I was growing up. A reservation is called a dead land. A place of death. They put you in a cage and put a number on you and keep an eye on you all the time. They kind of like put a string on you and they tell you what to do and who to do it.

The elders said, When you go onto the reservation, it's like you're giving your life away to someone else to control it. You don't have to be recognized by another entity. Our people say that you are who you are, because you already know and the Creator knows. And that's all you need.

It's like a cattle pen...the farmer comes to the pen, and the farmer throws a bale of hay in there, and then they all come running to it. Then after he feeds them, he does what he needs to do to them—milk, or meat. That bale of hay is the money, that housing, health service. I give you so much of this, if you do something for me.

Not only do they refuse to go to the reservation, they refuse federal recognition. "We know who we are, and the Creator knows who we are," Danny Billie explains. "We do not need the government to tell us that." Ironically, theirs is an immense struggle just to be left alone. To keep the federal and state government out of their lives. And to keep on answering the question of why they don't want to be like other Indians and go to the reservation, the place where Indians are supposed to go and be Indians.

The traditional Seminoles have lived for the past four generations on some land near Immokalee, land which, according to the white man's law, belongs to a family named English. In the 1880s, the first Englishes moved south from Georgia to grow winter vegetables and citrus crops. It was then, as the story is told, that some otherwise reclusive Seminoles, who used the name Billie in their interactions with non-Indians, were willing to help the English clan out, with some tips on how to make it in the subtropical jungle. That began a friendship and, a generation later, a deathbed wish that the Billies would always have a place for their chickees on the Englishes' property. Today, the traditional Seminole community is nestled in the middle of this citrus farm. The story is that the handshake has been replaced with a lease for a dollar a year. The English family is a friend of the Billies and, when the state of Florida and Collier County have shown up with complaints in the past, the family has stood by its friends. Ironic as it may be, the state of Florida is concerned about the health and environmental impact the traditional Seminoles have on the Everglades.

A few years ago, a Collier County code-enforcement housing official inspected the traditional Seminoles' village without a warrant and cited the Billies for housing code violations. The official claimed that their chickees had been constructed without proper building code permits and that the county was concerned about their way of life. The fire in the center of the cooking house, for instance, was a concern to the county—they threatened to fine the Seminoles $550 a day until the cooking fires were removed. The fire, in the Billies' eyes, is about who they are. Fire was a person once, an ancestor from long ago, Martha Billie Davis recounts. "My grandfather taught me that long ago. The fire is really important to me. All my kids are grown up. Sometimes I start missing my mother. I come at night and talk to her in the fire. It makes me closer to her. If you take my fire away, it's like taking my mother away from me. I don't think I could take that."[33]

The Seminoles fought the county's fine and found they had a lot of supporters, at least for this. In 1996, they mustered up a march to support their people: three days and 39 miles, from the village to the Collier County government building. Their legal help grew, and even local editorials in the *Naples Daily News* pointed out the county's discrimination. One editorial noted that "the embarrassment for all county citizens will end only when the government musters the skill to mind its own store and the grace to leave the Indians alone." After marches, press conferences, major articles, TV coverage, thousands of postcards, and legal gymnastics, the Billies fended off the county and eventually won a victory to preserve their way of life.

It is ironic that in the face of all the white man's laws and their alleged violation by Indians, it is the Billies who actually preserve the ecosystem. Their reverence for life is in stark contrast to the agribusinesses that encroach on their land. As Bobby Billie looked across the moat-like channel that separates one of their traditional villages of chickees from a freeze-burned field of a big farmer, he sighed: "You look out there, and everything is dead. But look in here, and everything is alive."

The Panther and the Seminoles

When we talk about the environment and our way of life, it is all connected. When red people talk of our ways, land claims, and rights to self-determination, some white people look at us as greedy, wanting everything. They don't realize where we are coming from. They don't have common sense. When we talk about saving our rights, we are protecting them, too. We are the caretakers of the Creator's creation. It is our job to follow the instructions that he has given us. If we don't do

our job, then we are going to get fired. If we don't follow our own
ways, our laws and ceremonies, the Creator is going to say that we are
not doing our job and will clear everything and start all over again.

—Danny Billie[34]

Most of the traditional Seminoles are Panther Clan. In their way, the panthers are saying the same thing as the traditional Seminoles. Let us be. Leave us
alone.

"There are 30 of them panthers left. And they're killing them. If they
would quit tinkering with them day by day, if they would just leave them alone,
and their environment and their habitat, they would regenerate this population,"
Bobby Billie explains.

> They're out there saying they want to help the panther population, but
> the way they're going about it is endangering and killing them. They're
> tranquilizing them, and capturing them, and putting collars on them,
> and doing whatever they do and that's what's killing them. Even when
> they're not doing that, they're killing the environment. And when they
> have those hunting seasons, they kill all the deer and the hawks. And
> when that happens, the panthers have nothing to eat. They starve and
> die. A lot of them they capture to look at, they're starving when they
> get them.

The analogy is quite apparent to Bobby. Bobby, Danny, and I were sitting
in a small backstage area at an Honor the Earth show, where the performers (the
Indigo Girls) and the Billies were working together to secure a state exemption
for their zoning. We talked, and two or three young Seminole women looked
over my shoulder as I furiously typed on my portable computer. Keeping up
with the Billies. That is a task. They all seemed to nod approvingly at my white
man's technology put to use. It may not be their path, but they can work with it.

"It's like our own people. There are certain things that they need in their
diet that keeps them in good health," says Bobby. "And their body functions in
the right balance. But once that food or whatever is in their own diet is taken
away, they start deteriorating inside. They say that the male panther can't reproduce with the females because they are not eating the things that they need. It's
no different with our people. Our natural world is disappearing. Our habitat, our
foods." Danny interjects: "Our elders talk about wanting to eat turtle soup or
garfish. They haven't tasted those kinds of things in years. But nowadays, you
know, everything is contaminated and polluted."

Bobby comes back again: "Now we have to eat these chemical-infested foods. Who knows what's in these foods? Even our people, some of them are getting sick. Their body organs are giving up, and it's the same with the panther."

Once they keep those collars on, they follow them around and chase them every day. Checking on them, and where they're at. That's another factor in their daily survival, stress. And just look at it. If someone put a big old collar on you, you aren't able to look down or twist your head the way you want to. The panthers go through thick woods and stuff, what happens if a big old branch gets caught and they'll get caught and struggle and get exhausted. And then they're going to die. They've been finding panthers dead with collars on.

The Panther Reservations

As it turns out, all this ecological maneuvering, all this playing god (in the "development" of the Everglades and all the subsequent managing that is then undertaken) has been a huge ecological mistake that, today, Congress, President Clinton, and a host of others are trying to unravel, in a twisted and complicated fashion. There are a range of ideas on how to preserve the ecosystem of the panther. Conservation biologists such as Larry Harris and Reed Noss at the University of Florida and Oregon State University are studying the state's endangered panther and its threatened black bear and hope to design nature reserves for the species that are more than outdoor museums or zoos. The plan requires the utmost care, since isolating small pockets of animals exposes them to additional threats: inbreeding can lead to genetic defects, and they are more vulnerable to extinction. A zoo is like a reservation to the traditional Seminole, a place of death. The panthers, like the Seminoles, need room to live.

The bravest proposals from Noss and others include a bio-reserve system with large wilderness cores, buffer zones, and biological corridors, which could be carefully managed to preserve habitat and species.

The politicized practice of panther-restoration work includes the sales of specialized license plates that go toward helping the panther and the endangered manatee. Funds from those sales go into special government bank accounts, which are supposed to be used to buy rights to the animals' natural habitats and support preservation of the species. However, according to reporters, the panthers aren't doing much better than Indians did in national Indian appropriations by the Bureau of Indian Affairs. Enviroworld, an environmental reporting service, noted in 1996 that less than 20 cents of every dollar raised for the animals had gone toward panther-recovery programs so far. The Florida Panther Research and Management Trust Fund (one of the state agencies charged with managing the money), according to newspaper reports, receives 45 percent of panther-tag revenues, or about $1.7 million a year. Nearly $1 million was stripped from the fund in 1997 to make up for a cut in the Florida Game and Freshwater Fish Commission's general operating budget. Another $675,000 went to pay for the tagging and monitoring of the panther, although money seemed to end up in multilingual environmental classes and courses in green construction for building contractors at the University of Florida.[35]

Here, in the so-called twilight of the panthers, there are a lot of interested players. Everyone comes in from a different angle. There are a host of proposals to save the Florida panther and to restore the Florida Everglades. The Army Corps of Engineers itself submitted ten different proposals to Congress, which ranged from a plan calling for only operational changes, which even the Corps admitted was inadequate, to full restoration alternatives. The most significant and comprehensive effort would reconnect Lake Okeechobee, Florida's great south central lake, to the Everglades; restore natural, seasonal waterflow from the lake; store water now dumped from the lake and from urban areas; restore sheetflow (waterflows that make a distinct channel) throughout the Everglades ecosystem; and improve water quality standards. Many environmentalists fear that the boldest proposals will end up being compromised, which, when there are only 30 big cats left, is a dangerous gamble.

As one reporter notes,

> In the end, the endangered cat's fate will likely depend on the goodwill of the orange growers and ranchers in southwestern Florida. They are receiving government overtures of possible tax incentives or cash payments to continue using their lands in ways that allow the panther to exist on their property. The trouble is, of 756 square miles considered prime panther land in Florida, one quarter has been permitted to grow oranges. And the panthers steer clear of orange groves due to the dearth of cover and food—such as hogs and deers—found there.[36]

On January 8, 1999, the South Florida Water Management District, the Nature Conservancy, and the St. Joe Company agreed to what some note as the largest single conversion of developed land back to its natural state. Over 60,000 acres were acquired by the federal and state governments in what was referred to as the Talesman Trade Agreement.

Additional proposals call for 251,000 acres of land to be acquired and for restoration of the Everglades back to pre-1950s channelization. These combined efforts would restore hundreds of billions of gallons of freshwater, which presently flows into the sea as a result of Army Corps of Engineers' projects of the past. Buttressed additionally by the Clinton lands legacy initiative, the federal government plans to use hundreds of millions of dollars collected from oil and gas leases to help pay for the Everglades Restoration Project.

Joining these initiatives is the Miccosukee Tribe of Indians of Florida (another Seminole entity), which had Clinton extend its 50-year lease on ancestral lands within the Everglades to "forever."

The People and the Ceremony

You cannot live in the modern way and think in the traditional way.
The way you live affects the way you think.

—Danny Billie

Where the people and the land are the same is in ceremony, Danny Billie explains. The Green Corn Dance is an annual cultural and religious ceremony of the Seminoles. Says Danny Billie, "It defines who we are and what we are as traditional Indian people. It is the heart and soul of the traditional Seminole way of life." That dance has taken place forever, and for around the past 250 years in the same area of cypress wetlands and pine forest north of Lake Okeechobee. In 1993, Seminoles were forced off the site, victims of progress, once again.

The Independent Traditional Seminoles in the 1990s have found that they have a group of allies. The Montana-based Indian Law Resource Center expanded their historically legal base into the policy and conservation arena and, with the guidance of the Seminoles and an amazing gift from a private Santa Fe–based philanthropic institution called the Lannan Foundation, orchestrated a solution. In late 1997, the Lannan Foundation purchased 1,750 acres of pristine Florida for a trust set up by the Indian Law Resource Center for the Seminoles, adding another 650 acres in February 1998.[37]

J. Patrick Lannan, the board chair of the Lannan Foundation, says the foundation's relationship with the Independent Traditional Seminoles

> inspire[s] us deeply in many ways.... In South Florida—the epitome of overdevelopment, mindlessness, and fast decisionmaking—the Independent Traditional Seminoles live their lives based on values and actions that are in direct contrast to everything else around them. Their struggle to survive has been surrounded by a world bent on destruction.

In spite of everything, they have continued their sacred ceremonies of renewal and their caring relationships to land, water, animals, plants, and other human beings.[38]

The new homecoming of the Green Corn Dance in 1998 lifted the spirits of many Seminoles and the Indigenous community everywhere. It is said by many Indian people that preserving the sanctity of the ceremony is the central responsibility for each subsequent generation and sustains all life.

"My oldest brother has this saying that explains it really clearly," Danny Billie explained to writer Dagmare Thorpe.

He says, "The way of life of the red people is like a clay cup, and the way of life of the white man is like a Styrofoam cup. The clay cup takes a lot of care because if you drop it, it is going to break. The Styrofoam cup does not take much caring; if you drop it it doesn't break. You have to be real careful with the clay cup because if you put something hot in it, it will burn you, compared to the Styrofoam cup, which you use once and throw away; it takes a lot of work to keep that clay cup intact. The Styrofoam cup is the white man's way. They have no rules or regulations in their way of life. They say they do but in reality, they do not."[39]

The big questions posed by the dilemmas of both the Independent Traditional Seminole nation of Florida and the Florida panthers are about exactly how much Florida, the developers, the citrus and sugar cane growers, the hunters, and the environmentalists are willing to back off. If Florida is willing to give up a culture of strip malls, then the panthers and the Seminoles might have a chance.

Danny Billie, talking with reporter Jordan Levin, did what the Seminoles do best. He pointed out, once again, that this whole discussion is really not about the Seminoles and the panther. It is really about America.

You know for a fact and I know for a fact that in reality we can't have what we want. You may sit there and ask what we want, but what we want is what you need, too. It's what this society needs, if they want to continue to stay alive on this earth. What we do is for all things, for all people. Because if you don't stop now with the destruction, with the development and the poisoning of the environment, we're all gonna go. So when you ask the question of what we want, you might as well go ahead and include yourself. Because not only do we want to survive as who we are, I'm pretty sure that you want to survive as who you are, too.[40]

As J. Patrick Lannan reflects, the Independent Traditional Seminoles "continue to teach us about how to be better citizens."[41] Perhaps, in the end, to be better humans.

K. Naeme Tuglavina from Nain, at the Innu and Inuit camp
set up to protest the Voisey's Bay Nickel Company.
CP Picture Archive (Jonathan Hayward)

Nitassinan

The Hunter and the Peasant

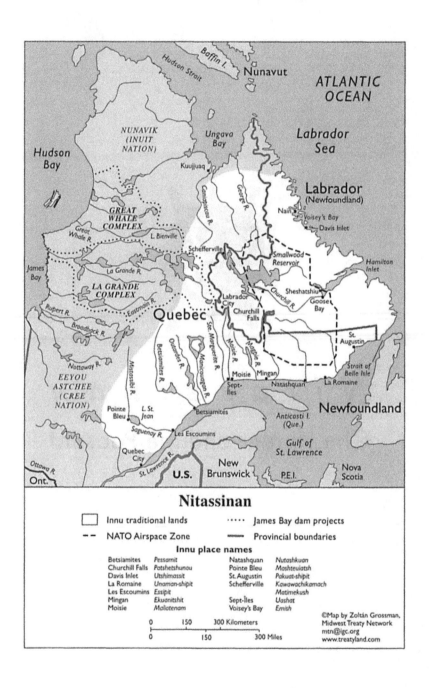

Nitassinan

☐ Innu traditional lands   ⋯⋯ James Bay dam projects

– – NATO Airspace Zone   ▬▬ Provincial boundaries

Innu place names

Betsiamites	Pessamit	Natashquan	Nutashkuan
Churchill Falls	Patshetshunau	Pointe Bleu	Mashteuiatsh
Davis Inlet	Utshimassit	St. Augustin	Pakuat-shipit
La Romaine	Unaman-shipit	Schefferville	Kawawachikamach
Les Escoumins	Essipit		Matimekush
Mingan	Ekuanitshit	Sept-Îles	Uashat
Moisie	Maliotenam	Voisey's Bay	Emish

©Map by Zoltán Grossman,
Midwest Treaty Network
mtn@igc.org
www.treatyland.com

0   150   300 Kilometers

0   150   300 Miles

Thre is a long-ago Cree and Innu story about Wesakejack and the Great Flood. It seems that, at that time, the people, the animals, and all of Creation were not behaving well. There was much arguing and fighting, and even children were doing what the grown-ups were doing. Badly. Wesakejack found this to be true for all the relatives, whether they had four legs or two, and the Creator also observed this. That is why the Creator sent the Great Flood—to make things new again. And that flood did just that. Afterward, there was nothing left, except for a few animals and Wesakejack. All clean. And with the breath of Wesakejack and some earth collected by the humble muskrat, the earth was made new again.

Wesakejack's dilemma is the dilemma we face today. Who has the right to make the earth anew, and how is it made so? There is a transformation going on in the North—in the subarctic from Nitassinan to Eeyou Aski, to Anishinaabe Akiing, Anishinaabe Aski, and beyond.[1] The military, miners, and dam-builders are "developing" the land, leaving a path of destruction in their wake. There is, by and large, no historical or scientific precedent for understanding the consequences of their actions, either collectively or in isolation. They are performing a great technological and geological experiment.

From the North looking south one finds a curious history, a series of cultural interactions driven by strange motivations. People from the temperate climes, motivated by fear, a perception of entitlement, and greed, have attempted to conquer the Arctic and the subarctic. This "temperate colonialism" is what is occurring in Nitassinan, a region the size of France in northeastern Canada. The military, the miners, the electric companies, and the loggers—along with their associated cultural baggage, technological accoutrements, and garbage—have been jackhammering this region for the past 40 years.

Nitassinan, which means "the land" in Innuaimun, is the wellspring of a culture and a way of life. On this peninsula spanning the Canadian provinces of Quebec and Labrador, almost 20,000 Innuaimun-speaking Innu live. Their land is a land of mountains, thundering rivers, vast boreal forest, sweeping tundra, and Atlantic seashore. Their colonial name, *Montagnais,* means "mountain people" in French. They are also known to other Native people as *Naskapi,* or "those beyond the horizon." The majority of the Innu people live in 11 villages along the north shore of the St. Lawrence River in what is now Quebec. Over 3,000 live in two villages in what is today Labrador. Their culture and language are much like those of their relatives, the Cree (Eeyou), Ojibwe (Anishinaabeg), and Mi'kmaq, all of whom are Algonkin speakers who maintain a northern harvesting and hunting culture.

Theirs is a rich land. The George River caribou herd of at least 700,000 animals roams Nitassinan, and many of the raging rivers are full of Atlantic salmon. The land has provided well for the Innu, and it could continue to do so. But only if a delicate balance between the animal world and the human world, the world of rivers and the world of canoes, is maintained. And if the humans continue to please the Caribou Master, *Katipenima*.

Seventeenth-century colonists documented the Innu's comfortable standard of living, describing robes of bear, moose, beaver, and bear skins covering floors; infants diapered in sphagnum moss, wrapped in soft materials, or moss-filled bags; and a diverse diet of moose, caribou, bear, beaver, porcupine, hare, marten, snow goose, eel, sucker, salmon, and a wide variety of berries. They remarked on the egalitarian nature of Innu life, reporting no class system in the bush or competition between the sexes.[2]

Innu elder Philomene Mackenzie said in a 1997 interview that

> Women and men both hunt. They have always been equals. When a woman delivered a baby, the next day she was up and ready to move onto the next camp. Today, she stays in the hospital for a few days, and she takes all kinds of medications. Women have lost their strength by this way of living.

> Since I lived the Innu way, I know how to deliver a baby myself. I delivered a baby myself, three years ago, in a tent. If the culture had not been broken, there would still be midwives here. We'd still have our babies in the bush, we knew everything about how to cure illnesses, to have our babies, we knew how to use the medicines of the forest.[3]

Egalitarianism and collective process are still revered today. "A hunter's prestige came not from the meat and goods he acquired for his family, but from what he gave away and shared with others."[4]

Each Spring and Fall many of the Innu travel far into the bush to hunt and fish. Their knowledge of hunting, trapping, fishing, hide preparation, cooking, snowshoe making, and rituals has been passed down from generation to generation. Their seasonal migration into the bush for fishing, hunting, harvesting, and trapping can last up to eight months. It is the essence of being Innu.

Surviving sustainably in the subarctic is a challenge mastered by northern Indigenous peoples. The hunting-and-harvesting way of life requires immense diligence, physical strength, and a vital relationship to the Creator and spirits. *Pimaatisiiwin*, which translates as the "good life" or, alternatively, "continuous rebirth," is a term used to describe the Innu practice of continuous balance, a balance maintained in ceremony. According to Daniel Ashini, the chief land rights negotiator for the Innu, the Innu religion is

> based on a belief in animal masters and other forest spirits. When we hunt we must show respect for the animal masters. We place the bones of the caribou, bear, marten, mink, and other creatures in tree platforms so the dogs do not eat them. We do not overhunt or overtrap areas where animals are scarce. If we do not show respect in this way, the animal masters get angry and punish us by not giving us any animals at a later date. Our elders communicate with the animal masters through dreams, drumming, steam tent, and a form of divination called Matnikashaueu. A caribou or porcupine shoulder blade is placed in the fire until it is charred and cracked. We read the marks to discover the future location of game.
>
> Our hunting culture thrives in the bush. We do things that very few non-Innu know anything about. Non-natives think they know us because they see us in their stores and at their hockey rinks, but they don't realize that there is another side to us, a side that they would have trouble understanding unless they spent time with us in the bush.[5]

The Peasants and the Hunters

> A colonial situation is created, so to speak, the very instant a white man...appears in the midst of a tribe...so long as he is thought to be rich and powerful...[and has] in his most secret self a feeling of his own superiority.
>
> —Octavio Mannoni, *Prospero and Caliban*[6]

According to anthropologist and cartographer Hugh Brody,

> The modern empires that now vie with one another for material and cultural domination of the world emphasize their historical and social differences. The rhetoric of global politics is replete with insistence by one or another of the superpowers that their institutions and points of view are underpinned by distinctive history and culture. Yet all these nations have in common one factor that provides a profound cultural

unity—namely an agricultural heritage. The commonality of social and mental form may be traced even more specifically to peasant forms of agriculture. This foundation of so many societies means that ideas about land, property, religion, sexuality, children, patriarchy, and social control are also shared. Urban and suburban attitudes to hunters are still shaped by an agricultural and peasant history that bridges other ideological chasms....

Hunters do not share peasant and urban consciousness. Their ideas and institutions, their views about property, children, sexuality, and social control are radically unlike those founded in settled, originally agricultural societies. Peasant attachment to specific plots of land, the wish to have a large number of children in short periods of time, emphasis upon marriage, subordination of women to men, preoccupation with private ownership, and bodies of explicit law that are enforced by some form of police—all these notions and practices are deeply alien to most hunting societies.[7]

Colonists from the temperate climates could not understand the North, which they found frigid and barren, a vast untamed wilderness. Jacques Cartier, a French explorer who hit the shores of Nitassinan in 1534, reported the doings of the Innu with great disdain:

These men may very well and truely be called Wilde, because there is no poorer people in the world. For I think all that they had together, besides their boates and nets was not worth five souce. They go altogether naked save their privities, which are covered with a little skinne, and certain olde skinnes that they cast upon them.[8]

Strangely enough, these skewed, negative perceptions of the Innu continue despite three centuries of interaction with them. There is a continuing presumption—subtle as it may appear at times—that hunting cultures are primitive and outmoded. This presumption is evident in current discussions with the animal rights movement and the Department of Indian and Northern Affairs (DINA) in Canada, for example. At various times, anti–hunting-and-trapping activists have callously called for northern hunting cultures to progress from their outmoded practices and away from the trapline, while DINA officials (until recently) heavily encouraged town wage-work (and dependency) over a bush lifestyle.

Often, the most sustainable economy and way of life in the northern ecosystems is based on hunting, not on agriculture or industrialism. The Innu's hunting economy and culture work with the land and allow the animals to remain on their own path.

If the vast ecosystem of the North rankled the European sensibilities, the religious practices of the Innu and other northern hunting cultures horrified them. Cultural practices central to the Innu, such as divination, recognizing animals as relatives, and holding feasts to honor spirits, became the focus of colonizing efforts. And so it was that the first of the Europeans to enter the interior of the region were priests, then soldiers and entrepreneurs.

Jesuit Father Paul Le Jeune recorded his experiences during the early winters he spent with Innu families on the south shore of the St. Lawrence River in 1633–34. He, like his religious brethren elsewhere in the world, was determined to change the Innu. In 1637, he attempted to encourage a group of Innu to settle and farm at his Sillery mission and created a prototype Canadian "Indian reserve." Like those which would follow, it failed, even though food, houses, and clothing were provided. The Innu preferred their own way of life and eventually moved back into the bush.

It was the Hudson Bay Company that unleashed the most economic strife in the North, and is likely the largest single exploiter of the region. The Hudson Bay Company created what scholars generally regard as an economic serfdom in the region. Canadian historian Alan Cooke, among others, argues that, during the 18th century, the traders deliberately set out to destroy the economic independence of the Innu by making them dependent on goods they could obtain only from trading posts and by cheating the Innu and other Native people on their price for furs and other trade items.[9]

At the close of the Second World War, the federal government decided that the North could be exploited for its land and its raw materials. The fur trade had collapsed, and the Hudson Bay Company's unfair practices with the Innu had left them hungry, dependent, and in some cases in servitude.[10] The new players in the North would be the military, the mining companies, and those who would take the rivers themselves.

The Military and the Bombs

Militarism is a form of colonization which takes away from our lives. That future is without hope for us. But we will fight for our rights. I believe in non-violence and civil disobedience. I am ready to go to jail, to take blows or die for our cause, because I believe in the struggle for the freedom of my people. I don't want your sympathy, I want your support. Your strong and collective support against the oppression of your government. What we need is your resistance.

—Penote Ben Michel, January 31,1987[11]

In the early morning at Nitassinan, the mist moves through the forest like an ancestor. The hunter walks carefully, yet still silences the animals. The animals watch as the hunter walks, acutely aware of each movement. The rustling of leaves and the sharp crack of a branch resonate against the quiet as the hunter walks. Something catches his eye, and he stoops to one knee to inspect a hoof print, the trail of a caribou.

As if from nowhere, the silence is shattered with an explosion of sound. A jet fighter screams 75 meters overhead, and the hunter presses his hands to his ears and throws himself to the ground. His head pounds, and he screams with pain. In a few seconds, the jet fighter is gone, but all the hunter can do is hear is his own heart beating and smell his own fear.

Monica Nui, Innu elder, tells a similar story.

> We were camping on the Kenamu River...we were overflown several times. What is the most scary is that the jets come in with no warning. They are very low, just above the trees, and the noise bangs inside your head for a long time after. In fact, you can see the treetops bending when they go over. If they pass over the tents, the tent canvas starts to shake, also. A little girl about five years old was so scared that she fainted. She had been playing near the lake, and she almost fell in. When this happened, they radioed another camp, and the other camp had been overflown as well. They had been making a fire outside the tents, and the coals from the fire had been scattered all over the ground. After the three jets went over, I could hear the ringing inside my head for at least a half hour.[12]

The sound of low-level flights overhead is the specter that returns day in and day out to the Innu, to the caribou, and to Nitassinan. Many of those flights are between 75 and 100 meters above ground, with some in Labrador as low as 30 meters. Their purpose is to penetrate unnoticed into enemy territory by passing below radar screens. Who is the enemy in the forest? That is what the Innu ask. Why use offensive rather than defensive weapons?

In 1941, the Canadian military claimed Goose Bay, in the heart of Nitassinan, as its own. Determined to have an outlying station linking North America and Europe during the Second World War, the Goose Bay base was established as the closest link to the old country from the continent. In 1952, the

U.S. Air Force signed a 20-year lease to use the base as a refueling station for interceptor squadrons. Before that lease expired, the United States generously lent these installations to the British Royal Air Force and its Vulcan Bombers. In the mid-1970s, European resistance to low-level flight training over densely populated areas was increasing. The physical and psychological impact of the flights had not gone unnoticed by others. West Germany and the other allies decided that it was better to fly somewhere other than their own backyards. They began to eye the vast territories of Nitassinan.

In 1980, NATO's military committee had sponsored a feasibility study on the construction of a fighter-plane training center in Goose Bay. Not to be outdone, then-Canadian Minister of Defense John Crosby announced in 1985 that the government would spend $93 million to modernize the existing base and encouraged new countries to join in the war games in the sky. Canadian government brochures and videos described the test area as "wilderness interior free of human habitation." Six countries—Belgium, Great Britain, West Germany, Netherlands, the United States, and Canada—joined in the flights over Nitassinan more intensely than ever.

By the mid-1980s, more than 4,000 "training flights" were being carried out over the 100,000 square-kilometer area. Between April and November 1989, there were 8,000 low-level flights: between 30 and 50 flights per day during the training season. But the worst was yet to come.

NATO's proposal would have increased the number of flights from 8,000 to 100,000 a year. And so it was that the Canadian government began a bidding war against Turkey for a NATO base on Nitassinan, in a long and protracted process.

The Innu believe that NATO's proposal would make their territory uninhabitable. There are some simple mechanics in their argument. The noise produced by a military aircraft flying at 30 to 75 meters is generally exactly at or above the human pain threshold of 110 decibels. The pounding of a jackhammer, for example, produces about 100 decibels of noise. Sonic booms created by military aircraft are in a different league. The sonic boom produces a constant shock wave, traveling along the ground like the wake of a boat over water. The power of the shock wave at close range can lift the water off the lake and tip a canoe and can drive animals insane: foxes have been known to eat their kits, geese to drop their eggs midflight, as a consequence of the sonic boom.[13]

Canadian journalist Robert Jobst describes the science: "The surface area affected by this shock wave is roughly one mile wide for every 1,000 feet of altitude between the aircraft and the ground. Therefore, a jet flying supersonically at 20,000 feet would produce a sonic boom 20 miles wide beneath it. Sonic booms are measured in pounds per square foot. The limit of human tolerance is less than two pounds per square foot. U.S. military aircraft produce sonic booms that average four to five pounds per square foot."[14]

The Innu had observed that caribou migration and social patterns were disturbed by the flights, that migratory birds seemed confused, and that the reproduction rates of the animals were low. But in 1990, the Canadian government concluded the opposite: that the construction of the NATO test base would not cause significant harm to the environment. The Innu testimony of massive disturbance and damage was dismissed as "unscientific," even though the Department of National Defense (DND) had already been forced to compensate people for the damage the flights had caused. The DND had paid over $145,000 to property owners, including $45,000 to a New Brunswick farmer whose foxes ate their newborn kits and whose pregnant foxes aborted their fetuses, as a result of similar flights. The Innu experience, the Innu observations, and the Innu pain, however, still have not been seriously acknowledged by the Canadian government.

Daniel Ashini wonders why Canadians don't see the "inherent bias of a process where the federal government is establishing the terms for a review of its own program. It's like asking McDonald's to conduct a study on whether or not it makes good hamburgers. Of course they are going to say they make the best hamburgers in the world."[15]

Next, the Canadian Federal Ministry of Transport established standards by which to judge the impact of low-level flights, sonic booms, and other forms of "sonorous aggression" on a given community. By their rather complicated mathematical calculations, the "noise exposure level" of a single flight of an F-4 jet was found to be higher than that allowed in Canadian suburbia, hotels, or stadiums. The Ministry's study found that exposing a community to such sonorous stress would provoke "energetic and sustained complaints by individuals. In addition, organized action and a law suit could also be expected."[16] Yet the flights over Nitassinan continued.

Shutting Down the Runway

In 1987, Rose Gregoire, Innu mother of four, her sister, Elizabeth Penashue, and friend Francesca Snow were among some of the first Innu to protest on the runway. The daring resolve of this small "mother-led band of peace warriors" as *Toronto Now* magazine called them, were truly a formidable force. Said Snow, "We are not afraid of anything, even if I get shot. We struggle all the way, no matter what happens."[17]

There is an image I cannot get out of my mind. It is of an 80-year-old couple shutting down the runway. They stand there as a 500-ton jet careens toward them and takes off above their heads. That image symbolizes the intensity of the commitment of the Innu and the story of their resistance to the military.

In 1988, Father Jim Roche walked onto the bombing range on the base as part of a protest. "On that bombing range," he said. "I really felt for the first time what it meant to the Innu. There were all these bomb shells and craters, and it hit me that what was really happening here was preparation for war." Roche spent five months in jail for his protests with 40 other Innu, a longer sentence than most, because he refused to sign a document stating he would not return to the runway. He told the judge, "We do not fear prison. There is no shame in being imprisoned for the pursuit of justice and the struggle for what we believe in."[18]

In 1989, Canadian authorities charged the Innu with trespassing on military land, and the Innu were hauled in front of a Newfoundland provincial court. On its face, the case was significantly biased against the Innu. The Canadian judicial system is foreign to the Innu's value system and way of life: English common law and Canadian law are not Innu laws. Plus, the court had an inherent interest in confirming the land title on which its jurisdiction is based. And the entire proceedings took place absent any simultaneous translation into Innuaimun. Finally, consider that to the Innu, the laws themselves make little sense.

But Judge James Ig(lioliorte agreed with the Innu claim that what the government called "military lands" were their own. The judgment acknowledged that the Innu had never signed a treaty or land-claims agreement, and the Canadian constitution states that aboriginal peoples cannot be deprived of their land except through just, equitable negotiations. According to Igliolorte's written decision,

> We are not dealing with land which has been the subject of divestiture through treaties...provincial and federal statutes do not include as third parties or signatories any Innu people.... All of the legal reasonings are based on the premise that somehow the Crown acquired magically by its own declaration of title to the fee a consequent fiduciary obligation to the original people. It is time this premise based on 17th-century reasoning be questioned in the light of 21st-century reality.

In the end, the court ruled that the Innu could not be charged with trespassing on their own lands.[19]

After almost a decade of repeated Innu occupations of the runway, in May 1995, the Canadian Environmental Review Panel released the conclusions of its eight-year, $16-million study: *that the evidence of low-level flights' negative im-*

pacts on the environment and on the Innu was still inconclusive. The panel recommended that the number of flights be doubled, a second bombing range be allowed, and the proposed avoidance program to avert flights over Innu and animals be essentially scrapped because there were too many sensitive areas to be practical.

And so the Innu stay on the runway, in a nonviolent campaign that may be the most persistent and longest-running in Canada's history. Entire communities have occupied the runways and fill the jails, as harsher and harsher sentences mount and the Innu enter their second decade of resistance to militarization.

"A lot of elders were taught that you never stand up against white people, you never challenge them," says Roche. "Since the protests started, that's been changing. They learned that they can fight back." [20]

The Liberation from Legal Colonialism

After the fear is quelled from your first arrest, the liberation of your mind from the legal colonialism begins. Facing down the white man's laws was indeed a process of unlearning oppression for the Innu.

It started with hunting. In the early 1970s, the Canadian government decided that the caribou of the Mealy Mountains needed a rest from hunting, and consequently the government banned Innu hunting in their traditional area for, they said, a few years. While American pilots stationed at the base had been known to make low passes over caribou to decapitate them for their antlers, it was deemed that the Innu shouldn't hunt from the same herd.[21] As the few years dragged on to 15, it became apparent to the Innu that Canada's laws didn't apply to all.

Finally, after their own ceremonies, prayers, and agreements with those they refer to as the Animal Masters, the Innu felt the herd had recovered enough in 1987 to allow for a limited hunt. And the meat-eaters were hungry for their relatives. Father Jim Roche tells what happened next. "I heard the older men talk about the pain of being treated as foreigners in their own land. They felt they had already lost so much...they were frustrated that they had to sneak around when they hunted caribou as though they were doing something wrong."[22]

And so they walked into the bush and took their animals. In April 1987, the Innu were charged with hunting violations. Ben Michel stood before the judge in Goose Bay to defend what the Innu were doing. "We are a hunting people," he declared. "It is this form of living which lies at the core of our identity as a people, which gives expressiveness to our language, which animates our social relationships, and which for thousands of years breathed life into our people. Without exception those who have categorized our hunting existence as primitive are those who have not tried to live it."[23]

Six years later, the Innu of another remote village, Davis Inlet, also liberated themselves from the white man's law, in a different way. The Canadian government historically had a provincial court in Davis Inlet. Many of the trials the court conducted were on charges that were 18 months to two years old. Few Innu could speak English, and the translator brought in to address this spoke a different dialect. Then there was the transportation challenge. On each of the four days the court was in session, the court party would fly into town, arriving in the morning, and spend the night in Goose Bay, to the south. The community found this schedule offensive, especially since prior courts took up residence in the town. Finally, virtually every case involved substance abuse, a fact that Chief Katie Rich and others considered to be symptomatic of deeper problems that the community ought to address over the long term, outside the Canadian court system.

In December of 1993, the Davis Inlet Mushuau Innu finally took matters into their own hands. They shipped out the judge and began to recover themselves, eventually reconciling with the court.

On the afternoon of December 13, 1993, Chief Rich, accompanied by a group of women, delivered a note to Newfoundland provincial court judge Robert Hyslop, who was presiding over Innu-related cases on Innu land in Davis Inlet. It read,

> This letter is to inform you that you are to cease and desist immediately the operation of the court in the community of Davis Inlet and to withdraw yourselves immediately from this community. You are further advised that no future holding of the court in our courtroom will be permitted until further notice by order of the councilors and community members.

After some back and forth discussions, the court left town.

Dams

> Soon there will be no great and beautiful wild rivers left in Quebec, the entire territory will be crisscrossed with a network of powerlines, which like spiderwebs will spoil the beauty of our mountains and valleys.

—Innu traditionalist

They called the great falls *Patshetshunau*—"steam rising." The white people called it Churchill Falls, named after a British guy who had never even seen them. Strange how that all works.

Larger than Niagara Falls, *Patshetshunau* seemed infinite. In 1895, the geologist A. P. Low visited the falls and wrote: "The noise of the falls has a stunning effect and although deadened because of its enclosed situation can be heard for more than ten miles away as a deep booming sound. The cloud of mist is also visible from any eminence within a radius of twenty miles."[24]

The Great Falls *Patshetshunau* are now silent. The long chute is dry, a result of the ambition of the Newfoundland and Labrador governments and the greed of Hydro-Quebec. In the 1960s, then-Premier of Newfoundland Joey Smallwood began a rather bizarre and co-dependent relationship with the province's wealthier cousin, Quebec, in an attempt to exploit the natural resources of Newfoundland (i.e., Nitassinan). First, he sold the idea of a hydro-electric power plant at Churchill Falls to a group of investors. His next obstacle was figuring out how to sell and distribute that hydro-electric power.

In what journalist R. John Hayes describes as a desperate move, "Smallwood signed over the right to sell most of the power to Hydro-Quebec at a fixed rate for forty years at a price of less than three-tenths of one cent per KWH. Hydro-Quebec has the option to renew the contract for another 25 years at only two-tenths of a cent per KWH. Newfoundland locked themselves in until the year 2044."[25]

Hydro-Quebec made a good chunk of change on the deal. The company has been able to sell the power at nine times its purchasing price. Not a bad deal. Newfoundland's revenues are estimated to be $70 to $80 million per year. Hydro-Quebec's revenues were approximately $750 million in 1976 from the same dams. Hydro-Quebec turned around and invested that income into new dams from James Bay to any available river in its presumed domain.

What it left in Nitassinan was ecological disaster. Joey Smallwood will always be remembered for this. The so-called Churchill River is the largest river in the area, draining 29,900 square miles and providing an inland route for the Innu. Dammed before its monumental 300-foot plunge, the river now squeezes through several shafts and tunnels, leaving a mere trickle for the lakes and rivers below. The Smallwood Reservoir floods 5,698 square miles of central Nitassinan and is half the size of Lake Ontario. Boastful politicians in the 1970s lauded it as the third largest artificial body of water in the world.[26]

When man does the Creator's job, it usually doesn't turn out right. The black spruce forest that was drowned in the flooding died slowly. Natural processes of decay seemed to pull the heavy metals, particularly mercury, out of the soil. And in its dying breath the forest killed the water. By 1977, studies determined that mercury levels in the Smallwood Reservoir were elevated. Thirty-seven percent of the Innu surveyed had elevated mercury levels.[27] The provincial government issued a bulletin advising people to limit their fish consumption to one fish per week. Since then, there have been no new studies done, almost as if the provincial government hoped that in not documenting mercury problems in the reservoir, the problems would disappear.

The Innu hunting, harvesting, and burial grounds flooded by the Smallwood Reservoir were of little interest to the electric company. River habitats of the animals were destroyed, and dams set in motion a process that threatens much of the commercial salmon fishery of the region. Hydro-Quebec kept on making dams in Nitassinan, on the Manicouagan, Outardes, Betsiamites, and Magpie Rivers. The utility sold the power to some industries that needed cheap power, then it turned to James Bay, in Cree country.

James Bay Dams

The settler's eyes see differently than the Native's. So it was that when Quebec Premier Bourassa looked to the north of Quebec, he saw a vast hydroelectric plant in the bud; for what he called a "tremendous waste" of resources crashed through gorges, and rivers meandered through vast forests, and finally made their way to the sea. The James Bay I complex was a result: the idea being to put 11,500 square kilometers of land behind the dams underwater and produce 12,000 megawatts of electricity. Ultimately, the initial project, concentrated along the Eastmain and Rupert Rivers, ruined the ecological balance of some 176,000 square kilometers of land, an area about two-thirds the size of the former West Germany.

The Cree, Inuit, and Innu of the northern villages whose land and lifeways were at stake did not hear about the project until the planning was well underway. The Native community, led largely by the Crees of James Bay, mounted an aggressive campaign to head off the project. After six months of testimony concerning the cultural and environmental impact of the project, in March of 1975, James Bay I was halted by a court injunction. A week later, the Quebec Court of Appeals overturned the lower court ruling, largely on the premise that too much money had already been spent on the project to abort it. The "balance of convenience," according to Hydro-Quebec and the government, rested in favor of continued development. That argument has been the bane of many northern development projects. The resulting "James Bay and Northern Quebec

Agreement," shoved down the throats of the Cree, Inuit, and Innu of northern Quebec, alleged to give the Cree and other Native people more power to determine the future of the North. That agreement has been continuously contested over the past two decades.

Within a decade of the completion of the La Grande Complex, signs of environmental disaster had become obvious. Massive flooding had once again leached methyl mercury from the soil, changing an inorganic mercury compound in the water into organic mercury. The result was mercury contamination in the reservoirs, with levels six or more times what was considered "safe." The most significant mercury contamination levels in North America—as pronounced as those found in Minimata, Japan, where thousands of people suffered severe neurological diseases—are now present in the waters of the La Grande Complex. To avoid its deadly impact, the Cree of the downstream villages had their hair tested for the presence of mercury and were advised not to eat fish from the dam complex.

Then there was the problem of the caribou and the water. The flow of water in the river has been radically altered from its natural path. At times, the flow may be increased or decreased by about 20 times the normal rate, according to the electrical demand at the end of the powerline. This situation carries obvious implications for fish, beaver, and other water-based creatures downstream. The Cree remember the picture of beavers, which in response to the dams built houses many stories high, and of dead animals floating in the toxic waters. In 1984 came the most deadly dam-release of water, precisely during the annual migration of the George's River caribou herd across the Canapiascau Reservoir. As a direct result, over 10,000 caribou drowned. Hydro-Quebec officials refused to accept responsibility, callously calling the deaths "mainly an act of God."[28]

So it was that when Hydro-Quebec came forward with a set of proposals known as James Bay II in the late 1980s, they were met with resistance. Their proposed new projects would have destroyed four major river systems: the Great Whale, Lower Broadback, Nottaway, and Rupert, and would have also flooded Lake Bienville. Further, James Bay II would involve the total deforestation of some 922,040 square kilometers of land, an area the size of Maine, Vermont, and New York State combined. That $60-billion mega-project, according to National Audubon Society's Jan Beyea, "would make James Bay and some of Hudson's Bay uninhabitable for much of the wildlife now dependent on it." According to the society, if James Bay II were constructed, "in fifty years, [this entire] ecosystem will be lost."[29]

The Cree and Innu and their Native and environmental allies began an organizing campaign, this time not only in Quebec, but in the Northeast, thus breaking the political isolation on which environmentally racist proposals are so often based. The James Bay project would only go through if Vermont, New Hampshire, Maine, and New York bought the power. Hydro-Quebec required American contracts and money to mount the project in the first place, and so the northeastern United States was where the organizing needed to take place. The Cree and their allies—such as the Vermont Natural Resources Coalition, the newly formed No Thank You Hydro-Quebec, the Conservation Law Foundation, the Natural Resources Defense Council, the Student Environmental Action Committee, and many Native and human rights organizations—put the James Bay projects on the public agenda.

Consumer groups pointed out that conservation practices could save 30 percent of presently used electricity, not to mention millions of dollars, for the taxpayers and ecosystems. The issue is not whether or not to use nuclear, coal, or hydro, the issue is conservation. Jim Huggins, a longtime organizer for No Thank You Hydro-Quebec, took a broader stance. "We must live within our means. We don't believe that we, as Vermonters, should be partaking in human rights abuses, even if they happen outside our borders," he said.[30] *The New York Times* referred to the resistance as a "rag-tag band of organizers." Those organizers, however, were successful. A multitude of student organizers successfully secured the divestment of their universities' stocks and bonds in Hydro-Quebec. Consumer groups, environmentalists, human rights organizations, and the Native community challenged state public utilities commissions to justify the power purchases in light of economic, human rights, and environmental impacts. And organizers broke the isolation by going to the press, to stockholders meetings, and to the American public about the project. After battling a six-year resistance campaign, Hydro-Quebec backed down. In November of 1994, James Bay II proposals were put on ice.

The utility, however, had a backup plan. In 1993, at the height of James Bay resistance, the utility announced that in addition to the 19 dams it had already built in Nitassinan, it would build another dam on the Sainte Marguerite River. That dam, with a price tag of $2 billion, would divert the Moisie River's two tributaries, the Pekans and the Carheil, and cut the river's flow by 40 percent at the confluence of the three rivers.

At the same time, Hydro-Quebec submitted new proposals to expand the Churchill Dam project again, in a combination of projects that environmentalists now refer to sarcastically as the Two Gorges Dam project. The new project is being called the second-largest construction project in the world, after the Three Gorges project in China.

The $12-billion, 3,100-megawatt complex would consist of dams at Muskrat and Gull Island Falls, an underwater transmission cable across the Strait of Belle Island to Newfoundland, and another high-voltage transmission line, carrying 2,000 megawatts of power, to the United States. Proponents once again lauded the project as a "clean" source of hydro-electric power for the northeastern United States.[31]

"Even though oil prices had dropped, there was the expectation that oil and gas were going to be scarce and expensive," says energy economist Ian Goodman. "The utilities in the northeast U.S. were reluctant to build power plants. 'We'll sell you power, it'll be easy, and it'll be cheaper than building your own power plants,' that's what Hydro-Quebec said."[32]

A lot of utilities were interested. Many of the nuclear power plants in the region had come under fire, and some had been canceled.[33] In Vermont, "the utilities managed to get most of their contracts approved, as a fast forward." Not surprisingly, the contracts were by and large uneconomical. Vermont is "paying on the order of 8 cents a kilowatt hour, and the price on the wholesale market is 3 cents a KWH," Goodman explains.[34] Other states canceled their contract negotiations after it became clear that Hydro-Quebec's offer wasn't a good deal. Vermont's Central Vermont Public Service and Green Mountain Power ended up holding the bag.

Goodman doesn't think any of Hydro-Quebec's new dams can provide electricity cheaply either, whether from the Nitassinan dams or the newly revived James Bay III project at Great Whale. But Hydro-Quebec is intent upon selling to the U.S. market and is hoping to have its entire scheme of new dams and power plants underwritten by American utilities.[35]

Since the Canadian fisheries collapsed, there is a driving political need for development in the region, says Goodman. The loss of fish stocks in Newfoundland and Labrador have left tens of thousands unemployed. Big dam projects bring jobs, and, as Goodman points out, by the time everyone figures out that the jobs don't last, the politicians who approved the projects are gone. "The benefits are up-front, the costs are long-term," says Goodman.[36]

In the year 2040, the colossal nuclear plants of the northeastern United States—Rowe, Seabrook, Indian Point, and Millestone—will be past their projected "lifespans." They will be either on the way to or in the process of "decommissioning." Hydro-Quebec will be ready. By that year, if they are able, Hydro-Quebec hopes to have dammed all the rivers in Quebec worth damming and most of those in Newfoundland and Labrador as well, positioning itself to become one of the largest energy brokers on the continent and possibly the world.[37] The utility's vision of the future hinges on an export market modeled after the rest of the provinces' plans for economic development—pillage natural resources, and sell them to the South, to the settlers.

In late 1996, Hydro-Quebec applied to the Federal Energy Regulatory Commission to secure unregulated exports to the United States. By mid-1997, the utility had signed five new contracts with U.S. utilities—Long Island Lighting Company, Montaup Electric Company, Boston Edison, United Illumination Company, and Central Maine Power Company—and had purchased controlling interests in Noverco, a natural gas interest with assets in Quebec and New England.

Given the current interest in environmentally safe products, Hydro-Quebec is marketing its higher-priced product as "green power." But hopefully, the "people that are interested in buying green power are not going to be interested in buying power with a high environmental and human rights price," such as Hydro-Quebec's, says Goodman. The reality is that the formula does not work and that, on a worldwide scale, people have found that mega-development projects usually entail various sorts of political injustices. "The politicians are slow in realizing the world is changing. Even in Quebec, there is beginning to be a realization that you're not going to get rich building dams," Goodman says.[38]

The Innu of the North Shore came out in strong opposition to these proposals in early 1998. Spokesman Guy Bellefleur denounced the proposals as "anti-democratic," since most were created during a state of emergency in response to the ice storm of the Winter of 1997–98.

> There exist already 15,000 megawatts of hydroelectric power from installations in Innu territory, and the reservoirs total approximately 4,500 square kilometers (excluding the 6,700 square kilometers in Smallwood). We have already paid too much. We were never consulted or even informed [when] the dam at Churchill Falls began, and we were never compensated for the damage from the flooding. Our people lost not only our lands and possessions when Mishikama was flooded to create the Smallwood Reservoir, but also a part of our history and identity as Innu. We will accept no more developments imposed from the outside. All discussions on the subject of development must include the Innu.[39]

In the decade ahead, this public policy debate and battle over Innu rivers will occur in the land, courts, and utilities of New England.

Voisey's Bay

There's only one road that transects Labrador, and it cuts it in half. That 500-kilometer, unpaved road links "developments" of the white people's iron ore mines in western Labrador to the Churchill River hydro project and the Goose Bay military base. Driving it is sort of a road trip of ecologically destructive projects. Beyond the tree line is where there is life: caribou, wolf, bear, and Innu. This is where the pristine rivers run from the mountains to the sea and are filled with salmon and char that live and die relatively free of the poisons of the rest of the world. All of this life is threatened now, not only from the air, but in the land and water.

Emish is what the Innu call the place, after the Emish River, "the land inside." "Voisey" is what the white people call the land, after an English trader by that name who, like other white men before him whose names mark maps of Nitassinan and other Native territory, only passed through the area.

In November of 1994, Diamond Fields Resources announced their "discovery" in Emish of the richest nickel ore body in the world. Six months later, when the snow had subsided, hundreds of mining companies descended upon the land. More than 50 companies remain today, all with the approval of the government of Newfoundland and without the approval of the Innu.

The newly created Voisey's Bay Nickel Company has moved to the top of the pile, a company now owned by Sudbury, Ontario–based nickel giant INCO. They began exploring the area in early 1995, proposing to build roads, airstrips, and loading docks without any environmental assessment. Innu and Inuit went to the courts to stop what the company called "advanced exploration infrastructure," which could have occurred without an environmental assessment. Their claims initially rejected by the courts, the Innu blockaded the site in the Summer of 1997, with some 300 protesters stopping the company's work. The blockade continued until the court finally ruled in favor of the Innu and ordered a stop to further construction, pending the completion of an environmental review.

Voisey's Bay Nickel Company has big plans. They propose to extract an estimated 150 million tons of nickel, cobalt, and copper ore from a massive deposit located in what is now a fertile valley. According to the Friends of Nitassinan, a Vermont-based support group, approximately 16 million tons of acid-generating waste rock will be discharged into presently pristine marine environments, and 55 million tons of waste rock will be spread over the land. The company, however, promises to "rehabilitate the site post-mining" to "approach predevelopment conditions." That is impossible. Studies by the Department of Natural Resources done in Wisconsin, for instance, indicate that there has never been a sulfuric ore mine in the history of ore mining that has been reclaimed. Rather, the ore will remain toxic for thousands of years. Mine wastes, or "tailings ponds," are pretty much an "ecological time bomb," the Innu contend, and the project remains a threat to the entire region's land and marine environment.

INCO is gambling on Voisey's Bay. With operations in 23 countries, INCO is the largest nickel producer in the world and sees Voisey's Bay as the cornerstone of its global expansion strategy. Some suggest it is a failed proposition from the start. In 1997, INCO, which operates the huge Sudbury, Ontario, complex, cut about 500 jobs from its Sudbury and Thompson plants, and saw a huge drop in profits. The international nickel market is glutted in production, equated with falling prices, and the remotely situated Voisey's Bay project will likely be a costly addition to an already precarious investment portfolio.[40]

Ironically, Canada uses its big dam projects and hydro-electric power plants as proof of its commitment to stemming global warming. Yet it skirts the actual price of this resource-intensive development policy, particularly in Nitassinan. First, consider that because of the dam's resultant flooding, Newfoundland will allow clearcutting of trees in the water's path, then additional pulp and paper mill capacity will be added to accommodate the new boom in logging. Then consider that INCO's Sudbury smelter is presently the single largest source of acid rain–causing emissions in the western world. The Voisey's Bay smelter, powered by the dams, will exceed the Sudbury smelter and will be located directly over the famed Grand Banks, once considered one of the world's richest fisheries. The Innu and their allies pledge to continue their resistance against the huge projects.

Davis Inlet: The Future for the Environmental Refugees

There is a term that has become increasingly common in this era: "environmentally displaced peoples." These are the refugees of industrialism's destruction. According to Julia Panourgia Clones, these displacements are

> the by-product of urban programs or of the construction of dams, highways, industrial estates, ports, agribusiness ventures, and so forth. It starts by taking away land, which is the main asset for family livelihood in poor countries, and, unless properly addressed by the states, it is certain to degenerate into processes of massive impoverishment and

social disorganization.... In China, more than 10 million people were involuntarily resettled over a period of 30 years as a result of dam construction alone. In India, the aggregate numbers are of comparable magnitude, about 15.5 million people over the last four decades including displacement from reservoirs, urban sites, thermal plants, and mines.[41]

It happened two years in a row, eerie as this may be, on the same night. Well past midnight in late January 1992, with the outside temperature around minus-35 degrees Celsius, four Innu teenagers intoxicated on solvents and gasoline fumes staggered and screamed their way down the littered dirt road of their village. Exactly one year later, the town policeman found six Innu teenagers sniffing gasoline in an unheated shed, shrieking that they wanted to die. The videotape of their torment was distributed nationally in Canada and brought subsequent national attention and media. It has only changed some things in Davis Inlet.[42]

The Innu call Davis Inlet *Utshimassit*, the place of the boss, the white man. It is aptly named. In 1967, the Canadian government forcibly relocated the Innu to this rocky island from their original lands inland. The Innu say that the provincial government and the Catholic priests moved them there so they would stop following the caribou and would live as the boss man would like them to. The reality is that the Innu of Davis Inlet are political and environmental refugees, forced out of their village by one bad development project after another. Their lives have been, by most measures, a living hell ever since. Before they moved to Davis Inlet, the Innu said that the "saltwater was no good." Now 84-year-old James Pasteen will simply say, "Davis is an evil place, eating away at the young people." James prefers the caribou and the bush way of life to village life. According to journalist Gavin Scott, "self-destruction is virtually a civic preoccupation in Davis Inlet." When Bill Partridge, a former police officer from Halifax, Nova Scotia, arrived in Davis Inlet in the early 1990s, he found himself involved in four suicide interventions a month. "Every adult in the community has contemplated suicide," he says, "Every second person has attempted it in one form or another." Partridge found that 95 percent of the adult population suffered from alcoholism and estimates that more than 10 percent of the children sniff gasoline.

It is not surprising. The Canadian government had forced the formerly self-sufficient Innu into a village, ice-locked from the mainland for most of the year, and then starved them, physically and emotionally, by disrupting their day-to-day cultural practices. A century ago, French sociologist Emile Durkheim documented how such forced, rapid transitions cause profound social disruption.

Records indicate that only a handful of the Innu at Davis Inlet have any kind of work. Many simply wait for their welfare checks in their cramped houses. Up to 20 people may live in a single, unpainted, clapboard dwelling. There is no running water or sewage system, and seldom is there garbage pickup, even though the Innu were promised acceptable housing, running water, and fishing boats.

After the story about the four Innu children found stoned out of their minds in minus-35 degree–weather broke in the Canadian press, planeloads of federal and provincial public servants, preachers, television crews, and private and public agency workers descended on the village. "No government likes to be affiliated with that kind of horror," explained Leslie Anderson, then-director of major projects for the Department of Indian Affairs. So they turned on the public faucet, doubling public funding for Davis Inlet, which shot up from a little over $4 million to a little over $8 million, translating into $16,730 for each Innu adult and child. For the six children and a dozen other youngsters addicted to solvents, $1.7 million was appropriated for drug treatment.[43]

The Innu of Davis Inlet want to go home, to a home that suits them well. In late 1996, two years after the children's tragedy, the government finally signed an agreement with the Innu allowing them to leave Davis Inlet. All 500 Innu were promised a traditional campsite on the mainland called Little Sango Pond, five miles away from Davis Inlet, but a different world. The relocation will cost the government $62 million, including the construction of schools, an airstrip, roads, housing, and other infrastructure.

Still, the Innu trust *Katipenima*, the Caribou Master, more than the Canadian government. The caribou can deliver more. That is clear after all these years. That is absolutely clear.

Ghost Dance
Two hundred seventy
Ghost Dancers
Died dreaming a world where the white man would drown
In a worldwide flood of their sins.

Where the earth,
Renewed
Would reclaim their

Cities and towns
Leaving only
The Ghost Dancers
Who lived by her laws.

History books tell us
The threat is gone.
The ghost dance
Died with the ancestors
Wovoka and his sacred dream
Destroyed.

Each time it rains
I go out to the sidewalk
Where tree roots have broken the concrete and listen to the water's
Whispering
"It is coming soon."

—Sara Little-Crow Russell (Anishinaabe)[44]

Bloodties

If the Innu constituted that 1 percent of the U.S. population that controls an estimated 50 percent of the country's wealth, they would certainly be left alone. Their lifestyle would be glamorized, the subject of tantalizing books, movies, and television series, their every move chronicled. Their land would be protected behind thick curtains of public policy, with tax write-offs for horse pastures.

If they were farmers, at least, close to that agrarian culture of temperate climates, they and other subarctic and Arctic peoples would at least be considered in public policy. Perhaps. However, they are neither. They are Innu, with a rich culture and history and a nuanced understanding of their ecosystem's land, water, and animals.

Out of sight, out of mind. The Innu are relentlessly jackhammered by those handmaidens of colonialism, neocolonialism and globalization. The military, mining, and energy capitalists always return. When they have every last river dammed, every last secret metal cached in Mother Earth carved out, every last bit of serenity shattered by a combustion engine, will they be happy? Can they contain themselves before they destroy the North altogether? *Pimaatisiiwin.* It is quite the time to reconcile the hunter and the peasant.

Gail Small. Photo courtesy of Native Action

There is no word in our language for mitigation. We cannot even understand the concept.

–Gail Small,
quoting Northern Cheyenne Elder[1]

N o r t h e r n
C h e y e n n e

A Fire in the Coal Fields

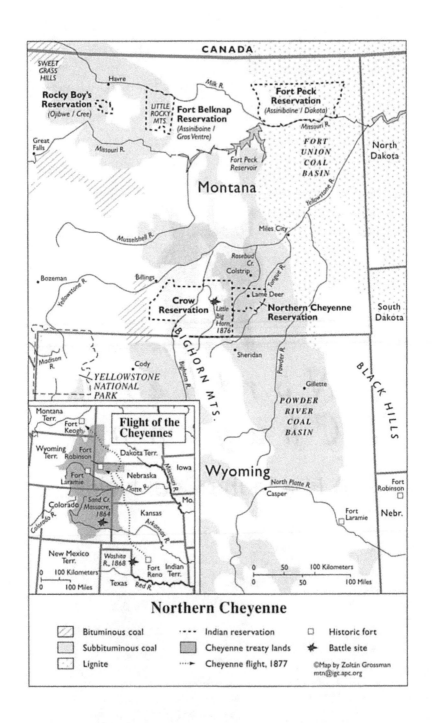

CANADA

SWEET GRASS HILLS

Rocky Boy's Reservation
(Ojibwe / Cree)

Havre

Milk R.

LITTLE ROCKY MTS

Fort Belknap Reservation
(Assiniboine / Gros Ventre)

Fort Peck Reservation
(Assiniboine / Dakota)

Missouri R.

Great Falls

Missouri R.

Fort Peck Reservoir

FORT UNION COAL BASIN

North Dakota

Montana

Musselshell R.

Miles City

Rosebud Cr.

Colstrip

Bozeman

Yellowstone R.

Billings

Lame Deer

Crow Reservation

Little Big Horn, 1876

Northern Cheyenne Reservation

Tongue R.

Yellowstone R.

South Dakota

BIGHORN MTS.

Sheridan

Powder R.

Madison R.

Cody

YELLOWSTONE NATIONAL PARK

Bighorn R.

BLACK HILLS

Gillette

POWDER RIVER COAL BASIN

Flight of the Cheyennes

Montana Terr.

Fort Keogh

Wyoming Terr.

Fort Robinson

Dakota Terr.

Iowa

Fort Laramie

Nebraska

Platte R.

Missouri R.

Mo.

Wyoming

North Platte R.

Casper

Fort Robinson

Colorado

Sand Cr. Massacre, 1864

Kansas

Colorado R.

Arkansas R.

Fort Laramie

Nebr.

New Mexico Terr.

Washita R., 1868

Fort Reno

Indian Terr.

0   100 Kilometers

0   100 Miles

Texas

Red R.

0   50   100 Kilometers

0   50   100 Miles

Northern Cheyenne

Bituminous coal	---- Indian reservation	☐ Historic fort
Subbituminous coal	Cheyenne treaty lands	✴ Battle site
Lignite	····▶ Cheyenne flight, 1877	

©Map by Zoltán Grossman
mtn@igc.apc.org

G ail Small is tall, lanky, and statuesque. She is quite a beautiful woman. She is also so direct and quick-tongued, she can make a federal official wince at the sight of her. She does have a big heart, and she has a hard line. For two decades I have watched her out of the corner of my eye, leading a small, reservation-based nonprofit on the Northern Cheyenne reservation in Montana, and I have admired her strength. Her path is different from mine, but she is always there, a keeper of the fire on Northern Cheyenne.

Gail is the kind of woman you'd want to watch your back at a meeting with dubious characters. She will watch it, and she'll guard your flank as well. And, when she is ready, she will send the opposition reeling. No matter how limited her weaponry, she is able to muster it. She is a trained sociologist, an attorney, and a 1997 appointee to the Federal Reserve Board's Consumer Advisory Panel.

Gail Small is one of ten children and the mother of four. She was a 1995 *Ms.* Woman of the Year and is a recognized leader in the Native environmental movement and the environmental justice movement, as well as in a host of organizing circles. Small's sophistication moves her deftly through courtrooms, the Federal Reserve Board, the picket line, and back to her herd of horses on the reservation. And, with a committed staff of six and many more volunteers, she directs Native Action, a grassroots organization that illustrates a unique, multifaceted strategy for reservation survival.

Native Action is one of the largest independent, reservation-based nonprofits in the country and has been around for over 15 years. That is an immense accomplishment in itself, given the tough nature of reservation politics and the whims of national foundations on which they rely. Gail and the staff of Native Action are survivors, in pretty much every sense of the word. They also highlight a Native politic directed from the grassroots, not from a posh national office in an urban area. That is their strength. Native Action does not *represent* grassroots Native America, it *is*.

"We understand our community's problems from the inside," Gail explains. "Our work directly reflects the history, experience, culture, and wishes of the unique people and community that it serves. We are concerned first and foremost with the continuation and well-being of our tribe and our community."[2] And, within that context, Gail Small, Native Action, and the Northern

Cheyenne find themselves in an ongoing set of battles to defend their community. They do so with dignity.

The Northern Cheyenne are in a tough spot, a hundred years or so of a tough spot. And the assaults on them and their land do not seem to relent. That is what makes your heart ache for them: that they must continue this struggle through each subsequent generation.

What is the value of your homeland? What is the value of land, traded and sold like so much dust and dirt? Companies, governments, and entrepreneurs sell grazing rights, mineral rights, and water rights and the land itself in a heartbeat.

These questions of value are unanswerable, unquantifiable. Yet all the same, the intensity of the Cheyenne relationship to the land is felt and realized each day, in each generation.

The Beautiful People

The Northern Cheyenne are *Tsetsestah,* the Beautiful People. (According to Northern Cheyenne historian Eric Spotted Elk, the word *Cheyenne* is likely an anglicized version of the Lakota word *Shyhela,* which is what the Lakota named them.) The most western of the Algonkin-speaking peoples, the *Tsetsestah* have been led by great prophets and leaders, including Maheo'o and Sweet Medicine. Sweet Medicine helped the Cheyenne organize themselves and develop a code by which to live, Spotted Elk continues. He gave them their first sacred items, the four sacred arrows. It was then that their hunting territory extended from the Platte River to what is now eastern Montana and the Cheyenne became a powerful force to reckon with. A southern group that had hunting grounds around the Arkansas River and another group known as the Sohtaio joined them.

Of all the prophetic teachings given by Sweet Medicine, his foretelling of the coming of the white man (*veho,* as one of Native Action's staff explains it to me, meaning "a spider in its cocoon") awakens the most fear among Northern Cheyennes today. As Spotted Elk explains,

> Before he died, he foretold of things to come. His people did not understand what he was telling them. He told them that they would meet the white people. They would have long hair on their faces. The white people would give them new things like sugar in return for things they want. They will try and teach the Cheyenne their way of living. The new way of life will take over. Sweet Medicine told them, when this

happens, you will become crazy, and will forget all that I am now teaching you.[3]

The Northern Cheyenne did not forget their teachings. They have tried to keep them and their land. The Cheyenne reservation of 500,000 acres stands on their homeland of ponderosa pine, deep valleys, beautiful rivers, and rolling plains, and is a testimony to their tenacity and sacrifice.

The Indian Wars: Land and Gold

We all fully realize that it is hard for any people to leave their homes and graves of their ancestors, but, unfortunately for you, gold has been discovered in your country, and a crowd of white people have gone there to live, and a great many of these people are the worst enemies of the Indians—men who do not care for their interests, and who would not stop at any crime to enrich themselves. These men are now in your country—in all parts of it—and there is no portion where you can live and maintain yourselves but what you will come in contact with them. The consequences of this state of things are that you are in constant danger of being imposed upon, and you have to resort to arms in self defense. Under the circumstances, there is, in the opinion of the commission, no part of the former country large enough where you can live in peace.

—John Steele, to the Southern Cheyennes[4]

In 1851, the Cheyenne, Arapaho, Sioux, Crow, and other tribes met at Fort Laramie with representatives of the United States to treaty on lands, passage, and mining. All present swore to maintain good faith and friendship in all their mutual intercourse and to make an effective and lasting peace. The treaty they negotiated at that time defined the territory of the Cheyenne nation as "commencing at the Red Butte and the place where the road leaves the north fork of the Platte River, thence along the main reign of the Rocky Mountains to the headwaters of the Arkansas River, thence down the Arkansas River to the crossing of the Santa Fe Road, thence in a northwestern direction to the place of the beginning."[5] The Cheyennes were divided into two main bands known to the white people as the Northern and the Southern Cheyenne.

Within a decade of this first Fort Laramie Treaty, the non-Indians, the *veho,* had driven a wedge into the heart of this territory, along the valley of the Platte River. Trains were followed by a chain of forts to protect the trains; then came the stagecoaches, pony express riders, and subsequently the telegraph riders. Settlers would follow and with them, the apologists from the federal government, explaining, once again, and wringing their hands about the bad white men. Then would come the cavalry. The first miners built mining shanties in the Rockies near present-day Colorado. The Pike's Peak gold run of 1858 brought thousands more miners. In 1859, they built a town called Denver City, and in blatant disregard for the treaty with the Cheyennes of less than a decade before, the United States created Colorado Territory from Cheyenne homelands. It was on these lands in November of 1864 that Colonel Chivington and the Colorado volunteers ruthlessly massacred over 100 Southern Cheyenne in what is known as the Sand Creek Massacre. There, some 105 women and children and 28 men perished while they stood under a white flag of peace. Chivington killed, in that massacre, virtually every one of the Southern Cheyenne chiefs who talked of peace with the white men. The Northern Cheyenne knew this story; it was their story as well.

Determined to defend their lands, the Cheyenne joined forces with others. The three allied nations (Cheyenne, Sioux, and Arapaho Tribes) came together for war and religious ceremonies. It was these three tribes that were celebrating summer ceremonies along the Bighorn River in southeastern Montana when George Armstrong Custer and his Seventh Calvary attacked in 1876. The three allied nations defeated Custer on that hot summer afternoon, and the story goes that when the American flag went down on the battlefield, the tribes picked it up and counted coup (victory) on the United States.

"I remember hearing the old people tell this story often when I was growing up in Lame Deer," Gail continues the story. "And it always ended with the moral that war does not bring peace." That seems always to be the case. The war stories of the Indian people's fight for their survival are retold on the reservations across the country as if they occurred yesterday. In a way, it is as if the Northern Cheyenne are caught in a time warp, in which they must keep fighting the Seventh Cavalry and its descendants for the rest of their history.

Dull Knife's Band

The story of Dull Knife's band is, in the end, the story itself.

It was a year after the great battle victory of the Northern Cheyennes and Lakota at the Little Bighorn. General Custer was long dead, as were many of the buffalo. Many of the bands had been pushed or forced on the reservations, and the military still held strongholds on the prairies. Both the Cheyenne and Lakotas were now on the verge of starvation. In the Spring of 1877, Crazy Horse shepherded his band of Oglala Lakotas into surrender at Fort Robinson, and several bands of Northern Cheyenne followed. The Cheyenne expected to live, as promised in the treaty of 1868, on a reservation with the Lakota. The Indian agents from Washington, D.C., however, ordered the Northern Cheyennes to march south to Oklahoma Indian territory and the camps of Southern Cheyennes already located there. There were 972 Cheyennes who started from Fort Robinson on the long trek to Fort Reno, in 1877. Some 937 of them reached Indian Territory. There they would find little: poor rations, starving and sick relations, and broken promises. Lieutenant Lawton wrote to Washington,

> They are not getting supplies enough to prevent starvation. Many of their women and children are sick from want of food. A few articles I saw given to them they would not use themselves, but said they would take them to their children who were crying for food. The beef I saw given them was of very poor quality, and would not have been considered merchantable for any use.[6]

The Northern Cheyenne chiefs, Dull Knife and Little Wolf, entreated Washington to let the Cheyenne return to their home in the mountains. But their pleas fell on deaf ears.

So it was that on the night of September 9, 1877, the Cheyenne stole out and headed northward across the sand hills: 297 men, women, and children, a third of them warriors. Ten thousand soldiers and 3,000 white vigilantes, who sought to chase them to their death, followed them.

After six weeks of running, the two chiefs split. Little Wolf was determined to return with his people to the Tongue River and live like Cheyennes again, and the next morning he led 53 men, 43 women, and 38 children north to their homeland. Those who were tired of running followed Dull Knife to turn themselves in at Fort Robinson, where they had been promised safekeeping. But within a few months after arriving at Fort Robinson, Washington ordered them back to the death camp in Oklahoma: Fort Reno. Dull Knife and his people again tried to flee. This time they did not make it. In the first hour of fighting, more than half the warriors died, and then the soldiers began overtaking scattered bands of women and children, killing many of them before they could surrender.

From the days when the Cheyennes numbered in the thousands, and they had more horses than any of the plains tribes, by the late 1800s, they were closer to obliteration than the buffalo.[7]

Some of Dull Knife's band would finally make it home 114 years later. On September 21, 1993, the National Park Service would issue a notice with regard to an "Inventory of Native American Human Remains." According to museum records the collection of remains was retrieved from a sinkhole in the vicinity of Fort Robinson, Nebraska, in 1879, about one year after Dull Knife's band was attacked while leaving the fort. Five skulls and one femur, along with "associated funerary objects" such as a leather knife sheath, a fragment of cloth, and some buttons, were deposited at Harvard University. According to the National Park Service, "The location and date of collection…and the evidence of violent death exhibited by the human remains support the identification of these human remains and associated funerary objects as being culturally affiliated with the Northern Cheyenne Tribe."[8] These ancestors have finally been allowed to go home to the Tongue River, home to their relatives.

Coming Home to the Coal Fields

In 1884, President Chester Arthur established a small, checkerboarded reservation along Rosebud Creek, which was expanded to the Tongue River and consolidated into one reservation in 1900. From there, Little Wolf's band of Cheyennes and their descendants slowly nursed their people back to health, all the while keeping those sacred bundles, their medicine items, and their traditional ways.

The Northern Cheyenne reservation lies in the middle of the Powder River coal basin, which extends across parts of southeastern Montana and northern Wyoming. The coal beds that lie within and around the reservation are some of the richest, highest quality, and most easily mined, from an economic standpoint. That coal has become the bane of their existence.

In the 1920s, a coal mine opened at the prophetically named town of Colstrip, just north of the reservation. That mine provided coal for the railroads and closed in the 1950s. Aside from this brief and relatively small-scale mine, the vast Powder River basin's coal reserves remained largely untouched and unnoticed until the late 1960s and early 1970s. Then, activities half a world away brought some of the largest transnational corporations in the world to the Northern Cheyenne reservation.

In June 1887, German, English, and American entrepreneurs formed a metals corporation called AMCO. Within a year, the British interest sold its shares to the Germans and the Americans. During World War I, the German interests in the company were seized, and the company was consolidated in American hands. In 1916, they acquired a controlling interest in various mining claims on Bartlett Mountain, and in the late 1920s AMCO joined interests with another big international mining company, Newmont Mining, to expand in Africa. After World War II, these two companies acquired mines in Namibia at a "bargain price after its appropriation from its defeated German owners."[9] The companies' subsequent expansion in Africa was extremely lucrative and allowed for the company to again expand—into coal—in the 1960s.

By 1974, AMCO, now renamed AMAX Coal Company, was the fourth-largest producer of coal in the United States.[10] Several factors combined with AMAX's expansion strategy to bring it to Northern Cheyenne lands: new legislation on air quality standards, the development of the national and international power grids, and the pressures of Third World nationalism. The passage of the 1973 Clean Air Act made the low-sulfur, high-quality coal of the West more attractive. Coal that could be mined on site and either moved by rail or burned in the rural area and then sent by high-voltage power line to consumers far away became increasingly plausible. Out of sight, out of mind.

While technology and domestic laws made the move to Northern Cheyenne (and with it a "domestic" energy supply) viable, Third World nationalism made it essential. As Richard Nafziger, an economist and former research director of Americans for Indian Opportunity, describes:

> Until recent years, British and American resource corporations, with the full backing of their home governments, roamed the world...plundering the raw materials of the people of Africa, Asia and America. Raw materials were extracted with little or no compensation to the people or governments in those areas. To secure control of these raw materials, a series of institutions were imposed on the people to foster dependency on the transnational corporations and their home governments. The raw materials became particularly important to the exploiting corporations and governments because of the high profits earned due to cheap labor and minimal royalties and taxes. In a sense, these resources fueled the industrial growth of the United States and Western Europe.[11]

This situation, history teaches us, was not without opposition. Third World nationalist governments challenged U.S. corporate dominance in their economies and were in many cases successful. Both the anti–Vietnam War movement domestically and the Cold War internationally made it difficult for the U.S. government to aggressively defend U.S. corporate interests abroad.

Finally, many resource corporations were interested in diversifying their resource base and expanding into coal and nuclear energy. All of these factors combined to bring the corporations to the reservation, to Native America, a place where, indeed, many of them had started initially.[12] So it was that the federal government began to eye the West and was pleased with what it found.

In 1971, the Department of Interior reported that the low-sulfur strippable reserves in the West were ten times more abundant than those in the eastern part of the nation.[13] By the mid-1960s, the federal government had determined that one-third of all strippable coal resources and one-half of the country's uranium was on reservation lands. That reality ultimately put Native communities, without infrastructure, attorneys, negotiators, environmental policy coordinators—without most of the strategic assets necessary to sit across the table from a multinational mining or oil company—face to face with the big companies and their own destinies.

The Northern Cheyenne and AMAX

"Before the mid-1960s, we were a small, isolated Indian tribe living on a small piece of land in one of the last and least settled regions of the continental U.S.—land for which our ancestors fought and died," Gail explains. "Our ancestors left that land to later generations in sacred trust. By the 1960s, we had just begun to recover somewhat from the awful destructive reservation policies that characterized the period from the late nineteenth century through the termination policy of the mid-twentieth century. Around 1950, our population halted a long downward spiral and began to recover." Then came the next wave.

The Bureau of Indian Affairs (BIA) is the trustee of the Indian estate. This relationship is a colonial holdover from when responsibility for Indian peoples, lands, territories, and political rights was moved from the Department of War to the Department of Interior. The BIA has always suffered from a little conflict of interest problem, in that it cozied up to the Interior Department's Bureau of Mines, Bureau of Reclamation, and other bureaus managing natural resources. The BIA has always been a stepchild of the Department of Interior and has stumbled through its existence with the mandate of taking care of something the U.S. government pretty much doesn't want—Indians.

Not surprisingly, the BIA found itself wooed by some big corporations into giving away the North Cheyenne reservation to AMAX. Actually, the BIA found it couldn't help itself and during a short period gave away much of Indian country to a few corporations, signing leases on tribes' behalf and pretty much squandering most of the assets of tribal peoples. "The average Indian lease covers 23,523 acres, or nearly 37 square miles and is 15 times larger than the average public land lease."[14] This is in spite of the fact that the BIA was only allowed to approve leases for tracts larger than 2,560 acres if more land was needed to construct thermal electric power plants or other facilities near the reservation. In fact, it might be argued that the BIA leasing policy facilitated the development of the mega-structures near the reservation.[15]

Nor were the terms equitable, as even the federal government itself acknowledges. According to the 1976 American Indian Policy Review Commission Report, "Measured by international standards, the leases negotiated on behalf of Indians are among the poorest agreements ever made."[16] According to the commission, the royalties were too low and fixed, ignoring the increase in the value of production. Hence, many leases were signed for between 15 and 35 cents a ton for coal, which had a market value between $4.67 (1968) and $18.75 (1975). Another problem was the fact that most lease provisions allowed for the continuation of mining "as long thereafter as minerals are produced in paying quantities."[17]

According to Ken Peres, a former economic planner for the Northern Cheyenne, "In the 1970s, the BIA and the energy corporations brought a money economy to the reservation lands. They also brought unemployment and poverty. The corporations wanted the coal under the people's land, so they signed leases with the BIA that gave them the right to mine. Of all the acreage on the reservation, 64 percent was leased to such corporations as Chevron, AMAX, Consolidated Coal, and ARCO in the early 1970s. Most of these leases were set up to give the Cheyenne Nation a 17.5 cent royalty on the coal removed."[18]

When AMAX ambled onto Northern Cheyenne in 1973, they had three billion tons of coal reserves; they bought purchasing permits for 1.9 billion more tons of coal on the Northern Cheyenne reservation. Although previously the company's strongest coal holdings were in the Midwest, that coal had a high sulfur content, and most of AMAX's mines had a short life span—around 11 years. The company saw the writing on the wall of Third World anti-colonialism against its properties abroad and expanded its investments into its coal subsidiary, investing some $212 million in a few short years and projecting that annual production of coal would reach 50 million tons by 1978.[19]

Coal strip-mining is about as destructive as it gets. There is a term used in the strip-mining business for everything that is on top of the coal, or, perhaps, whatever else it is you want to get from under the ground. That term is "overburden." That term, in itself, encapsulates the divergence between industrial development and Native society. Coal strip-mining, whether in Appalachia or on Northern Cheyenne and Crow territory, is destructive, but in the government's own research, the more arid the land, the more damage strip-mining wreaks. According to a 1973 National Academy of Sciences report that sent shivers up the backs of Native people in coal-rich reservations,

No issue associated with the current energy debate is more in the center of this conflict between demand and conservation than is the surface mining of coal. Our most abundant domestic fossil fuel is coal, and much of it occurs at depths where it can be mined by surface methods. Surface mining destroys the existing natural communities completely and dramatically. Indeed, restoration of a landscape disturbed by surface mining, in the sense of recreating the former conditions, is not possible.[20]

The problem was so dire, according to the academy, that in those areas receiving little rainfall (i.e., less than seven inches or so), the academy recommended that reclamation not even be attempted. They noted that

The coal lands of the western United States are quite different from others in the nation.... The ecological process of vegetative succession, or the orderly process of community change, is extremely slow under such arid conditions. Where natural revegetation of a disturbed site may develop in five to twenty years on a high rainfall eastern U.S. site, it may take decades or even centuries for natural vegetation to develop in a desert. The precarious nature of these dryland ecosystems should suggest caution by prudent men in any deliberate disturbance of an arid site.

The academy suggested that if such lands were mined, it was more feasible to deem the land "National Sacrifice Areas."[21] That same year, the government itself issued an urgent warning to arid, coal-rich areas of the West, recommending that reclamation not be attempted.

These conclusions, however, were not initially presented in the negotiations, not by the federal government, which had contributed to the study, nor by the companies. Nor would the impact of the coal development be exclusively on the environment. The mining would affect a nation of people, with some 3,000 residents on their pristine reservation. The influx of workers, machinery, and infrastructure all would impact the community socially, politically, and culturally. Sociologists refer to the ramifications of such development as the "boom town syndrome." It is not considered to be a healthy environment for the host population and is exacerbated when the local host community is a different color, race, and culture from the newcomers. These cultural, political, social, and environmental impacts all were concerns to the Northern Cheyenne. But while they fought coal development on their reservation, they found that their neighbors, the Crow, were also faced with coal development, and the areas adjoining the

Crow and Cheyenne reservation lands were, too. Hence, while the Northern Cheyenne could potentially fend off development on the reservation, they might still find themselves in the midst of coal exploitation and *coal culture*, just the same. Over the next decade, four large power plants, Colstrip 1-4, and the Rosebud power plant, were built in Colstrip, all adjacent to the reservation.

"We were in high school," Gail explains. "While the Tribal Council was looking at these leases and horrified at the agreements, we had to deal with it face to face. We were bussed off-reservation into the border town, and all of a sudden, there were all these new kids there—miners' kids. Those kids didn't like Indians at all. I never experienced so much racism before and never heard some of those words before. Never got called those names until that time." Gail pauses, the memory still painful. "They called us prairie niggers. That's what they called us. *Prairie niggers.* I had never heard anything like it."

"I feel like I have lived a lifetime fighting coal strip-mining, and I long for a better life for my tribe," says Gail. The fact is that Gail's entire adult life has been spent fighting coal strip-mining, all by virtue of the fact that she was born a Northern Cheyenne.

Since I was in high school, I have been involved in my tribe's fight to protect our reservation and the environment of southeastern Montana. It was during this time, the early 1970s, that the Cheyenne people learned the horrifying news that our federal trustee, the BIA, had leased over one-half of our reservation to the coal companies for strip-mining. Cheyenne coal was sold for 11 cents a ton, and no environmental safeguards were on the coal leases. The fight was on, and every resource our small tribe had was committed to this battle. I was with a group of young Cheyenne whom the tribe sent to the Navajo coal mines and then on to the coal fields of Wyoming. The enormity of our situation frightened and angered us. After college, I served on the tribal negotiating committee charged with voiding these coal leases. I was 21 years old, the youngest on my committee, and the only one with a college degree. We were fortunate to find a very capable young attorney with a passion for Indians and for justice because we were suing our federal trustee and the coal companies, both formidable opponents.

They were also facing utilities as far west as San Francisco, which through the regional power grids could contract for power from Cheyenne coal. The odds were not good.

What the Northern Cheyenne did stunned the federal government and the mining companies. It was in 1973 that Gail and the rest of the Northern Cheyenne sparked off a virtual revolt against the substandard mineral leases concluded by the federal government on their behalf. Their legal research revealed numerous violations—at least 36—of federal leasing procedures in the execution of mineral permits and leases. The Secretary of the Interior was forced to suspend the leases pending tribal and corporate negotiations with the Northern Cheyenne.[22] Congress voided the leases and paid compensation to the leaseholders, in the form of federal bidding rights for Montana coal in the future. (Some of these compensation agreements would come back to haunt the Northern Cheyenne years later in the form of what would later become Montco, an entity created by Billings coal mining speculator Mike Gustafson.)

According to Richard Nafziger,

> The Northern Cheyenne action put in motion a domino effect and set a precedent for other tribes to take on the big companies and the government. Their neighbors, the Crow Tribe, also found numerous irregularities in their leases. They invalidated a lease with Westmoreland Resources and then signed another one raising royalty rates from 17.5 cents to 40 cents per ton. On the basis of the violations, the Crows filed suit in the Ninth Circuit Court to cancel two other leases with Shell and AMAX. The court ruled in favor of the Tribe. Both companies returned to the bargaining table, but their tactics differed considerably. Shell tried to push through a new lease by offering a $200 to $400 gift to the Tribal members just before Crow Fair, an annual celebration that is one of the largest powwows in the nation. The Crow Tribe protested such divisive tactics. A tentative agreement was finally reached reducing Shell's leased acreage from 33,000 acres to 7680 acres and increasing the royalty rate to 12.5 cents per ton.[23]

Then the Northern Cheyenne went a step further. In 1978, the Cheyennes took advantage of that year's amendments to the Federal Clean Air Act, which allowed them to redesignate their entire reservation to class-one air quality. The amendments are referred to as Prevention of Significant Deterioration Regulations, or PSD and would apply to all government agencies (i.e., National Parks, refuges, etc.) The Northern Cheyenne were the first entity in the United States to redesignate, Gail explains. That redesignation required that the government fund and enforce an air quality program. However, the EPA never gave the Northern Cheyennes enough money to manage their air quality program. Funding to tribes represents less than 1 percent of the EPA's budget, even though Native people bear a disproportionate share of the burden of environmental devastation between Superfund sites, strip-mines, and abandoned uranium mines. "We were eventually forced to settle with the coal companies in a lawsuit over Colstrip," Gail explains, "just to get the equipment for our air quality monitoring program on the reservation." Some Native activists argue that tribal governments are considered sovereign by the federal government only if they want to put in a dump or open a casino, not if they want to protect their air quality. Regardless, by designating their air of high quality, they forced nearby Colstrip to modify its *modus operandi* and likely curtailed some development.

It took almost 15 years before the Cheyenne Tribe convinced Congress to void all the present coal leases and compensate speculators with other potential sites or money. "Fifteen years of anxiety and sacrifices by the people," Gail explains, and sighs. "It has been an immense struggle and sacrifice, and one which seems to go on and on. I wish I could tell you that we have a happy ending; unfortunately the battle is still waging because the Cheyenne coal is now even more valuable and sought after." And the Cheyenne face powerful adversaries. "The political and economic power of the coal and utility companies is so great," Small explains, that "they basically rule the state of Montana."

The Native community's battles with the big energy companies led to the creation of the Council of Energy Resource Tribes, CERT, in the early 1970s. CERT was a collective effort of several influential tribal chairmen (i.e., Floyd Correo [Laguna Pueblo] and Peter MacDonald [Navajo]) and Native leaders like LaDonna Harris (wife of former Oklahoma senator Fred Harris), funded by federal and corporate grants. CERT was intended to level the playing field for tribes who went face to face with the big corporations interested in their resources. CERT has played an historic and important role in the leasing process by securing better prices for Native resources, but since its inception has been mired in controversy and criticism. Many Native people question whether CERT was engaged in the process of brokering of Native resources, when in fact many tribes have actually opposed development. Subsequent federal funding to CERT and other national organizations in various roles in this energy-and-environment equation has brought criticism from Gail and others. "Rarely is there money in the federal bureaucracy for cultural and environmental needs of tribes," she points out. "I find it ironic, however, that federal monies always miraculously appear to study and develop coal strip mines, uranium mines, and nuclear waste dumps on reservations." Most of CERT's resources have been focused on fossil fuel and nuclear power development, despite the immense environmental impacts of these technologies and the vast potential for alternative energy development.

America is the single largest energy market in the world, and consumption is not, at present, dwindling. Some people call Montana the "boiler state of the West." Actually, it is one of a few. Coal exports from Montana are lower than those from Wyoming, but thanks to those big power grids Montana power can keep the lights on in Los Angeles and Seattle. The Colstrip 1-4 power plants, adjacent to the Crow and Northern Cheyenne reservations, are owned by various interests with Montana Power Company, including Pacific Corporation, Puget Sound Power and Light, Pacific Gas and Electric, Western Washington Power, and the Los Angeles Department of Water and Power. Although these utilities may perceive that they have externalized their environmental problems far away, it may be argued that they are culpable for the environmental problems in Montana and the struggles of the Northern Cheyenne.[24]

The national power grid looks like a big *veho* spider web, and it links the Northern Cheyenne to the rest of the country through high-voltage transmission lines. The western portion of the National Electric Reliability Council's electric grid system includes Montana and hooks it up to Washington State and the rest of the West, in a rather uneven interdependence in which Montana produces power and Portland receives it. That's perhaps one of the reasons why Native Action and the Northern Cheyenne find it frustrating that many presumed allies like environmentalists and foundations are so sporadic and fickle with their support. Everyone seems to benefit from the Northern Cheyenne, but few want to change their relationship with them. "Americans would rather fight for the rainforest than deal with their own backyards," Gail says. "Because of the teachings of one of my past elders, a tribal chairman, since deceased, I've learned to strategize based on the premise that we have few allies." That is a political tragedy in its own right, but it is also a pragmatic reality.

The broader environmental movement often misses the depth of the Native environmental struggle. Although it has been romanticized historically and is often considered in some New Age context, the ongoing relationship between Indigenous culture and the land is central to most Native environmental struggles. Gail concurs:

> Environment, culture, religion, and life are very much interrelated in the tribal way of life. Indeed they are often one and the same. Water, for example, is the lifeblood of the people. I recall taking a draft tribal water code for public input into the five villages on my reservation when I was a tribal sociologist. Protection of the water spirits was a

major concern throughout the reservation. And the water spirits varied depending on the water source being a river, lake, or spring. I reported back to the attorneys, and they laughed at my findings. However, it was no laughing matter a few years later, when an elderly Cheyenne man held off the drilling team of ARCO from crossing his water spring with his rifle. "Today is a good day to die," he said as he held his own hunting rifle before him.

I defended him in tribal court the next morning, and I cried with him when he told me how the water spirits sometimes came out and danced at his spring. Indeed, there is a profound spiritual dimension to our natural environment, and without it, the war would not be worth fighting.[25]

Native Action's strategies to fight the coal development and to ensure the survival of the Northern Cheyenne community have been diverse and sophisticated. As an attorney, Gail Small, on behalf of Native Action and a number of individual plaintiffs, has been through the courts and administrative processes, down virtually every avenue open to her community.

To some, though, because there is coal in the ground, it should be mined. Mike Gustafson, a minerals speculator from Billings who had been compensated in the 1973 congressional lease cancellation, had new plans that would affect the Northern Cheyenne and in particular those homelands on the Tongue River. His proposal came in the form of Montco, and he had over time become, according to Gail, one of the last great railroad and coal-mining barons in the country, "amassing" both political and economic wealth that Gail equated to a "little dynasty." "Even though we got our reservation's mineral sites cleared, we ended up with a formidable opponent in the form of Montco." For almost 20 years, Gustafson and Montco have sought to open a rail spur along the Northern Cheyenne reservation, ostensibly to haul coal from Wyoming coal fields to Montana markets, but also to service new mines in the Northern Cheyenne homeland. Thus far, all have been averted.

In a seemingly relentless onslaught of battles spanning almost two decades, Native Action has organized and coordinated hearings on the reservation and played a central role in litigation related to the proposals for the Tongue River Railroad and Montco Mine. Their work resulted in the state of Montana denying a request by the company for an extension of their mine permit. The significance of this case lies in part in the fact that the land that the companies wanted to mine is the land on which Little Wolf's band originally settled upon their return from the death camps of Indian territory. It is an extremely important historic site to the Northern Cheyenne, not a suitable location for yet another strip mine.

Each year, it seems, the Cheyenne face a new development project that will tear away at the social and cultural fabric of the community. As I was completing the interviews and research on Native Action, I had to call and clarify the status of three different mining projects the grassroots organization was currently fighting. In a related action in Fall 1997, President Clinton issued a line-item veto of the transfer of federal coal lands to the state of Montana as a tradeoff for Montana not devastating Yellowstone National Park with a new gold mine. The Great White Father helped out his Northern Cheyenne children. For once.

"That there are not more mines in Montana is in part due to Gail's work," explains Jeff Barber of the Northern Plains Resource Council, a non-Indian advocacy group composed primarily of ranchers and farmers. The group ends up working with Native Action on a number of issues every year. As Barber explains, "about 25 percent of the nation's coal is out here, and there are only five major mines in Montana, producing an average of 30–40 million tons of coal annually. That compares to the 300 million tons annually produced in Wyoming, a steady increase since the 1980s. That is, in part, because of Gail. Otherwise, we would have the same kind of rape and run that they have in Wyoming. That is no small feat."[26]

Economic Justice and Ethnostress

Agnes Williams, a Seneca social worker, came up with a term in her practice on the Cattaraugus reservation: "ethnostress." That's what you feel when you wake up in the morning and you are still Indian, and you still have to deal with stuff about being Indian—poverty, racism, death, the government, and strip-mining. You can't just hit the tennis courts, have lunch, and forget about it. You will still have to go home. That reality of ethnostress pretty much sums up life on the reservation, perhaps more so at Northern Cheyenne.

Ethnostress comes from the structural issues that affect every reservation, Northern Cheyenne included. Most statistics place reservations in the Third World economically, something that the energy and mining corporations understood when they negotiated leases on Native lands. Land- and natural resource–rich, the Northern Cheyenne continue to live in immense material poverty. As Gail describes it, "The current profile of our reservation is characterized by a 60 percent unemployment rate, alcoholism, drug abuse, suicide, violence, a 57 percent dropout rate, apathy, and a sense of powerlessness." All of this is especially disturbing considered along with the fact that the tribe's population is young: 42 percent of the total population are less than 21 years of age. Alarmingly, approximately 250 Cheyenne youth, or 57 percent, had in 1995 already dropped out of non-Indian–controlled high schools. These statistics indicate a deep and chronic cycle of underdevelopment, as well as the structural racism of the region.

The Northern Cheyenne realized that unless there was some long-term work done to address these symptoms, each time the coal companies came back to the reservation, the community would be prey. In response, Native Action took on two strategies—economic justice and education. Since the tribe had been aggressively fighting the coal mines and the companies, the local pro-development townspeople and businesses were hostile towards tribe members. As Gail explains it, non-Indians in the bordering towns rarely hire Cheyennes. There is no bank on the reservation, and very few Indian-owned businesses. Very little money generated from the reservation stays on the reservation, with most going to the off-reservation coal towns. The Cheyenne also found that there were virtually no loans going to the reservation, although a good portion of tribal members operated ranches. Native Action took on the bank.

The Northern Cheyenne do not want to live in poverty, nor should they be forced to trade their ecosystem for some economic justice. They decided they needed some alternatives. Native Action opposed an interstate bank merger on the grounds that the banks were in violation of the Community Reinvestment Act (CRA). This act requires that banks loan to the communities in which they do business, but as it turned out there had been less than a half-million dollars' worth of loans to Northern Cheyennes over the previous decade. In December 1991, the Federal Reserve Board of Governors shocked the banking industry by denying the merger application of the First Interstate Bank System based solely on Native Action's CRA appeal. Three years later, the bank and Native Action settled the appeal and entered into a CRA agreement.

In the 20 months that followed, over $3.8 million was loaned to residents of the Northern Cheyenne reservation. Almost $2 million was loaned to young people working to re-establish ranches and farms on the reservation. In early 1997, Gail Small was appointed to serve on the Federal Reserve Board's Consumer Advisory Council, the only Native person ever to have served on one of the federal bank's committees. To others, another important benchmark occurred when an automated bank machine was installed in 1997 at Lame Deer. That meant to Gail that they were coming of age.

Return to High School

In the last few years, Gail has gone back to that border-town high school that caused her so much anguish. For decades, the majority of Northern Cheyenne students were bussed to the border-town high schools, meaning that the Cheyenne lost control over their children's educations. Not surprisingly, most Native students dropped out. The local school districts adjacent to reservations get around $6,000 per student to teach enrolled Native students, according to Gail. That is money the school districts don't want to lose, so they fought the Northern Cheyenne community's initiatives to start their own school district. But in 1993, after almost 30 years of fighting, the state superintendent of public instruction granted the Northern Cheyenne's petition for a high school because of the hard work of Native Action and the community at large. In 1997, the Northern Cheyenne broke ground for the Morning Star High School.

Gail Small sits in an office overlooking her town of Lame Deer, Montana. During the course of her life, she has pretty much done everything in her ability to ensure some quality of life in the town, on the reservation, and in the region. She would like to take a breather. One day, she might. Maybe. In the meantime, the largest coal strip mine in the United States looms like a great shadow over her. The Northern Cheyenne beat the latest proposal to mine their territory, but there will be another. There will most likely always be another proposal. She takes another breath and thinks about her four young children. She wants them to be happy to be Cheyenne. It is not so much to ask.

This America
has been a burden
of steel and mad
death,
but, look now,
there are flowers
and new grass
and a spring wind
rising from Sand Creek.[27]

Virginia Sanchez. Photo © Susan Alzner.

Nuclear Waste

Dumping on the Indians

Nuclear Waste

Existing nuclear waste dump

Proposed nuclear waste dump

Uranium mining

Tribal government pursuing Monitored Retrievable Storage

Tribe formerly considered for Monitored Retrievable Storage

Affected Native community

CREE Affected Native nation

0 200 400 Kilometers
0 200 400 Miles

©Map by Zoltán Grossman, mtn@igc.apc.org

Alaska Native villages not shown
△ Akhiok-Kaguyak
△ Tetlin

Oklahoma tribes
1 Absentee Shawnee
2 Apache
3 Caddo
4 Chickasaw
5 Eastern Shawnee
6 Ponca
7 Sac and Fox

Т he United States today hosts 104 nuclear power plants. Thanks to the anti-nuclear movement, it is a far cry from the 1,000 nuclear power plants the Nixon administration envisioned in 1974. Canada today hosts 22 Candu nuclear reactors, which provide 15 percent of Canadian electricity.

Much of the world's nuclear industry has been sited on or near Native lands. Some 70 percent of the world's uranium originates from Native communities, whether Namibia's Rossing Mine, Australia's Jabulikka Mine, Cluff Lake, or Rabbit Lake Mine (in Diné territory). *Tletsoo,* as uranium is known in Diné, comes from Native America.[1]

> The Navajos ...were warned about the dangers of uranium. The people emerged from the third world into the fourth and present world and were...told to choose between two yellow powders. One was yellow dust from the rocks, and the other was corn pollen. The people chose corn pollen, and the gods nodded in assent. They also issued a warning. Having chosen the corn pollen, the Navajos were to leave the yellow dust in the ground. If it was ever removed, it would bring evil.

> —Grace Thorpe,
> founder of the National Environmental Coalition of Native Americans[2]

The nuclear reaction that releases so much power also creates profoundly hazardous wastes—compounds so dangerous to life forms that they must be isolated for 100,000 years. To date, 30,000 metric tons of nuclear waste have been generated by the U.S. nuclear industry. If today's reactors are operational until the end of their licensing periods, the nuclear industry will have created 75,000 to 80,000 metric tons of nuclear waste. For this reason, among others, harnessing nuclear power was "a bad idea twenty years ago," says longtime anti-nuclear activist Faye Brown. And "it's still a bad idea now," she says.[3]

There is pretty much no knowledge in the human repertoire on how to handle such long-lasting toxic substances, so industry relies on that old standby, computer projections, and counts on the Earth to take care of it.

As a result of this neglect, over 1,000 abandoned uranium mines lie on the Navajo reservation, largely untouched by any attempts to cover or cap or even landscape the toxic wastes.[4] Vast areas of both the Spokane reservation in Washington State and the Yakama Reservation, which includes the Hanford Nuclear Reservation, have been contaminated with mine wastes and byproducts of the military's nuclear experiments. Stretches of northern Canada from Ontario's Serpent River to the Northwest Territories' Baker Lake are inundated with radioactive waste, a legacy of decades of uranium mining and an absence of virtually any environmental regulation or protection.

The nuclear industry is perhaps the most highly subsidized industry in the United States. The federal government doled out some $97 billion in subsidies for the nuclear industry between 1948 and 1992, including over 65 percent of the Department of Energy's (DOE) budget for research and development.[5]

"The utilities don't care," says Harvey Wasserman of the Nuclear Information and Resource Service. "They spent more than they were originally costed out. But they figured they would pass the price overruns on to the consumers."[6]

The Nevada Test Site and the Western Shoshone

In 1951, the Atomic Energy Commission set up the Nevada Test Site within Western Shoshone territory as a proving grounds for nuclear weapons. Between 1951 and 1992, the United States and Great Britain exploded 1,054 nuclear devices above and below the ground. The radiation exposure emanating from these tests was only fully measured for 111 tests. Within just the first three years, 220 above-ground tests spewed fallout over a large area.[7]

The government maintained that the maximum radiation exposure from the tests was equivalent to that of a single chest x-ray. But in 1997, the National Cancer Institute made public a study of radiation exposure from above-ground nuclear tests that showed that some 160 million people had suffered significant radiation exposure from the tests, on average 200 times more than the amount indicated by the government. In some parts of the country, the exposure was found to be 2,000 to 3,000 times that amount.[8]

The institute estimated that as many as 75,000 cases of thyroid cancer may have been caused by atmospheric testing. Since the incidence of thyroid cancer is highly age-dependent and has a long latency period, children born prior to the 1950s—people in their 40s or 50s today—are still at risk. The radiation exposure is linked to other thyroid disorders, as well.[9]

None of that is news to Virginia Sanchez, a Western Shoshone woman who has grown up in the shadow of the Nevada Test Site. When the nuclear tests were exploded, "in school, [we would] duck and cover under the desk, not really understanding what it was."[10] Now she understands all too well. Sanchez lost her 36-year-old brother Joe to leukemia a few years back. Her grandfather died of bone cancer. She has seen the impact of the test site ravage her community.

In 1993, she began a new project at the Reno-based Citizens Alert Native American Program called Nuclear Risk Management for Native Communities. In that work, she began to grapple with what the federal government had done to her community.

According to Sanchez, the Atomic Energy Commission and then the Department of Energy would deliberately wait for the clouds to blow north and east before conducting above-ground tests, so that the fallout would avoid any heavily populated areas such as Las Vegas and Los Angeles. This meant that the Shoshones would get a larger dosage. They literally had no protection.

> We weren't wealthy, you know, our structures weren't airtight. Besides, our people spent major amounts of time outside, picking berries, hunting, gathering our traditional foods.... At that time we still ate a lot of jackrabbits.... [In] Duckwater, which, as the crow flies, is 120 miles directly north of the test site, the people in that community didn't have running water or electricity as a whole community until the early 1970s, so they would gather water outside.

> And so, we received some major dosages of radiation. When the federal scientists began to look at the Department of Energy's dose reconstruction of the off-site fallout, [they found that] we were put under the shepherd lifestyle. So we weren't even looked at at all. The scientists...figured that a one-year-old child who ate a contaminated rabbit within a month's time after the test probably had six times the dose of what DOE's figures were saying.

Virginia recorded many stories that the federal agencies missed. People outside seeing the clouds coming over and gardens turning black. "People [were] working outside when the clouds went over. [There were stories of] getting sick with leukemia or doctors writing blisters off as some sunburn. There was a county school about three miles from the reservation, and all the kids wore the film badges [issued by federal officials to document the gamma rays], and they were never told the results."

The Western Shoshone territory on which the test site resides consists of about 24.5 million acres of traditional homeland, as recognized in the 1853 Treaty of Ruby Valley. The government has for decades been trying to secure title to the Shoshone land. As Virginia explains it, in 1979, the Claims Commission recognized Shoshone title and offered to buy the land based on its 1873 value. "The traditional people blew apart the hearing," Virginia says. The federal government awarded $26 million on behalf of the Shoshone, but has never been able to get the Shoshone to accept the money. The latest estimate of its accrued value is $91 million. So here we have some of the poorest people in the country who are refusing to accept a $91 million settlement for their land, because they want their land even if the federal government has put radiation on it. They want their land, and they want to heal their community.

Pressures Build to Dump on the Indians

In addition to the problem of already extant nuclear waste contamination, many of today's American reactors have almost run out of space for their used fuel rods and their on-site waste. In the next decade most of the nation's reactors will experience a shortfall in their space. This space "crisis" has pushed the discussion around handling nuclear wastes forward.

The growing environmental justice movement, coupled with the sovereign status of Indian lands and their frequent lack of infrastructure, mean that the nuclear industry has increasingly targeted Native lands for dumps. Besides that, by the 1990s, it had become "conveniently politically incorrect" to argue against a tribe's autonomous decisionmaking, says Winnebago attorney Jean Belile of the Rocky Mountain Land and Water Institute.[11]

During the early and mid-1990s, the federal government and the nuclear industry offered seemingly lucrative deals to Native communities willing to accept nuclear waste dumps on their lands. A few big Native American organizations took the bait and worked on or at least provided the forum to discuss the dumping.

The federal Administration for Native Americans (ANA) and the Department of Commerce funded Indian consulting firms to promote the waste industry in Indian country. A big chunk of their money went to the Council on Energy Resource Tribes (CERT), an organization of 50 member tribes founded in 1975 to assert control over the development of Native mineral resources. In 1987, CERT received $2.5 million, over half of their total income, from federal nuclear waste contracts.

During the late 1980s, the National Congress of American Indians (NCAI) joined in nuclear waste research. Founded in 1944 to "work toward the promotion of the common welfare" of Native Americans, NCAI cooperated with the Department of Energy to ensure participation of Indian tribal governments in the siting and transportation of high-level nuclear waste.[12] Between 1986 and 1990, NCAI received nearly $1 million, over one-fourth of their total income, from Department of Energy nuclear waste grants. In 1992, the DOE and NCAI signed a five-year cooperative agreement for $1.8 million. The

NCAI's nuclear waste program, initiated largely with federal funds, provided tribes with a steady stream of information on radioactive wastes.[13]

At a 1991 meeting of the NCAI, the Mescalero Apache Chairman explained that it was easy to get $100,000 by signing up for a grant for no-strings-attached research into the feasibility of siting a Monitored Retrievable Storage (MRS) facility for nuclear waste on tribal lands. In 1992, the Mescalero Apache Tribe and CERT publicly advocated that Native communities host nuclear waste dump sites on their lands. Fourteen tribal councils, along with pro-nuclear government representatives and nuclear industry salespeople, attended the meeting.

That influential meeting was essentially about the philosophical underpinnings of hosting nuclear waste sites on Indian lands. David Leroy, DOE's nuclear waste negotiator, aggressively courted tribes with nuclear waste proposals. According to Nilak Butler, a former Indigenous Environmental Network council member, Leroy and the DOE argued that Native responsibility to hold nuclear waste emanates from the "superior Native understanding of the natural world" and the fact that we are "our brother's keeper."[14]

Grassy Narrows

Judy De Silva is a softspoken Ojibwe woman from the Grassy Narrows reserve in northern Ontario. The administrator of the band's day-care program and mother of three young children, she is angry at the Canadian government's mid-1990s announcement of a proposal to dump nuclear waste in her community.

"We've been through so much," she said, sounding both disgusted and weary at the scope of the problems in small Grassy Narrows, a community of 500 residents 55 miles northeast of Kenora, Ontario. "We've learned to accept this kind of abuse from the system.... I could stand up to the big lumber trucks and the other trucks, but.... I have more fight now because of my children, because of my baby."[15]

Not unlike other communities under consideration for nuclear dumps, Grassy Narrows has pretty much seen the bad side of development. In 1960, Dryden Pulp and Paper started contaminating the nearby Wabigoon River in Canada with suspended solids. In March 1962, Reed Paper opened a plant that released an estimated 20 pounds of mercury into the river every day.

In 1963, the government relocated the entire village so as to push more water through the dams to provide power for other communities. "They did it under legislation," says Grassy Narrows Chief and spokesperson Steve Frobisher. "It took sort of an army to move us."[16] The Grassy Narrows band didn't get power from the three dams up the river and two dams down the river. Yet their land and their cemetery were flooded, and their ancestors' corpses floated in the reservoir. Grassy Narrows was no longer a narrows, it was a vast lake.

Meanwhile, mercury contamination was killing the fish. "We knew there was something wrong that the fish were floating within the whole river system. The marine life was dying, and the fish tasted funny. It tasted like oil or something that had rusted," says Frobisher. It took a university student from Boston, Massachusetts, to uncover the scope of the mercury releases. On September 28, 1975, the Ontario Minister of Health publicly admitted that 20 to 30 of the Native people living on the Grassy Narrows reserve showed symptoms of mercury poisoning.

As a result, commercial fishing by area Anishinaabeg was closed down, and unemployment on the reserve rose to over 80 percent. Their attempt to procure rights to uncontaminated fish from a nearby lake was defeated by non-Native lodge owners who wanted to use the lake for sports fishing. Between 1969 and 1974, welfare tripled on the White Dog Reserve and quadrupled at Grassy Narrows. Mercury discharge continued virtually unabated until 1970 when, after more than 50,000 pounds of mercury had been dumped into the Wabigoon River system, the plant stopped the discharge.

The poison devastated the Anishinaabeg community. "The consequence was that there was a disruption of our ways of living, the ways that our people used to live before: [our] spirituality, culture, self-esteem, and all of that. Because the work didn't mean anything anymore. That mercury killed everything," says Frobisher.

> We lost everything.... It took 30 years for them to even acknowledge what they had done to us. They compensate [other] people for natural disasters, but they don't compensate us for what they did to us. Ours wasn't an act of the Creator, it was the act of man.

The infrastructure on the reserve is minimal. Running water and a sewer system were installed in 1994. There is a nursing station, but no nurses. There is a recently built high school and a volunteer fire department with a fire truck, which Frobisher calls the "noise truck." The hard rock road into the reserve turns to gravel seven miles before the reserve entrance.

Today, this transformed community is suffering. About 95 percent are on welfare. In the 1970s, it was about 50 percent. The incidence of alcoholism is about 50 percent, but "you wouldn't find anybody sober in the 1970s," says

Frobisher. "We are still tested today for mercury. That is a program that's going to be here forever," he says.

The Canadian government is spending $10 billion to study the nuclear waste dump site on Grassy Narrows. "White people don't usually spend billions to do a study unless they're doing something with it," says De Silva. "There are so many environmental things that have happened here that we never yelled about, because we just settled for compensation. Because we're poor, we just settled for money. That's probably what the government is counting on."

Resisting the MRS Program

The work of Native anti-nuclear advocates during those years—when a good deal of money and influence was intended to persuade tribes to accept the waste—was especially critical. Grace Thorpe is one such activist.

Grace is a bear of a woman. She was a U.S. corporal stationed in New Guinea at the end of World War II when the first atomic bomb was dropped in Hiroshima. She is also a veteran of most domestic Indian wars in the past decades, including the occupation of Alcatraz Island and the struggle to reinstate the decathlon and pentathlon medals of her father, Jim Thorpe, which were won and confiscated in the 1912 Olympics. This veteran emerged victorious from a battle in her own territory, the Sac and Fox nation of Oklahoma. In 1992, she, along with other community members, convinced her tribal government to withdraw their application for study of a nuclear waste repository in their homeland.

Grace found out that her tribe had signed up for an MRS grant in a newspaper article. "Nobody in the tribe knew anything about it," she says. "I was shocked.... The treasurer of the tribe told me that they got more phone calls that day than in the history of the tribe."

> I knew diddly-squat about radioactivity. I went to the library right away and got some books out. When I read that you can't see it, can't smell it, and can't hear it, but it was the most lethal poison in the history of man, I knew that...our sacred land shouldn't even be associated with it.

> I'm on the health council and am a part-time district court judge in our tribal court. So I started talking with everyone about it. Finally, we brought it to a vote of the people, and there were 75 votes in attendance of this special meeting. Seventy voted against it; five were for it. The

five who were for it were the tribal council. We voted them out. The
money was there, [but] they had to return the check.

All of a sudden, I was a kind of hero. Now I've been getting calls from
all over asking me to talk [to] their community about what we did.[17]

In 1993, she founded NECONA, the National Environmental Coalition of
Native Americans. Through her stature as an elder and statesperson in Indian
country ("Having a dad like mine didn't hurt much," she says), Grace was able
to participate in most national Native meetings and talk about the hazards surrounding nuclear waste.

I caught up with Grace one day on her way back from the Ft. McDermitt
Paiute Reservation in Nevada. She'd just been attending a community meeting
on the second phase MRS research grant the tribe was considering. Local
Paiutes had asked Native people who had faced the nuclear industry to come in
and tell both sides of the story. Grace and a half-dozen other grassroots activists
had found their way to the Nevada reservation to address the Paiutes' concerns.
After the forum, it looked like the Paiutes would have a referendum.

Ultimately, community work such as Grace's and NECONA's on most of
the MRS's proposed reservation sites doomed the program. In 1996, Congress
withheld funding for the program.[18]

NECONA urged tribes to institute nuclear-free zones on their lands, and,
by 1997, 75 tribal governments in both the United States and Canada had
agreed.[19] By 1998, there were only two tribes who had not removed themselves
from the MRS program: the Ft. McDermitt Paiutes and the Skull Valley
Goshutes.

A Private Initiative in the Goshutes

In 1996, a group of utilities—New York's Con Edison, Georgia's Southern Nuclear, Pennsylvania's GPU, Illinois Power, Indiana's Michigan Power,
and Wisconsin's Genoa Fuel Tech—under the leadership of Northern States
Power chartered a new corporation called Private Fuel Storage (PFS), incorpo-
rating it in the state of Delaware.

The PFS facility would function pretty much like a nuclear waste condo-
minium owned by a consortium of utilities. And PFS, as a limited liability corporation, conveniently shielded the individual companies from any liability
arising out of the subsidiary's actions. If there was an accident at PFS, in moving nuclear waste, for instance, only the parent company (PFS) and not the individual utilities could be sued.

In 1997, PFS signed a lease with the Skull Valley Goshute Tribal Council for 40 acres of the 180,000-acre reservation. That land would become an above-ground storage facility, a kind of nuclear parking lot on the reservation. Jean Belile is working with *Ohngo Guadableh Devia,* a Goshute community group opposed to the dump. She is skeptical about the PFS deal. "I think it's the government that's pushing the whole thing; they tried to do an MRS there, and this is one way to get around the [opposition to the] whole thing."

Margene Bullcreek is the main organizer for *Ohngo Guadableh Devia.* "Our forefathers passed on our history," she says. "It tells us how we are to live in the world if we are to continue as a people. It is still being told in our homes—of our feathered friends, the birds of all colors, who at one time fought for our land and our people. It is our responsibility to continue to fight for the protection and preservation of our homeland.... The waste will damage our plant life, water, air, and spiritual atmosphere as well as future generations."[20]

Margene is a tiny Goshute woman in her mid-50s who is taking on some big companies. As we sit together outside in a tent, I ask her what her village looks like. She draws me a little map that looks like a skimpy telegraph pole. About six or seven families live there. "We really don't have anything here, we have a community building we got ten years ago and a paved road that goes to the proving grounds," she says.

Characterized by one reporter as the kind of place where Mad Max might find a home, the Dugway Proving Ground is where, until 1969, the U.S. military conducted open-air testing of chemical and biological weapons. In August 1996, Dugway began burning up its stockpile. Nearby, in Tooele, Utah, are two commercial hazardous-waste incinerators. On the reservation itself, a private company test-burns rocket-motors under a deal with tribal members. Then, as Cherie Parker reports in the *Twin Cities Reader,*

> There are the sheep carcasses. Nearly 30 years ago, 6,000 sheep reportedly died after being exposed to nerve gas. The details are a bit hazy due to an *X Files*-type reluctance on the part of the military to admit just what went on at Dugway. Initially the military blamed the mass deaths on pesticide poisoning, but an autopsy reportedly revealed a nerve agent. The Goshute had to broker a deal with the U.S. Department of Defense to disinter the sheep bodies. According to Utah state officials, the military has neither confirmed nor denied the nerve gas accident, but the U.S. Army Corps of Engineers recently has undertaken what it terms the Tooele County Sheep Project, to clean up the contaminated site.[21]

Tribal politics are tough at Goshute, as on most other reservations. The numbers are small, so it's usually a few families or a family who end up with the most influence. When the tribe voted on whether to consider the PFS dump, half the participants walked out of the meeting. Those who remained voted in favor of the dump. "It's family against family now," says Jean Belile. The pro-dump advocates are "punishing the people who are against them. For instance, they get a dividend from the tribal treasury every year at Christmastime; some of the people got $200, and some got $1600."

In 1998, the BIA approved a lease for PFS that provides little protection for the tribe, should the dump pose future risks. Says Belile, "The lease...gives the tribe no out, ever. It's horrible. I don't think the bureau has met their obligations [of] trust responsibility for the tribe."

The community's lack of infrastructure makes them even more vulnerable. "If anything does happen," says Jean, "it's going to take 45 minutes to an hour for someone to respond to anything. They have to rely on Tooele County for help. They have to go through the mountains or clear around the mountains to get there." PFS did agree to provide the tribe with a new fire truck in case of emergencies.

The tribal chairman promised each tribal member $2 million if the dump gets built.[22] That kind of money, in a poor community like the Goshutes, has a lot of sway. Margene, however, and a lot of others, hope that the Goshute traditions and the loyalty to an ancestral homeland will be more persuasive. And that somehow, some of the money might be put into cleaning up the present mess, before any new toxins come into their territory.

Prairie Island

The Prairie Island nuclear facility is composed of two nuclear reactors built by Westinghouse for the Minnesota-based utility Northern States Power (NSP) in 1973 and 1974. Located on a sandbar in the middle of the Mississippi River, the reactors have the dubious distinction of being situated in a flood plain and on the Mdewakanton Dakota Prairie Island homeland. The facility sits a few hundred yards from the homes, businesses, and childcare center of that community, a historic site of a traditional village and burial mound dating back at least 2,000 years.

The plant went up just next to the reservation boundary, but was technically in the city of Red Wing, Minnesota. Ironically, although the plant produces an estimated 15 percent of Minnesota's power, not a watt of it goes to the Mdewakanton community.[23] While the city negotiated a deal that included tax benefits and other income from the plant, the neighboring Mdewakantons couldn't even afford to hire an attorney to help decipher the contracts. The Bureau of Indian Affairs negotiated on behalf of the Mdewakantons, selling right of way along the only road running through the reservation for $178, with neither a discount on the plant's power nor a portion of the $20 million the plant would pay in property taxes to Red Wing.[24]

It is likely that the plant has contaminated Prairie Island residents, who have been poorly informed of even those safety breaches that the facility acknowledges. For 30 minutes in 1979, the plant leaked radioactivity into the environment, and most of the staff were rushed off-site. The Dakota people of Prairie Island heard about it on the radio. In 1989, radioactive tritium was found in the community's wells. The utility blamed the contamination on bomb tests from the 1950s to 1960s. In 1994, the Minnesota Department of Health found that the plant had exposed Prairie Island residents to six times greater risk of cancer.[25] Local people say that almost every family has lost someone to cancer.[26]

The problem is that the facility doesn't have enough space to store its wastes. According to the Prairie Island Coalition, formed in 1990 to oppose bad nuclear policy in Minnesota, the company "has known with increasing certainty during each of those past 20 years that the day would come when no waste storage space would remain in the plant's spent fuel pools."[27]

Each year, NSP found itself with a massive pile of radioactive waste and no place left to put it. By 1986, the storage problem had become acute. Finally, they piled the fuel into tall, reinforced-steel cans set outside the plant, in effect creating an on-site nuclear dump. In 1988, they had to request permission from the government to store more fuel above ground in what's called "dry cask storage." This type of storage is a sort of parking lot full of big cement casks full of waste, which would significantly expand the risk to the tribe.

According to Faye Brown, the tribe took an active role in disputing the request. "The tribe said, 'This isn't going to happen. We don't want it next to our land.'"

> This was environmental racism.... [They thought] it was somehow acceptable to do this to Indian people. This would never ever have been tolerated in...the rich suburbs of the Twin Cities. They actually started building the damn thing before they [had state authorization].

And so began a six-year battle, one of the biggest fights in the Minnesota legislature ever. The fight was watched with great trepidation and interest by

utilities and anti-nuclear activists across the country, because the battle over nuclear waste storage was raging in every state that had a nuclear reactor.

Although the tribe was able for the first time to hire a lobbyist and a few
attorneys, Northern States Power was sure to spend more. During the six-month
period that included the 1994 session, NSP volleyed about $1.3 million into the
legislature "to influence legislative action." As journalist Monika Bauerlein
notes,

> Almost $1.1 million went into an advertising campaign that blanketed
> newspapers with full-page testimonials attesting to the dump's safety.
> The company also listed two dozen lobbyists on its payroll, and [they
> had] hired guns with political connections on both sides of the aisle.[28]

In 1994, the Minnesota legislature authorized an interim dump and the
placement of 17 casks of nuclear waste on a concrete pad on that sand bar in the
Mississippi River, three blocks from the tribe's childcare center. The Prairie Island band fought to the end, even refusing an offer of $220 million from NSP.

There were some small victories for the Mdewakanton. The legislature
mandated that the facility would be closed down unless there was a permanent
storage facility operating by 2004. That, according to Brown, "is precedent-
setting. That's the first time a state legislature mandated the shut down of a nuclear reactor if they didn't have a nuclear waste dump."

Before 2004, the utility would have to find a better solution for its waste
storage problem.

Yucca Mountain

The debate over nuclear power's final resting place is becoming increasingly volatile. Despite the back-room dealings of Northern States Power and the
other big utilities, an increasingly concerned public is slowly becoming aware of
a bill pending in Congress known derisively as "Mobile Chernobyl." That bill
has perhaps one of the largest potential ecological impacts of any piece of legislation ever presented to the U.S. Congress. It would authorize the transportation
of up to 90,000 shipments of nuclear waste on America's highways and rail-
ways across the country. That, according to many Americans, whether doctors,
firefighters, or residents of the small towns along the major interstates, is a public health hazard of monstrous proportions.

Pushed through with some heavy lobbying by the nuclear industry and a
sentiment in Congress of "get it out of my backyard," the bill authorizes the
transport of nuclear waste from 108 nuclear reactors to Yucca Mountain in

Western Shoshone territory. As Senator Rod Grams of Minnesota, a co-author of the 1997 Nuclear Waste Policy Act, explains it, "We in the Senate have done our part in trying to restore the promises made by the federal government to the ratepayers of this country to move nuclear waste out of our home states."[29]

To start with, Northern States Power put about $171,000 into its congressional delegations' coffers, and the other members of the Nuclear Energy Institute also anted up, sending about $12.8 million to their congressional delegations to set up the interim site at Yucca Mountain. That money is almost three times the amount utilities have spent on Congress in nearly a decade.

The problem is that Yucca Mountain doesn't really get the waste out of the senators' backyards. Yucca Mountain would create yet another nuclear waste site. Operating reactors would still have to store waste on their sites, because the radiation is so hot that it has to chill in liquid for five to ten years before it can be transported. Perhaps most alarming, the waste would be moving on U.S. highways. More than 50 million Americans live within a half-mile of the most likely route, near some of the nation's largest cities: Chicago, New York, Los Angeles, Houston, Baltimore, Jacksonville, Denver, Portland, and others.

Nuclear Information and Resource Service director Michael Marriote outlined some of the problems in his congressional testimony on the act. First, there will be some potentially disastrous accidents. According to the Nuclear Waste Strategy Coalition, there have been about 2,400 shipments of high-level nuclear waste in the United States (most of it in small quantities from submarine reactors). There have been seven accidents associated with those shipments, none of which involved the release of radioactive materials. This rate of one accident per 343 shipments translates into, at the very minimum, 268 accidents resulting from the 15,000 to 90,000 shipments of nuclear waste to Yucca Mountain.

Second, the act's designation of acceptable radiation exposure is dangerously high. The act establishes a radiation standard for Yucca Mountain of 100 millirems per year, or what the Nuclear Regulatory Commission calculates is the equivalent of a 1 in 286 lifetime risk of fatal cancer. Yet, Marriote observed, "our nation typically regulates pollutants to ensure that exposure to them will cause no more than a 1 in 10,000 to 1 in 1,000,000 lifetime risk of fatal cancer."[30]

The Need for Alternatives

It was that Indian

Martinez
from over by Bluewater
Was the one who discovered uranium west of Grants.
That's what they said.
He brought in that green stone
into town one afternoon in 1953.
Said he found it by the railroad tracks
over by Haystack Butte.

Tourist magazines did a couple spreads
on him, photographed him in Kodak color,
and the Chamber of Commerce celebrated
that Navajo man,
forgot for the time being
that the brothers from
Aacque east of Grants
had killed that state patrolman,
and never mind also that the city had a jail full of Indians.
The city fathers named a city park after him
and some even wanted to put up a statue of Martinez but others said
that was going too far for just an Indian
even if he was the one who started that area
into a boom.

—Simon Ortiz, Acoma Pueblo[31]

"The nuclear industry is hoping for one last twilight dance," says Harvey Wasserman. "It's dying in the United States, in western Europe, and Japan." The big producers are "banking on the hopes of sales to India, China, Iran, and maybe Turkey," he says.

The problem of nuclear waste, according to Wasserman and others, is "unsolvable." The only solution, he says, is to "let the stuff sit where it is, then 50 years from now, hopefully [we'll] have better technology to deal with it. George Crocker, executive director of the North American Water Office and a key force in the Prairie Island Coalition, echoes Wasserman. "We're basically trying to figure out the best way to bequeath [nuclear waste] to the next generation.... The more we produce, the more overwhelmed [the next generation] will be," he says grimly.[32]

For now, the waste debates in this country always seem to end up with the Indians. That is the reality that Virginia Sanchez continues to struggle with. "We have been violated, but we don't have to get stuck in that rut of victimization," Virginia says. "We've got our grandmothers, our spiritual people, tribal government representatives, all of them...work[ing] together and hav[ing] ceremony together.... We do have a lot of power. Knowing that we're making progress —it may be in little bits and pieces, but we are definitely making progress. That's how you begin the healing."

This struggle to resist and to heal should not be placed solely on the shoulders of women like Virginia Sanchez, Margene Bullcreek, or Judy De Silva. The question of where to dump the nuclear waste generated over the past 20 years is a question that anti-nuclear activists like Faye Brown, George Crocker, Harvey Wasserman, and others believe should be opened up to a full public debate.

"It's a way to engage this country in a larger political debate on how we're going to meet this country's energy needs," says Brown. "Are we going to rely on this type of energy that kills people and poisons things, or are we going to engage in a discussion about alternatives?"

Pat Wichern with John and Waseyabin, and horses
Rosebud and Aandeg, on White Earth, March 1998.
Photo by John Ratzloff

Now the white people claim everything that the Indians used to use in the olden days…. If they could do it, they'd take everything…the only thing they'd leave us is our appetites.

–Lucy Thompson, White Earth elder, 1983.

White Earth

A Lifeway in the Forest

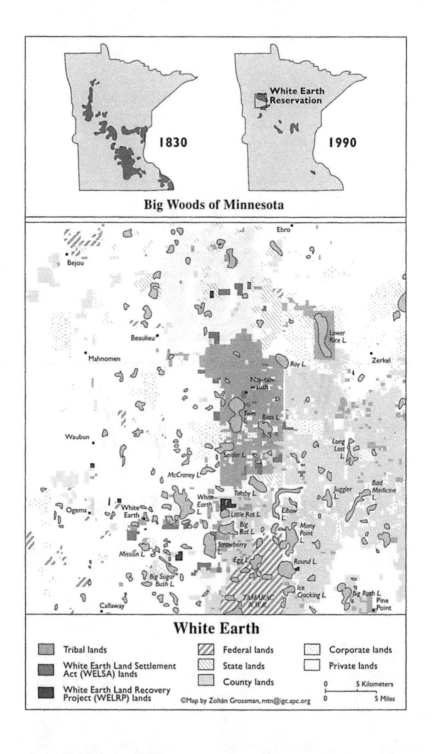

Big Woods of Minnesota

1830

1990

White Earth
Reservation

Ebro

Bejou

Beaulieu

Mahnomen

Waubun

Ogema

Callaway

White
Earth

Mission L.

Big Sugar
Bush L.

Lower
Rice L.

Roy L.

Zerkel

Nay-tah-
waush

Twin

Bass L.

Long
Lost
L.

Snider L.

McCraney L.

White
Earth
L.

Tulaby L.

Little Rat L.

Big
Rat L.

Strawberry

Egg L.

Juggler

Bad
Medicine
L.

Elbow
L.

Many
Point
L.

Round L.

Ice
Cracking L.

Big Rush L.

Pine
Point

*TAMARAC
N.W.R.*

White Earth

Tribal lands

White Earth Land Settlement
Act (WELSA) lands

White Earth Land Recovery
Project (WELRP) lands

Federal lands

State lands

County lands

Corporate lands

Private lands

0   5 Kilometers

0   5 Miles

©Map by Zoltán Grossman, mtn@igc.apc.org

I t's mid-September in northern Minnesota. Somewhere on one of the many lakes Lennie Butcher and his wife Cleo are making wild rice. *Manoominikewag.* That is what they do.

It's a misty morning on Big Chippewa Lake. The Anishinaabeg couple drag their canoe toward the water's edge. The woman boards in the front and sits on her haunches. The man pushes the canoe offshore and jumps in the boat behind her. As they pole toward the wild rice beds, they can feel the crisp dampness of September on their faces. The man rises to stand, his head visible just above the tall stalks of rice. The woman pulls the rice over her lap with a stick and gently raps it with another one. This is a thousand-year-old scene on Big Chippewa Lake. And there is a community that intends to carry it on for another thousand years.

There are many wild rice lakes on the White Earth reservation in northern Minnesota; my community, the Anishinaabeg, calls the rice *Manoomin,* or a gift from the Creator. Every year, half our people harvest the wild rice, the fortunate ones generating a large chunk of their income from it. But wild rice is not just about money and food. It's about feeding the soul.

On the White Earth reservation's 1,300 square miles, prairie, maple-basswood forest, and boreal pine forest intersect. This land was chosen by the headspeople a century ago for this very reason and was named "White Earth," or *Gahwahbahbahnikag,* for the white clay that underlies part of it. In Wintertime, or *biiboon,* below deep snows and layers of ice, the reservation's 47 big lakes teem with life. The remains of an indigenous prairie and its attendant grasses slumber through the dormant season, preparing for the Spring, *ziigwan,* and new life. This wealthy, diverse ecosystem has been called the Medicine Chest of the Ojibwe. It is the wellspring of a traditional way of life, one that has nurtured biodiversity for thousands of years.

The Anishinaabeg migration story, retold in winter stories and in ceremonies for countless generations, dispersed the Algonkin language throughout the continent.[1] The Anishinaabeg world undulated between material and spiritual shadows, never clear which was more prominent at any time. It was as if the world rested in those periods rather than in the light of day. Dawn and dusk, *biidaabin* and *oshkidibikad.* The gray of sky and earth just the same, the distinction between the worlds barely discernible. The small camps, villages, and bands would plan their hunts by dream and memory, fill their birch-bark *makakoon* with wild rice, maple sugar, berries, dried corn, and squash. By snowshoe, canoe, or dogteam, they moved through the woods, rivers, and lakes. It was not a life circumscribed by a clock, fence, or road. But there was a law just the same. Natural law, Creator's law.

There is no way to set a price on this way of life. That simple truth more than anything else encapsulates the Anishinaabeg people's struggle with the federal government, the miners, and the logging companies. For the past hundred years, Native people have been saying that their way of life, their land, their trees, and their very future, cannot be quantified and are not for sale. And for that same amount of time, government and industry accountants have been picking away, trying to come up with a formula to compensate Indians for the theft of their lands and livelihoods. So long as both remain steadfast, there appears to be little hope for a meeting of minds in the next generations.

Gitchimookomaanag, the White Man

> Religion, morality, and knowledge being necessary to good government and the happiness of mankind, schools and the news of education shall be forever encouraged. The utmost good faith shall always be observed towards the Indians, their lands, and property shall never be taken from them without their consent, and their property, rights and liberty, they shall never be involved or disturbed, unless in just and lawful wars authorized by Congress. But laws bounded in justice and humanity shall, from time to time be made for preventing wrongs being done to them, and for preserving peace and friendship with them.
>
> —Northwest Ordinance, Act of Congress,
> July 13, 1787, Section 14, Article III.[2]

Land has always been a source of wealth and power, and the issue of land rights and ownership is a central point of contention between settler and Indigenous governments. Between 1784 and 1894, the U.S. government signed 371 treaties with Native people and made some 720 related land seizures on Native territory. For what today would be about $800 million, the United States "bought" over 95 percent of its present continental territory from Native people. Of the remaining Native-held lands within U.S. borders, the federal government continues in most cases to exercise "trust responsibility" and "plenary power" over these lands and peoples—a double-edged sword. Legally this means the government, as the "trustee" of the Native estate, is mandated to protect Native interests. However, as this chapter illustrates, this responsibility is often unfulfilled, as the government has frequently moved instead into the realm of takings, plenary power, and acquiescence to the greed of economic interests.

Beginning at Fort McIntosh in 1785 and ending in 1923 at Georgian Bay, the United States, England, and Canada entered into more than 40 treaties with the Anishinaabeg, the bases for some of the largest land transactions in world history. Anishinaabeg original landholdings included millions of acres around the Great Lakes; today, the Anishinaabeg traditional homelands consist of close to ten million acres in 100 reserves and reservations in the lakes region, and a sprinkling in the great prairies, in total spanning the northern part of five American states and the southern part of four Canadian provinces.

The U.S. government never claimed to hold or control Anishinaabeg land "by right of conquest." Rather, it claims to have legally acquired Anishinaabeg and other Native lands by mutual agreement. Some of the first incursions onto Anishinaabeg land were to secure access to iron and copper deposits. By 1800, representatives of both the Queen of England and the emerging United States had "discovered" a 2,500-pound boulder of naturally occurring copper called the "Ontonogan Boulder" resting on the south shore of Lake Superior in Anishinaabeg territory, in what is now known as the Kewanee Peninsula. By the 1820s, the federal government had decided to do a comprehensive study of "mineral assets" of the Lake Superior area and a study of Indian title to the land therein. Within a very short period, four treaties were signed by the United States, each providing for access to and mining in Anishinaabeg territory. These treaties covered both the Kewanee Peninsula and the Mesabe "Sleeping Giant" iron-ore belt in northern Minnesota.

In the Summer of 1837, Governor Dodge of the Wisconsin Territory signed a treaty with the Anishinaabeg to secure the beginning of the pine lands in the St. Croix Valley. With that treaty, lumber interests secured the last outpost of the great white pine forests that had once extended from Maine to Minnesota. By mid-century, more than 100 copper companies had been incorporated in Minnesota, Wisconsin, and Michigan Territories. As early as 1849, copper production at Kewanee Peninsula—"ceded" by the Anishinaabeg in the treaty of 1842—led the world. Similarly, beginning in 1890 and continuing for nearly 50 years, mining at Mesabe accounted for 75 percent of all U.S. iron ore production.[3] Many of today's U.S.-based transnational mining corporations were founded on their exploitation of these natural resources.[4]

In 1867, the White Earth reservation was created, reserving some 36 townships of land for the Anishinaabeg, a land of natural wealth and beauty, over two-thirds of which was covered with huge white pines and beautiful maples. Twenty-two years later, the 1889 Nelson Act opened up the White Earth reservation to allotment and annexed four townships with the most white pines for the state of Minnesota; in the 1930s, more lands were taken to form the Tamarac National Wildlife Refuge.

In 1889, Minnesota ranked second in the country in logging, with the northwestern portion of the state leading the state's production. In 1889–90, 11 million board-feet of timber were taken from the White Earth reservation. In the next year, 15 million board-feet were cut, followed by another 18 million in the 1891–92 season.

Some are made rich and some are made poor. In 1895, White Earth "neighbor" Frederick Weyerhauser owned more acres of timber than anyone else in the world.[5] The self-made German was considered "the richest and brainiest" of the lumber millionaire kings.[6] His logging company sawed enough lumber "in one season to six times encircle the globe if it were cut up into inch strips, to build a baseball fence from here to San Francisco, or to construct two or three cities the size of Little Falls," enthused the local newspaper.[7] Weyerhauser's Pine Tree Lumber Company, the *Little Falls Daily Transcript* wrote in 1893,

> is eating a big hole in the forests of northern Minnesota, as it runs steadily, rarely meeting an accident.... The Weyerhausers have secured a monopoly of the Mississippi River so far as the driving of logs is concerned, but if they carry out their present plans, it will work good to both the millmen and lumbermen, great and small.[8]

In 1893, Weyerhauser and other lumber interests secured funding from public and other sources to build a railroad from Little Falls into Leech Lake reservation, where Weyerhauser had access to 800,000 board-feet of standing timber.[9] But in October 1898, the Anishinaabeg people on nearby Leech Lake reservation resisted the further encroachment. The military came to the defense of the lumber companies, and the uprising was staved off. Later, Private Oscar Buckhard was awarded a medal of honor for "distinguished bravery in action against hostile Indians."[10]

In 1897, 50 permits were issued for 70 million board-feet of timber from the reservation. By 1898, in excess of 76 million board-feet were being cut annually.[11]

Not content to take just the great pines, the lumber companies and land speculators set their eyes upon the land itself. Mechanisms were set in place to pry land from children at boarding school, blind women living in overcrowded housing, soldiers at war, veterans, and those who could not read or write English. A common saying describing what happened sprung up in nearby Detroit Lakes: "Fleec[ing] the Indian."[12] A quarter of a million acres of White Earth land were taken by the state of Minnesota as tax payments. In other cases, minors were persuaded to sell their land illegally.

Some land transfers were facilitated by a miracle of blood quantum transformation that occurred largely at the hands of Dr. Ales Hrdlicka, a physical anthropologist from the Smithsonian, who measured heads, nose bridges, and chests to determine the "Indianness" of the Indians. In his theory, the Pima Indians of Arizona were an example of "the most Indian of all Indians." Hrdlicka developed a "full blood" physical standard against which he could measure the Anishinaabeg. In his work, families were often divided into different "blood quantums," conferring "mixed blood" status to many, who were then considered "competent" to sell their land. In some cases, full blood children were attributed to mixed blood parents and vice versa.[13]

Through almost every conceivable mechanism, the land changed hands. As one Anishinaabe elder, Fred Weaver, recalls,

> We used to have a lot of them lands here around Pine Point. We had eight 80s [80-acre allotments]. Them land speculators came and tricked us out of them lands. My mother had an 80 on Many Point Lake. They tricked her out of that for $50. Now that's a Boy Scout Camp. And my father-in-law, Jim Jugg, he had land, too. The County says it owns them lands, too. All of them. We lived poor a long time, and we should've had all of them lands.[14]

By 1904, 99.5 percent of the remaining reservation lands were allotted, and ten years later, just 14 percent of the original White Earth land was still in Indian hands.

The newly acquired land was a bonanza to the border towns and the timber industry. Land companies emerged overnight, fly-by-night mortgage outfits held deeds for thousands of acres of lands, and timber companies closed in on leases to clearcut almost a third of the reservation.

"There is a myth, which was created at that time," Bob Shimek, a local Native harvester turned forest activist, reminds me. "It was this Paul Bunyan myth, Paul and Babe, and their ability to change the landscape. That myth is in the center of America, and that myth is what we are dealing with today."[15]

White Earth: The Appropriation of a Homeland

The stripping of the great forests of White Earth began a process that would be devastating to the Anishinaabeg forest culture. Great maple trees and maple sugarbushes moved horizontally toward logging mills, clearcuts replaced biodiverse groves of medicinal plants and trees, basket-makers searched for materials, and birch-bark canoe-makers couldn't find the huge trees for the great Anishinaabeg canoes. The Anishinaabeg had become "painfully aware of the mortality of wealth which nature bestows and imperialism appropriates," as Latin American scholar Eduardo Galeano wrote in 1973.[16]

"There was quite a forest when I left, before the war started," recalls Bill Gagnon, a White Earth elder, "and when I came back on furlough, there was just a desert. There was no timber left."[17] Another notes how

> the clearcut logging just hurts everything.... I have a place I like to pick strong woods medicines. The medicine I pick in the jackpine forest, it's a lifesaver. The jackpines, they've been butchered. Where they've been butchered, the medicine's gone.[18]

In the beginning, the Anishinaabeg people simply crowded together in the remaining houses, as one family was pushed off the land into another family's house. This adaptation was not without consequences, as the recently traumatized refugee population was susceptible to illness. From 1910 to 1920, epidemics of trachoma and tuberculosis swept through the villages on White Earth. Every family was affected, and some families disappeared altogether. As Minnesota historian William Folwell reports,

> The principal conditions of the Indians at White Earth the inspectors found to be "very bad." Fully 60 percent of the people were infected with tuberculosis, from 30 to 35 percent with trachoma, and from 15 to 20 percent with syphilis; and the diseases were on the increase.[19]

After a few years, the federal government came to view the social experiment of White Earth as a failure and sought to relocate the White Earth people to urban areas. This was perceived as the final assimilation and the end of a long road for the White Earth people. By 1930, of the total enrolled population of 8,584 persons, only 4,628 remained on the reservation, slightly more than half. In the mid-1930s, more White Earth land was annexed to form the northern half of the Tamarac National Wildlife Refuge, which ostensibly became a hunting area for non-Indians from the South. By 1934, only 7,890 acres, or less than ten percent, of the reservation was in tribal trust, and Indians were being arrested for traditional harvesting on White Earth land that was now considered "private property" requiring permits. In a harvesting economy that had existed for eons, this was a strange transformation.[20]

Removals continued under the so-called Relocation Act of the 1950s, under which tribal members (and native people across the country) were offered one-way bus tickets to major urban areas.

The Land Struggle Continues

In 1966, as a result of mounting criticism of its management of the estate of Native peoples, the "wards of the federal government," Congress decided to look at the problem of loss of land and other assets in Native America. It had become clear to the public that in spite of the supposedly vast Native landholdings, Indian people were not doing very well. Every economic, social, and health indicator showed Native people at the bottom.

Title VIII of the U.S. Code, section 2415, mandated a federal investigation into land and trespass issues since the turn of the century on some 40 reservations in the United States. It wasn't until 1978 that what became known as the "2415 investigation" came to White Earth, and it was 1981 when federal investigators began to interview elders on the reservation, who had first-hand knowledge of how the land had been plied, stolen, or taken.

However, the investigation did reveal the tangled mess that each title to Anishinaabeg land had become. For over 60 years, the Bureau of Indian Affairs hadn't properly recorded the many complex transactions that had occurred during the great transfer of land from Indian to non-Indian hands. Ultimately, it was revealed that the state of Minnesota's claim to White Earth lands and their subsequent sales and transfers of those lands were, in fact, illegal. Further damning the state's Native land transactions, the Minnesota Supreme Court ruled, in the 1977 case *State of Minnesota v. Zah Zah,* that the tax forfeitures that removed the Indians from the lands in the late 1800s were also illegal. According to the court, "the removal of the U.S. government's trust responsibility under the 1889 Nelson Act should not have occurred unless the allottee applied for such removal."[21]

In 1982, with less than a third of its research complete, the 2415 investigation team published a preliminary list of several hundred land parcels with questionable title transactions. The title to such parcels was "clouded," they wrote, and thus could not be legally sold or transferred until the title was cleared. This meant that thousands of acres of Minnesota's land, much of which was owned by farmers, could not be used by their erstwhile owners as collateral to secure mortgages or other sorts of loans.

The White Earth Land Settlement Act

It was at the same time that the northern rural farm economy was begin-ning its cycle of failure, primarily as a result of bad government policies and, some would say, corporate subsidies. While some farms were not affected by the initial federal title determinations, others were implicated with clouded title on all or parts of their land, further deepening farmers' already precarious finan-cial situation.

There has always been an anti-Indian sentiment in America. Over time and with awareness and the arrival of new immigrants to serve as scapegoats, those sentiments have waned in segments of the population. In areas adjacent to and within Native communities, however, anti-Indian racism has often remained and at times flourished.

A 1995 paper by Rudolph C. Rÿser of the Center for World Indigenous Studies in Olympia, Washington, chronicles the growth of the anti-Indian move-ment, from vigilante groups in the 1980s to white-supremacist and wise-use groups in the 1990s. According to Rÿser, since the 1970s,

> resident and absentee non-Indian landholders and businesses objected to the growing exercise of general governmental powers by tribal gov-ernments. This is...true in the areas of taxation, zoning, construction, and land use ordinances.... When tribal governments began to exercise the will of tribal members, tribal officials used governmental powers to restrain the actions of persons who depended on reservation land and resources for their personal wealth, but were not willing to share with other members of the tribe.[22]

The few court cases decided in favor of Native people fanned the anti-Indian sentiment. In the 1974 *Boldt* decision in Washington State, Native peoples' right to fish was recognized. For some non-Indian people in the region, this was perceived as a "gift" to Indians at the expense of personal property rights.[23] Anti-Indian organizations such as Interstate Congress for Equal Rights and Responsibilities, Protect American Rights and Resources, Stop Treaty Abuse, and Totally Equal Americans were formed.

A subsequent decision in Wisconsin, the *Voigt* decision, a decade later es-calated the movement. This time, the controversy was over the court's affirma-tion of the Anishinaabeg right to harvest a multitude of natural resources, including walleyes—the preferred fish of sports-fishermen in Wisconsin and Minnesota. The court held that Anishinaabeg did not relinquish their reserved rights to harvest when permanent reservations were established.

The sports-fishing and hunting industries were some of the most vocal proponents of anti-Indian sentiments. Bumper stickers that read "Save a Deer, Shoot an Indian; Save a Walleye, Spear an Indian" began appearing on cars. Paul Mullaly from Wisconsin claimed that the *Voigt* decision "discriminates against white people in the area and is not the kind of thing that should occur in a democracy." Mullaly founded the anti-Indian organization Equal Rights for Everyone, which claimed 31,000 members, many in Minnesota.[24]

The racial slurs, intimidation, and threats Native people experienced led the FBI to investigate the potential for violence. Resort owners were investigated to determine if they might be implicated in threats to "kill Indians if they came on certain lakes."[25]

Many of these groups moved to White Earth or emerged anew on the reservation, as the land issue became more visible. United Townships Association emerged, and chapters of Totally Equal Americans and Protect American Rights and Resources were opened. These groups were concerned with the protection of their "private property" and the exercise of Native rights on the reservation, whether to land or to natural resources. As reservation resident Bruce Berg, a vocal opponent of Native rights, wrote in a letter to the editor of the *Detroit Lakes Tribune*,

> The time for treaty abuse of fish and wildlife has long since vanished. Treaties enacted 125 years ago when wildlife and fisheries management were unknown concepts must not be used as an excuse to neglect conservation practices, or as a tool to raid state treasuries.

Many of these groups eventually coalesced with the national "wise-use" movement, in coalition with county governments who sought to abrogate Indian treaties and the far right and white-supremacist groups.[26]

It was in this climate that Minnesota's Republican Representative Arlan Stangeland moved to terminate Anishinaabeg rights to land on the reservation. In 1983, Stangeland forwarded a bill calling for Congress to "clear title" to White Earth lands retroactively, by compensating Indian people for the land and confirming the titles of non-Indian landholders. His bill, the White Earth Land Settlement Act (WELSA), was to pay the White Earth people $3,000,000. "The Indians will get the land back when hell freezes over," he flippantly noted to the press, on more than one occasion.[27]

But by couching the idea of returning land documented as stolen or otherwise illegally taken to Native people as a "misbegotten" congressional effort to render "after-the-fact justice," Stangeland was able to attract some support for his proposal.[28] In 1982, the 2415 investigation at White Earth was suspended "indefinitely," with only one-third of the titles researched.[29]

Stangeland entreated the White Earth Tribal Council to settle. The council, influenced by Stangeland's threats and his political power as a multi-term Republican Representative, initially agreed, until approximately 500 tribal members, and then hundreds more, demanded that the offer be rejected. By 1985, the federal government's offer was for $17 million. But it was rejected again by community people who maintained that the "land is not for sale." For the Anishinaabeg, it had been clear for centuries that "cash payments for land mean little if a tribe has no political power," as Wabunoquod, headsman of the Mississippi band, had put it in 1874, "and consequently no control over the money paid for the land."[30]

The volume of community resistance to the settlement grew. But in 1986, tribal chairman Darrell Wadena (a.k.a. Chip)—who was later ousted on corruption charges—overrode his community, flew to Washington, D.C., and secured passage of the bill. It was passed in an unusual move, known as "suspension of the rules," in a voice vote with only 12 members of Congress present. The final bill offered approximately $17 million, or the 1910 value of their titles, without interest or damages, in paltry compensation for 10,000 acres of land.

WELSA was a slap in the face to the people of White Earth. It left our people with little choice. In June 1986, a organization dedicated to the White Earth land struggle, Anishinaabe Akiing, supported 44 plaintiffs in a class-action suit, *Manypenny v. United States,* challenging the legality of reservation land takings. In 1987, another suit was filed, *Little Wolf v. United States,* which argued that the WELSA violated the Fifth Amendment guaranteeing just compensation, due process, and equal protection under the law—rights that Stangeland would apply to some citizens but not to Native people. A third suit, *Fineday v. United States,* was filed on the same grounds as *Manypenny.*

The federal circuit courts ruled against the Anishinaabeg. In *Manypenny* and *Fineday,* the courts decided that the statute of limitations on the titles in question had expired. In *Little Wolf,* the court decided that since Native people had the right to sue, they also had an option not to accept the WELSA; in other words, they had redress if they felt their constitutional rights were violated. And so, Congress's policies of land seizure and paltry compensation remained standing, and the land tenure crisis on White Earth continued.

In 1990, U.S. Census data indicated that the unemployment rate for non-Indian people on the White Earth reservation was 12.6 percent, but the unemployment rate for Indian people on the reservation was almost 50 percent.[31]

Poverty rates for Indian people on the reservation were a third higher than for non-Indian people, and the overall social and physical health of the community was in decline.

The majority of the white population on White Earth is landed farmers, while the majority of Indians on the reservation lives in government housing projects. Most of the lake shore is owned by absentee landlords, as are some of the larger landholdings, including the 5,000-acre Oxley Cattle Ranch, whose corporate headquarters are located in Tulsa, Oklahoma. But while the landed white farmers age, retire, and emigrate out of the area, the landless Indians get younger and more numerous. The average age for a non-Indian farmer on the reservation is 57 years, while the average age of a Native person on White Earth is 18 years. The Native birth rate is three times the non-Native. These trends—fewer non-Indian residents, more absentee owners, and a growing, mostly landless Indian community—are projected to continue over the next decades. The crisis between who lives on the land and who owns it will continue.[32]

Extra-Territorial Treaty Rights

Non-Indians dominate hunting and fishing on reservation lands. Non-Indians on the White Earth reservation harvest roughly twice as many deer as the Indian people on the reservation. Inside the Tamarac National Wildlife Refuge, white deer hunters took nine times more deer than tribal members. Fishing is not much different. The White Earth Reservation Biology Department reported, for instance, that tribal members took just 3.3 percent of the walleye catch at one major reservation fishing lake. The remaining walleyes were taken by non-Indian fishers.[33]

Yet even though the Anishinaabeg take of the harvest is relatively small, many of the hunters and fisherman who dominate the lands have opposed Anishinaabeg attempts to discuss recovery of land, exercise of jurisdiction, or traditional harvesting. There is an assumption of entitlement to the reservation lands that these non-Indian sports-hunters and fishers seem to have, that the reservation lands should continue to be their hunting and recreation area.

In the past two decades, U.S. courts have recognized the "extra-territorial treaty rights" of Anishinaabeg people in the region. Most notably, the 1987 *Voigt* and 1997 *Mille Lacs* decisions upheld Anishinaabeg rights to harvest fish, animals, or whatever else they deem appropriate, from lands in the northern third of Wisconsin and Minnesota.[34]

The five-to-four decision by the Supreme Court in the *Mille Lacs* decision ended a pitched battle between the state and the 1,200-member Mille Lacs band. The court recognized a continuation of Anishinaabeg harvesting rights to hunt and fish on 13 million acres of "ceded land" in east central Minnesota and western Wisconsin, as had been upheld in the *Voigt* decision. The Mille Lacs band is allocated some 40,000 pounds of walleye on Mille Lacs Lake, for instance, one of the most plentiful walleye fishing lakes in Minnesota. In 1998, non-Indian sports-fishers harvested over 355,000 pounds of fish from the lake, while the Mille Lacs tribal members took some 38,000 pounds.[35]

White Earth Land Recovery Project

> We do not have thousands upon thousands of dollars. We do not have great mansions of beauty. We do not have priceless objects of art. We do not lead a life of ease nor do we live in luxury. We do not own the land upon which we live. We do not have the basic things of life which we are told are necessary to better ourselves. We do not have the tools to be self-sufficient. But today, I want to tell you that we do not need these things. What we do need, however, is what we already have. What we do need has been provided to us by the Great Spirit.... We need to realize who we are and what we stand for.... We are the keepers of that which the Great Spirit has given to us, that is, our language, our culture, our drum societies, our religion, and, most important of all, our traditional way of life.... We need to be the Anishinaabeg again.
>
> —Egiwaateshkang, George Aubid, Sr.[36]

In 1989, to directly address the crisis of land tenure on White Earth, we founded the White Earth Land Recovery Project (WELRP) with the proceeds of a Reebok Human Rights Award. The WELRP works to return White Earth land to the Anishinaabeg by supporting the transfer of public lands back to the White Earth tribal government, buying land from willing sellers, and other mechanisms. To date, we have purchased over 1,300 acres of land—primarily maple sugarbush, the most endangered ecosystem on the reservation—which is held in a conservation land trust. The project also seeks to preserve White Earth land, even when held by others, including Native cemeteries, forests, and other endangered ecosystems. The project works aggressively to preserve Native languages and culture, restore traditional seed stocks, and reinstate self-determination and self-reliance. The WELRP is the largest independent reservation nonprofit in the state of Minnesota and is one of the four largest nationally.

In 1920, half a world away in India, Vinoba Bhave, the leader of the land reform movement, argued that "it is highly inconsistent that those who possess the land should not till it themselves, and those who cultivate should possess no land to do so."[37] Through the work of Bhave and others, millions of acres of land were returned to the people. The WELRP sees the situation at White Earth as the same as that in any poor community with absentee landholdings and takes the victories of land reform movements across the globe as inspiration.

In 1993, the WELRP launched its Sustainable Communities initiative. Its goal is to meld the useful and meaningful aspects of both traditional Anishinaabeg and Euro-American culture into a truly sustainable way of living for willing Anishinaabeg people. The four areas we focus on are forestry, energy, agriculture, and culture.

Noopiming: In the Woods

> My old hunting grounds are all damaged. It's all clearcut. I hunted there my whole life, so did my dad. Now it's like hunting in a strange country.
>
> —Gordy Goodman, Ponsford hunter and traditional harvester[38]

The struggle to preserve the trees of White Earth is not solely about forest preservation and biodiversity. It is also about cultural transformation, for the Anishinaabeg forest culture cannot exist without the forest.

Non-Indians, the federal government, the state, the county, and tribal members all own lands adjoining the reservation. This puzzle of land-ownership means that while one landowner may limit logging on his or her land to some 20- or 40-acre slot, clearcuts (or "patch cuts" or "contour cuts" as they are also called) may well adjoin another clearcut on someone else's land, increasing the ecological damage to the region. For instance, in July 1995, high winds exacerbated by the clearcuts flattened over 100,000 acres of trees on the reservation.

When the high winds hit the reservation, the press called it a "natural disaster." But when lumber companies similarly vanquish the trees, it is commonly called "progress." All across the region, lumber companies are expanding, a result, many Anishinaabeg say, of heightened resistance to logging elsewhere in the country. The Minnesota lumber industry cuts 4.1 million cords of wood every year. This industry has turned its attention to the boreal forest, which still covers most of northern Minnesota, Wisconsin, and Michigan, and much of the Canadian provinces of Ontario, Manitoba, and Quebec. This land is largely Anishinaabeg Akiing, Ojibwe country.

Since 1983, the lumber company Potlatch (a descendant of Frederick Weyerhauser's empire) has operated a lumber-processing plant in St. Louis County, northeast of the reservation. Potlatch is the largest clearcutting operation in the area. In June 1995 the company sought state approval for an expansion that would allow it to double the plant's manufacturing capacity, increasing its wood consumption from 178,000 cords per year to 355,000 cords per year. The expansion would result in the loss of approximately 7,600 mature-forest acres per year, primarily from northeastern Minnesota. If the company successfully completes its expansion plans, the lumber industry will be cutting a square mile of Minnesota's northwoods every day. Six timber-rich reservations lie within the borders of the state, as do three proposed huge pulp and paper mill expansions.[39]

Federally managed lands are equally problematic. President Bill Clinton, early on in his administration, talked about providing economic opportunity for Indian tribes, by "bringing backlogged Indian timber to market," something Native forest activists have referred to as "equal opportunity clearcutting." Federal officials prioritized logging and cultivation of aspen in the Tamarac National Wildlife Refuge, which spans some 21,000 acres of the reservation. Between 1982 and 1992, 97,970 cords of wood were taken from refuge lands, 83 percent of it "popple," or aspen. The vast majority of the harvest was taken from the areas of the refuge that fall within the reservation borders, and 66 percent of the total harvest was designated for Potlatch and other paper mills in the region.[40]

Forest preservation work at the WELRP is multifaceted, involving both litigation and organizing to preserve the forests of the North and to show that our forests are worth more standing. In the Summer of 1994, Potlatch attempted to cross WELRP land and roads to access adjacent forests for clearcutting. After the county refused to stop the trespassing, the community members and WELRP staff blockaded the road the loggers had used, which as it turned out was the WELRP driveway, only to be undercut by the tribal council, which allowed the company access across tribal land.

We have seen another way. The Menominee reservation in Wisconsin successfully fought off termination and allotment and kept their forests, which today stand as a testimony to what could be. According to their booklet on sustainable forest development:

> To many, our forest may seem pristine and untouched. In reality, it is one
> of the most intensely managed tracts of forest in the lake states. During the
> past 140 years, we have harvested more than two and one-half billion

board-feet of lumber from our land. That is the equivalent of cutting all the standing timber on the reservation almost twice over. Yet, the saw timber volume now standing is greater than that which was here in 1854 when the Wolf River Treaty defined the reservation.[41]

As with the Menominee and our other Algonkin relatives, determination and dignity motivate the people of White Earth, ensuring that the way of life continues. In 1998, we began work with a multitude of agencies to develop a forest management plan similar to that utilized at Menominee.

Gaa-Noodin-Oke: The Windmaker

By the 1990s, the Minnesota Department of Health and the Clean Water Action Project found that the area lakes were contaminated with mercury and heavy metals, including PCBs. The primary sources of the contamination are coal-fired power plants and incinerators often located hundreds of miles away. The entire food chain is exposed to the mercury; people are exposed primarily by consuming contaminated fish. The effects of mercury poisoning include nerve and kidney damage, muscle tremors, and fetal abnormalities.

Annually since 1993, Minnesota's Department of Health has advised a consumption limit of just one walleye per week for seasonal fish consumers and one walleye a month for year-round fish consumers at many lakes on or near the White Earth, Red Lake, Leech Lake, and Mille Lacs Lake reservations, which are extensively fished by Indigenous people. Surveys and tribal data indicate that while non-Indians take more fish from White Earth than Indians do, most White Earth Anishinaabeg consume more fish per capita than non-Indians.

In response, a cooperative program between the WELRP, Indigenous Environmental Network, and Clean Water Action Project has been established to increase awareness of the link between the power plants and the mercury poisoning in the lakes and, in the case of White Earth, to counter it directly with an alternative source of energy: wind power. And in 1996, the WELRP erected two wind anemometers to test wind energy potential, with hopes that by 2000, a 20-kilowatt wind turbine can be erected on the reservation.

Other WELRP programs have focused on restoring traditional farming. The Anishinaabeg people are traditionally strong agriculturalists. But traditional agricultural practices on the reservation have diminished, as non-Indians and corporate interests have controlled more and more reservation land. Over a third of the reservation is under increasing industrialized and chemically intensive agricultural development, with devastating consequences. Since 1858, some 50 percent of the reservation's wetlands have been lost, largely due to ill-founded agricultural practices. Between 1955 and 1975, Mahnomen County lost more than 30,000 acres of wetlands, or over 60 percent. Between 1987 and 1992, over 1,800 tons of fertilizer and over 110,000 gallons of pesticides and herbicides were applied to White Earth lands every year.[42] Over 12,000 acres of reservation land are held by RDO Offutt, the largest potato grower in the world, which has contaminated the groundwater with herbicides and fungicides. As more and more small farmers leave the reservation lands or fall into economic hardship, corporate interests such as this one are increasingly dominant.

In the face of globalization, we have moved toward recovery of local self-reliance. In the mid-1990s, the WELRP began restoring the traditional hominy crop and purchased an organic raspberry farm. The project also began Native Harvest, a community development project, to restore traditional foods and capture a fair market price for traditionally and organically grown foods. Along with hominy corn and organic raspberries, Native Harvest sells wild rice, maple candy, buffalo sausage, and maple syrup.

There is nothing quite like walking through a small field of hominy corn, corn you know your ancestors planted on this same land a thousand years ago. Corn is in the recipes and memories of elders. That inherited memory is the essence of cultural restoration and the force that grows with each step toward the path—"the lifeway"—as some of the Anishinaabeg call it.

Finally, at the center of WELRP's cultural work is language. While most North American Indigenous languages are expected to be extinct by the year 2050, the Anishinaabeg language is one of approximately five expected to survive. That is because there are an estimated 50,000 speakers, most of whom live the process of reaffirming the traditional way of life and its ceremony, dances, songs, and prayers to which the elders refer.[43]

Since 1995, the WELRP has worked on a range of language restoration projects. The WELRP's Wadiswaan Project is an early-childhood language-revitalization program in one of the tribal schools. The WELRP also organizes adult/family language-immersion retreats and takes children out of school into the woods, the sugarbush, the corn fields, and the heart of cultural practice. All of this is a slow process, but in the WELRP philosophy it is thought that these children will be leading our community in 20 or 30 years and that we need to ensure that they know something about who they are, why we are here, and how we talk to the Creator. Renewal is a central part of each generation's responsibility.

Noojwiijigamigishkawajig: Finding Neighbors (Friends)

When the Anishinaabeg discuss land return, as with other Native people, lines are often drawn between those environmentalists who can support Indigenous rights to self-determination and those who fundamentally cannot. Some call it environmental colonialism, others call it plain racism and privilege. The underlying problem is often quite basic, revolving around historic views of who should control land, perceptions of Native people, and ideas about how now-endangered ecosystems should be managed. Most disturbing is the widespread absence of any historic knowledge of traditional Native tenure on these lands and the demise of Native ecological and economic systems.

There are many ways in which these lines are drawn. The National Wildlife Federation, for instance, sued the Bureau of Land Management (BLM) to make it stop leasing five canyons in southern Utah to the Ute. According to environmental writer Mark Dowie,

> Native Americans thought they had seen all the callous discrimination and insensitivity they could imagine. They were shocked, then, when, two centuries later, white environmentalists took positions that jeopardized their survival.... [In response to the National Wildlife Federation suit] the tribe, which had been grazing about 200 head of cattle in these canyons for generations, intervened on behalf of the BLM, which lost the suit. The Utes lost another piece of their livelihood.[44]

The Nature Conservancy, a wealthy national environmental organization with chapters across the country, likes to buy land and preserve it. The conservancy holds over one million acres of land in the United States. In 1983, the Nature Conservancy purchased 400 acres on the White Earth reservation in order to preserve it. Then they gave that land to the state of Minnesota, with not so much as a by-your-leave to the Native community that lived there. Although the conservancy recognized their *faux pas* in internal briefing documents, the organization has expressed no interest in working collaboratively with the reservation to restore and preserve its ecosystems. When approached to consider collaborative ventures with the Native people of White Earth, the conservancy has thus far shunned us as marginal to the conservancy's priorities. According to the conservancy, its resources are allocated in other areas, presumably based on the interests of its primarily white, urban, middle-class membership. The endangered maple-basswood ecosystem of the reservation has not appeared on their radar screen.

In 1992, on behalf of the WELRP and the White Earth reservation, I asked the Sierra Club to support the return of the northern half of the Tamarac National Wildlife Refuge to the White Earth band. A number of Minnesota's environmental, social justice, and other organizations gave their support to the effort, and about 4,000 individuals sent supportive postcards to the U.S. Department of Fish and Wildlife. But the Sierra Club Northstar Chapter would not lend its support because, its representatives explained, if the lands were returned to the White Earth band, the club (and its primarily non-Indian constituency) would not have a say in refuge management.[45]

Elsewhere in the Great Lakes area, organizations such as HONOR (Honor Our Neighbors' Origins and Rights), Midwest Treaty Network, and many others have come to the support of the Anishinaabeg and their rights to land, harvesting, and a future. And the growing environmental justice movement combines anti-racism with environmental work.

Minobimaatisiiwin: The Good Life

There is no way to quantify a way of life, only a way to live it. *Minobimaatisiiwin* means "the good life." Used in blessings, thanksgivings, and ceremonies, it refers to the lifeway, evoked in the words of Fish Clan elder and scholar Jim Dumont:

> Our ways are still there, our way of life. Here we are in the dying moments of the twentieth century, almost into the twenty-first century, and we say the reality that we live within is totally different from anything we ever knew. It is just a different environment, a different context. Not a very good one, not a very harmonious or balanced one, not a very healthy one, but this is the environment that we live in today. The lifeway that spoke to our people before, and gave our people life in all the generations before us, is still the way of life that will give us life today. How it will manifest itself and find expression in this new time comes as a part of the responsibility of how we go about the revival and renewal.[46]

"You can cut a tree once and get some money," explains Ronnie Chilton, "but if you make syrup every year, you will get money, you will get food, a sweet taste, you will smell Spring, and you will get food for your soul."[47] True to form, in 1999 Ronnie Chilton was in the maple sugarbush, where he, Pat Wichern, Paul Jackson, Wanda Jackson, and a host of others waded through snow to set 4,400 taps in the trees. A team of coal-black Percheron horses,

Rosebud and Aandeg, hauled the bobsled full of sap and sap haulers to the evaporator: a 20-foot-by-4-foot monstrosity, which steams through the crisp Spring's sleet, sun, and wind. There was once a time when all the maple sugar and maple candy in North America was produced by Native people. Now, less than 1 percent of commercially available syrup is produced by Native people, although many families still make their annual trek to the sugarbush for a time of reawakening and of the return of Spring.

By 1999, the WELRP had purchased almost 300 acres of maple sugarbush. The lands will be protected from the butchers with chainsaws, and the sugarbush will be maintained for generations to come.

That year, Native Harvest started selling maple sugar candy, its taste reminding people of the sweetness of life. WELRP staff returned four sturgeon to a reservation lake and, with the Tribal Biology Department, began a long process of bringing back the fish. In 1999, 50,000 sturgeon hatchlings returned to White Earth. *Azhegiiwewag.*

The WELRP is only a small part of the White Earth community. While all the white man's laws have made it difficult to be Anishinaabeg, this community, like many others along the trail of migration laid by long-ago ancestors, is maintaining its way of life. Surveys conducted in the late 1980s, supported by interviews in more recent years, show that at least 65 percent of the people on White Earth hunt for deer and for small game. Forty-five percent harvest wild rice, with somewhat fewer engaged in subsistence fishing. Most of those who do not themselves harvest traditional foods trade with others who do. In spite of all the laws, all the time, and all the historic clearcutting, the land is still here, and the land is still good.

Lennie Butcher lives on a side road on the outskirts of Bemidji. His front yard is occupied by a partially constructed wigwam. Lennie is a man of the woods of White Earth. He harvests most things in season and raises his four children to live a traditional life as much as possible. Right now, he doesn't live on the reservation, but just the same, he continues the traditional way of life, undaunted by the white man's laws and practices.

I interviewed him in 1997, after he had been arrested, yet again, for his harvesting activities, this time for shooting deer in the four townships area, which the state considers its property.[48] In a consistently thoughtful, slow, and contemplative stream of consciousness Lennie began talking:

> I wasn't born to be rich. I was born to live a good life.... I hunt all
> over. I don't believe the white man has a right to stop us and don't understand what they say and what they do. Moose travel down to Min-

neapolis…. That's the way we used to move…where the food went. Now they kill the moose if they think it's a nuisance. And the honkers down in the cities, they shock them and kill them, yet they won't let us get to them. The white man kills the deer that eat the shrubbery, yet they won't let us hunt them, we people that are connected to them…. I just want them to live up to this land, to what they said and to themselves…. I don't mean to disrespect anyone, just to be who I am.

They cut down all the trees, the fir trees, all of them, and then they say we can't practice our way of life. All these plants are given to us as medicines from the sweatlodge, and this is who we are. We are this land, and everything that comes from it. There is no freedom, no sovereignty…. Freedom is living how I choose to in my people's way.[49]

In the dying moments of the twentieth century, a spirit and a lifeway prevail in the northwoods. Not in spite of it all—the rapacious culture eaters, the loggers, the miners—but because that spirit and lifeway have sustained a community for generations. Like the eternal Spring, after the freezing Winter, there is always a rebirth. *Minobimaatisiiwin. Mi'iw.*

Rosalie Little Thunder. Photo by Susan Alzner

The four leggeds came before the two leggeds. They are our older brothers, we came from them. Before them, we were the root people. That is why we are spiritually related to them. We call them in our language Tatanka, *which means "He Who Owns Us." We cannot say that we own the buffalo, because he owns us.*

—Birgil Kills Straight, Oglala Lakota[1]

7

Buffalo Nations, Buffalo Peoples

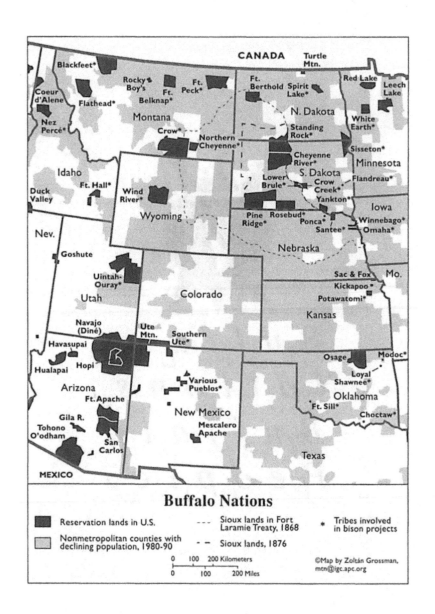

Buffalo Nations

- **Reservation lands in U.S.**
- Nonmetropolitan counties with declining population, 1980-90
- - - - Sioux lands in Fort Laramie Treaty, 1868
- - - Sioux lands, 1876
- * Tribes involved in bison projects

```
0      100    200 Kilometers
0       100        200 Miles
```

©Map by Zoltán Grossman, mtn@igc.apc.org

Buffalo peoples dream of their buffalo, their older brothers. They dream of them, and through those dreams, ceremony, and hard work, they are bringing back those herds, bringing back the buffalo. "If I had my way, I'd turn the whole upper Midwest into a buffalo area," Birgil Kills Straight explains. I'm talking to him in Pine Ridge, South Dakota, where, under the auspices of the Oglala Lakota Natural Resource Management Program, the 500-strong Oglala buffalo herd is roaming, with about as little bothering by humans as is possible in this day and age. The Oglala Lakota, in *tiwahe* (families), in *tiosapaye* (extended families), and as *oyate* (a nation), are one of many native nations that have begun restoring their herds. As the herds grow, the collective mental and spiritual health of the people, many say, is being restored as well.

"The buffalo have the right to be here, they were here before we were; this is their land as well. Just because we can articulate some of our needs and wishes and we seem to have some sort of intelligence and intellect, we think we're better," says Birgil. He pauses, thinking again about his relatives. "If you communicate with a buffalo, you'll see that they're much more intelligent than a human, just that they can't articulate it as humans. [We] rely on the buffalo. As long as the buffalo live, we can also live."

It is not far down the pothole-marked roads that Buzz Ironcloud's family has its own dreams of buffalo. Buzz Ironcloud's family welcomed back their first buffalo calf in late 1997. It was like welcoming home a long-lost relative. Ironcloud, who heads the Knife Chief Buffalo Project near the village of Porcupine on the Pine Ridge reservation said that before then, "we only saw buffalo at state parks or in pictures. It was really good to actually be close to one."[2]

To the north of Pine Ridge is the Standing Rock reservation, and there, too, an innovative, community-based project is underway to restore the buffalo. In the Seventh Generation Buffalo Cooperative, ten individuals—representing as many member families—are sweating on weekends to fence 2,000 acres of land for their collective buffalo herd. By 1998, they had 21 animals. The cooperative hopes to have 150 animals in the next few years, explains Shilo Comeau, and to support a number of families by loaning them young cows in return for future offspring. The goal is to foster a diverse buffalo herd, collectively held by a number of Lakota families.[3]

Amidst all this, there is Rosalie Little Thunder, a Lakota grandmother who lives on Rosebud reservation and is standing up for the buffalo spirits, and the buffalo themselves. The state of Montana slaughtered and auctioned off over 2,500 buffalo between 1995 and 1997. A third of the herd from Yellowstone National Park was shot when it crossed the invisible border between park and state land.[4] In 1998, however, only 11 buffalo were killed, largely due to Rosalie's vigilance.[5] Rosalie and a resolute group of friends called Buffalo Nations have, through direct action and civil disobedience, put themselves between the buffalo and the guns of Montana's state officials, part of this century-old, seemingly continuous slaughter. By acting as a human shield, they have asked a simple question: When will the buffalo be allowed to return to their past prominence, and when will their spirits be free?

It is said that should the Earth, the mother of all life, ever be shaken to crisis by the people living upon her, then the White Buffalo Calf Woman will return. In the Summer of 1995, a white buffalo calf was born in southern Wisconsin. Called "Miracle," the calf has brought new hope to the buffalo nation and the buffalo peoples of the Great Plains. The return of the White Buffalo Calf Woman symbolizes the beginning of a new time, a new era, and with it the promise of restoration.

That is the process unfolding in the Great Plains today, a place where the grass calls to the buffalo, and their hooves respond with thundering, it is said, that resonates in the vast underground water table. The buffalo were made for the prairie, and the prairie for the buffalo.

Buffalo and Prairie Ecosystems

In 1800, 40 million buffalo roamed the North American plains.[6] They were the most numerous grazing animals on earth, their numbers surpassing even the immense wildebeest herds in Africa. Buffalo, prairie ecosystems, and Indigenous peoples have co-evolved in the center of North America for thousands of years.

Bisons' massive heads are uniquely equipped to plow through snow. The hardiness that enables bison to survive the severe climate of the plains is especially impressive when compared to cattle's vulnerability. The deep snow and searing cold of the Winter of 1996 killed over 450,000 head of livestock out of approximately 45 million. (Similar deaths had occurred in the Winters of 1885-86 and 1906-07.) Cattle could not break through the snow. Many would call this evidence that domesticated livestock do not belong in the ecosystem. Buffalo in these same circumstances fared much better in 1996: fewer than 20 out of about 10,000 were lost in all tribal herds within the blizzard zone, and those mostly from wandering over drifted fence lines and into traffic.[7] The buffalo peoples will say that there is a lesson in all that death. (Even in death, there are lessons.) The prairies are where the buffalo are intended to be.

Land Grabbing and Buffalo Killing

> These men (the buffalo hunters) have done...more to settle the vexed Indian question than the entire regular army has done in the last thirty years. They are destroying the Indians' commissary.... Send them powder and lead if you will, but for the sake of lasting peace let them kill, skin, and sell until the buffalo are exterminated. Then your prairie can be covered with speckled cattle and the festive cowboy who follows the hunter as the second forerunner of an advanced civilization.
>
> —General Philip Sheridan, Commander of the Armies of the West, in remarks at the Texas legislature, 1875[8]

During the 1800s, buffalo killing was part of military policy, and land grabbing was part of America. Treaty after treaty was signed during the great buffalo slaughters. These two policies were key to the colonization of the plains: the expansion of the cattle and beef empires and, of course, the industrialization of American agriculture.

During the mid-1800s, federal and private encroachment into Native areas protected by treaty increased dramatically and pushed Native nations and buffalo into smaller and smaller areas. During the 1860s, Abraham Lincoln signed the Homestead Act, granting 90 million acres of western lands to railroad companies to persuade them to push into the West. By 1867, market hunting of the bison was growing exponentially. The extermination proceeded in three distinct phases, precisely corresponding to the extension of the railroads—the Union Pacific and Central Pacific (1869); Southern Pacific (1883); Northern Pacific (1883); Atchison, Topeka and Santa Fe (1885); and Great Northern (1885)—into three broad sections of the country. Those railroads moved the hunters in and the hides out, and were the vehicle for an astonishing slaughter. The speed of passenger trains was slow at that time, and, as historian Tom McHugh wrote, "it often happens that the cars and buffalo would be side by side for a mile or two...during these races, the car windows are opened, and numerous breech-loaders fling hundreds of bullets among the densely crowded and flying masses. Many of the poor animals fall, and more go off to die in the ravines. The train speeds on, and the scene is repeated every few miles."[9] Colonel Richard Irving Dodge reported that near his army post in Kansas, buffalo were limitless in number as late as the Winter of 1871.

By the Fall of 1873, Dodge wrote, "where there were myriads of buffalo the years before, there was now a myriad of carcasses. The air was foul with a sickening stench, and the vast plain, which only a short twelve months before teemed with animal life, was a dead, solitary, putrid desert." Dodge estimated that over four million buffalo had been slain.[10]

When the dust settled, almost 50 million bison were gone—their spirits left to wander the Great Plains without the benefit of ceremony. And the small surviving groups would be left in isolated enclaves, some eventually ending up at Yellowstone.

"To settle the vexed Indian question," buffalo hunters killed the buffalo and thereby destroyed the major food source for the Native people of the prairie—and then set upon their land. Feeding those whom the government had deprived of food and sustenance became a major business and a new commercial opportunity for the fledgling western cattle industries. The Indian Department purchased a large amount of beef from western ranchers, setting the precedent for future price supports. This relationship continues to this day. The federal commodity program (a.k.a. "commods") allocates canned beef, pork, and other food to Indian families. Ironically, many of these products originate from livestock raised on Native lands. This intergenerational distortion of subsistence, and its replacement with industrialized dependency, continues today.

Jeremy Rifkin reports that in 1880 alone, the government bought 39,160,729 pounds of western beef for 34 Indian agencies in ten western states, at prices from $2.23 a hundred-weight at Fort Belknap Agency in Montana, to $3.74 at Los Pinos Agency in Colorado. Some estimates of the amount of beef purchased by federal agencies for distribution to the reservation communities are as high as 50 million pounds annually. According to Edward Dale, "a number of important cattlemen laid the foundations of their large enterprises by securing lucrative government contracts to supply Indians with beef."[11]

Concurrent with the rise of the beef market was the pressure on Native reservation lands. In 1875, four years after Congress had ended formal treaty-making with Native nations, the total reservation land base stood at 166 million acres, or 12 percent of the continental United States. In 1887, with the passage of the General Allotment Act, that would end. Under the act, 118 reservations were "allotted"—that is, the collective landholdings were dissolved—and of those, 44 were opened to homestead entry under public land laws. Approximately 38 million acres of reservation land were "ceded" outright to the government. Another 22 million acres of so-called surplus lands existed after allotments and were opened up for settlement by non-Indians. Within a few years, Indian landholdings had diminished to less than 137 million acres. By 1934, less than 52 million acres of land were retained by Native people.[12]

From 1936 to 1974, an additional eight million acres of land were taken, not including lands taken for right of ways, roads, pipelines, and other power projects. During those years, Indian people lost 13,000 acres of land a year to diversion projects, largely to benefit the farmers and ranchers who had moved into the reservation lands, and those adjoining them, 70 to 100 years before. Remaining reservation lands have been largely allotted. In many cases of so-called fractionated heirship, hundreds of individuals hold title to one allotment, making much of the land inaccessible. More than ten million acres of reservation lands are burdened by this bizarre pattern of land-ownership. Faced with these circumstances, and constant pressure from the Bureau of Indian Affairs and agricultural interests, it is not surprising that non-Indian farmers cultivate, lease, and graze cattle on about 63 percent of Indian agricultural lands.[13] Today, on Cheyenne River reservation in South Dakota, for instance, it is estimated that 50 percent of the reservation is retained by tribal members, with some 80 percent of those tribal holdings leased out directly or indirectly to non-Indian ranchers.[14]

The Buffalo Are Prairie Makers

> For it was the White Buffalo Cow Woman who in the beginning brought to us our most sacred pipe, and from that time, we have been related with the Four-Leggeds and all that moves. Tatanka, the buffalo, is the closest four-legged relative that we have, and they live as a people, as we do.
>
> —Black Elk, Oglala healer, 1863-1950

Buffalo determine landscapes. By their sheer numbers, weight, and behavior, they cultivated the prairie, which is the single largest ecosystem in North America. The destruction of the herd set in motion the ongoing ecological and, now, economic crisis that afflicts the Great Plains. Think of it this way: in 1850, 50 million buffalo ranged the prairie system and left it in excellent shape. One hundred percent of all plant and animal species were present without the "benefit" of fences, federal subsidies, elaborate irrigation systems, or powerful pesticides. Today, a century and a half later, the environment is quite different. Industrialized agriculture has transformed land, life, and water. Forty-five and a half million cattle live in this same ecosystem now, but they lack the adaptability of buffalo. Industrial agriculture determines the entire ecosystem, from feed crop monoculture to feedlots, from underpriced public grazing permits (a holdover

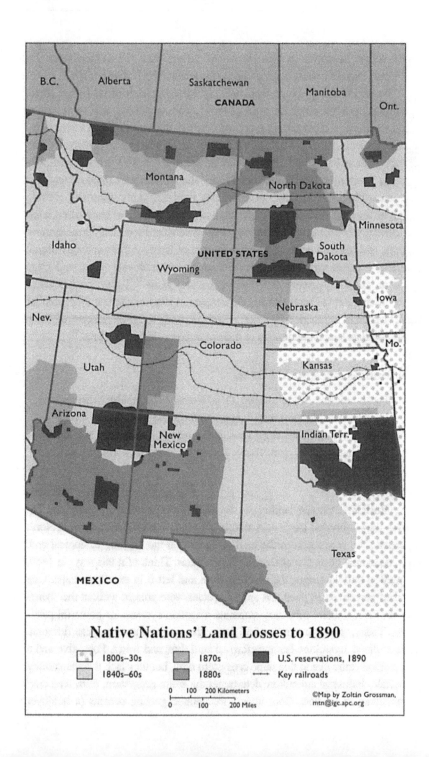

Native Nations' Land Losses to 1890

▦ 1800s–30s	▨ 1870s	■ U.S. reservations, 1890
▨ 1840s–60s	▧ 1880s	┄┄ Key railroads

0   100   200 Kilometers

0   100   200 Miles

©Map by Zoltán Grossman, mtn@igc.apc.org

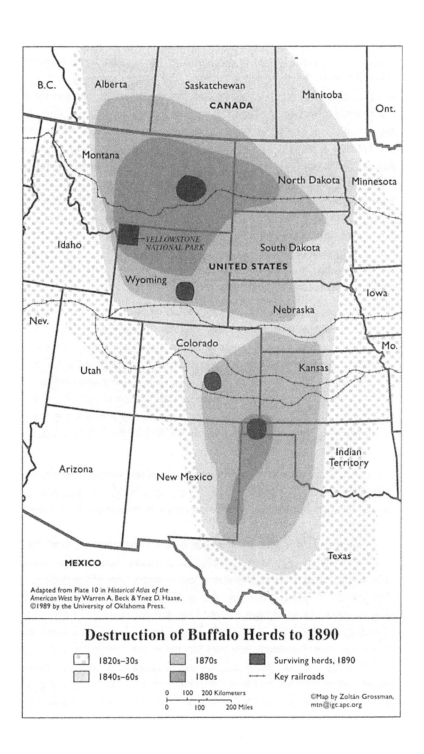

Destruction of Buffalo Herds to 1890

1820s–30s	1870s	Surviving herds, 1890
1840s–60s	1880s	—— Key railroads

0   100   200 Kilometers

0   100   200 Miles

Adapted from Plate 10 in *Historical Atlas of the American West* by Warren A. Beck & Ynez D. Haase, ©1989 by the University of Oklahoma Press.

©Map by Zoltán Grossman, mtn@igc.apc.org

from old reservation leases) to drawdown of the aquifers, agricultural runoff, and soil erosion. Much of this is for cows. The prairies today are teeming with pumps, irrigation systems, combines, and chemical additives. Much of the original ecosystem has been destroyed. The Great Plains have been stripped of their biodiversity. This biome that covers more area than any other in North America has suffered a massive loss of life. As *Grasslands* author Richard Manning writes, "if one can find an ungrazed stretch of native high plains, one can identify as many as 250 species of plants inhabiting a single site. On a site that has been grazed by domesticated livestock, that count would drop to about four; a wheat farmer drops the count to one species. On grass land, soil erosion is virtually nonexistent. On wheat land, it is constant." Manning quotes the Pawnee: "Grass no good turned over." Simple, and to the point.[15]

According to Jeremy Rifkin, cattle are a primary cause of much of the ecological destruction of the western half of the United States:

> Let loose on public lands, each animal eats its way through 900 pounds of vegetation every month. They strip the rangeland of its forage of grass and herbage, and browse on shrubs, trees, cactus, and tree bark. Their powerful cloven hooves trample and compact plant and soil with a pressure of 24 pounds per square inch. The soil compaction reduces the air space between soil particles, reducing the amount of water that can be absorbed. The soil is less able to hold the water from the spring melting of snow and is more prone to erosion from the flash floods that run along the surface.[16]

Over 270 million acres of federal range land are presently leased to cattlemen, often at a highly subsidized rate. Given the subsidy, it is unclear who will pay the long-term cost of the loss of biodiversity in those areas, a direct result of overgrazing.[17]

Cattle and other domestic livestock destroy ecosystems and limit the ecosystems' ability to support wild species, from native birds to large mammals such as elk, bighorn sheep, pronghorn, and antelope. One of the reasons is the sheer amount of land and resources that are allocated for livestock. In the Burns, Oregon, district of the Bureau of Land Management, about 252 million pounds of herbage were allotted to livestock, leaving fewer than eight million pounds for wildlife. Not surprisingly, there are few indigenous species left in the region. A 1990 study, for instance, found that only 20 percent of the Great Plains remained sufficiently unaltered to be potentially capable of ever supporting natural plant communities. No other system has suffered such a massive loss of life.[18]

Then there is the water needed for agriculture and for the cities located in places with little water, which require huge diversion projects. The United States (and Canada, on an almost corresponding scale) has created the world's largest water distribution system ever. The Bureau of Reclamation has irrigated 9.1 million acres and constructed 322 reservoirs, 345 diversion dams, 14,490 miles of canals, 34,990 miles of laterals, 930 miles of pipelines, 218 miles of tunnels, 15,530 miles of drains, 174 pumping plants, and 49 power plants in the United States, much of it in the arid West.[19]

Under the surface of the land, the water is also being pillaged. The Ogallala Aquifer is a cache of ancient freshwater that underlies most of the Great Plains region. The crush of industrialized agriculture in the 1970s is sucking the reservoir dry. Between 1959 and 1977, for instance, Nebraska farmers increased the amount of acreage under irrigation by sevenfold, to seven million acres. By 1975, farmers in the region pumped more than 27 billion gallons a day from the Ogallala Aquifer. Drawdown rates today continue to drop the aquifer level by four feet per year. The recharge of this aquifer is estimated to be one-half inch a year. Today, 20 percent of nationally irrigated cropland is serviced by the Ogallala, but hydrologists suggest it will be depleted within 30 years.[20]

It is also not surprising that we are losing the topsoil in the region. This country has lost nearly one-third of its prime topsoil. Two hundred years ago, most of the prairie region had over 21 inches of topsoil. Today, in some regions, less than six inches remain. The United Nations discusses this phenomenon internationally in terms of desertification. Desertification is attributed largely to overcultivation of land, overgrazing of livestock, deforestation, and improper irrigation techniques. All of this is occurring on the Great Plains, and much of it is underwritten by American taxpayers. Collectively, diversion projects, below-market-price grazing fees on public lands, salvage logging, and subsidies to industrialized agriculture continue to dominate the policies of the region.

The ecological crisis of the region, however, is not a result of one decision, such as that to graze cattle. Many would argue that the ecological future of the Great Plains is intertwined with the psychological and spiritual relationship the prairies and the people of the prairies have with the buffalo, and with American culture and mythology. Cattle culture's takeover of the prairie and the subsequent destruction of the buffalo herds is a multifaceted mistake, and one whose significance is becoming increasingly apparent. At its foundation, many would say, is a spiritual mistake: killing without reverence.

When you take a buffalo, there is a Lakota ceremony, the Buffalo Kill ceremony. In that ceremony, the individual offers prayers and talks to the spirit of the animal. Then, and only then, will the buffalo surrender itself. That is when you can kill the buffalo. That was not done for the 50 million buffalo decimated by U.S. agriculture and buffalo hunters, nor for the present Yellowstone herd, except, that is, for those commemorated in recent times by people like Rosalie Little Thunder, Birgil Kills Straight, and others. To kill incorrectly, many would say, affects and disrupts all life.

Community Health and Buffalo

Pine Ridge is a testimony to survival. It is also a testimony to genocide. From the survivors and descendants of the Wounded Knee Massacre, who to this day cannot get an apology from the federal government for the 1890 massacre, to the stark brutality of a prairie midwinter—frozen cars in snow drifts—Pine Ridge is all of it. The Oglalas are survivors. They are like the Yellowstone herd: besieged, shot down, but still alive. (The Wounded Knee Descendants Association requested an apology and has received "an expression of regret" by Congress, according to Mario Gonzales, Lakota attorney for the association.[21])

Most Indigenous cultures of the western hemisphere suffer from a historical unresolved grief. That is a grief that is accumulated over generations of trauma. Maria Yellow Horse Brave Heart-Jordan chronicles this grief in her study of the Oglala Lakota of Pine Ridge, which has broad implications for the experience of Native peoples, in particular the buffalo peoples and the buffalo nations.

According to Brave Heart-Jordan, despite 54 years of studies on the notorious social, economic, health, and legal problems of the Lakota, there have been few proposed solutions. Alcoholism, unemployment, suicide, accidental death, and homicide rates are still well above the national average. Indian Health Service statistics indicate that alcoholism death rates in the Aberdeen, South Dakota, area are seven times the national average and almost three times that of all Indian people. The suicide rate on one of the Lakota reservations is almost seven times the national average and generally is at least three times the suicide rate of all non-Indians in the state of South Dakota.[22]

Brave Heart-Jordan, who is from Pine Ridge, argues that the Lakota's unresolved grief, what she describes as "a repercussion of the loss of lives, land, and aspects of culture rendered by the European conquest of the Americas," is a "significant factor contributing to current Lakota social pathology."[23] In addition to obvious factors such as massacres, forced attendance at boarding schools, and starvation policies, Brave Heart-Jordan notes specifically that the allotment process (the removal of Indians from their land); the flooding of the Cheyenne River, Standing Rock, Crow Creek, and Lower Brule reservations; and the subsequent leasing of those lands to non-Indian ranchers have all contributed significantly to the loss of self-sufficiency and self-esteem in these communities.

Psychologist Utng Erickson's analysis of Lakota communities documents in part the internalized impact of constantly degrading and "disempowering" federal policies on Indian people. He considers the modern Lakota to "have a group neurosis, with identity being formed upon the status of being persecuted and due compensation." Erickson contrasts this "cultural pathology" with the absence of "individual psychopathology." Erickson specifically discusses the impact of the loss of the buffalo economy on the Lakota people, noting that "the decimation of the buffalo led to the spiritual and ethnic death of the Lakota. The Lakota attempted to recover from this tragedy through embracing the cattle economy, but again government prohibitions removed cattle from the Lakota to serve white ranchers' interests and devastated the growing economy." Erickson writes, "Step for step, the Sioux have been denied the basis for a collective identity formation and with it that reservoir of collective integrity from which the individual must derive his stature as a social being."[24]

The lesson is that the war on nature is a war on the psyche, a war on the soul. It is seen in the faces on Pine Ridge. It is seen in the monocropped field awash with chemicals and in the blood of a slaughtered Yellowstone calf. Healing in buffalo cultures must be multi-dimensional. It is not enough to provide detox centers and job-training programs. One must courageously venture to the heart of the whole to heal the individual. To heal the soul.

The Wild Herds: Wood Buffalo and Yellowstone

When the buffalo guns quit shattering the peace of the prairie with death at the turn of the century, there were very few survivors. An estimated 26 animals remained within the U.S. borders, and perhaps some 500 in what would become Canada. The animals had watched their 50 million relatives disappear, and had hidden away. Today, there are two herds that are direct genetic descendants of the original herds: the buffalo herds at Wood Buffalo National Park in Canada and Yellowstone National Park in the United States. These herds are arguably critical to any buffalo restoration efforts. Spiritually, native people maintain that these are the elders.

The Wood Buffalo herd is presently estimated to consist of 3,500 animals, descendants of the northern variety of buffalo that survived the great

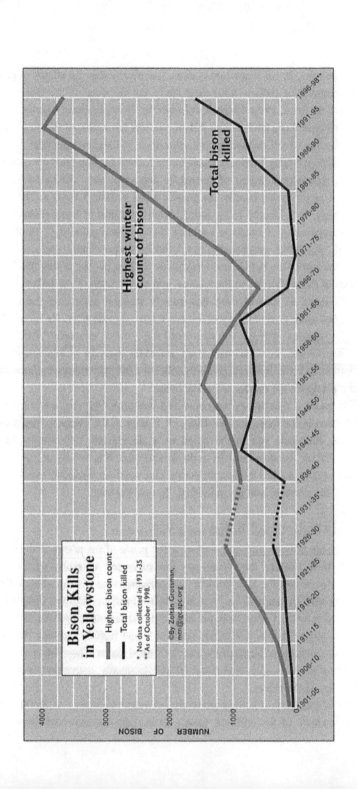

Bison Kills in Yellowstone

— Highest bison count
— Total bison killed

* No data collected in 1931-35
** As of October 1998.

©By Zoltan Grossman,
mrn@igc.apc.org

Highest winter count of bison

Total bison killed

NUMBER OF BISON

massacres and plains buffalo that were shipped to the park in 1925. Inter-mixing the northern variety of buffalo with the plains buffalo was controversial, but more controversial has been the fact that the plains buffalo introduced cattle-based disease into the herds, and infected buffalo have been destroyed by park officials. The government agencies that manage the herd have been accused of managing the disease poorly, slaughtering the animals to provide meat to local communities, destroying the herd's habitat, and losing animals to drowning by building a dam.[25]

The second most genetically important herd is the Yellowstone herd, living on 2.2 million acres of national parkland. The land itself was promised as "Indian territory" by the U.S. Congress, but in 1872 was seized from the Native people to create Yellowstone National Park, with a mission to "protect native species," thus allegedly assuring the survival of the Yellowstone buffalo. By the late 1880s, the Native people who lived in Yellowstone were forced from their lands within the park's boundaries and restricted to reservations.

In 1902, 23 bison were counted in the Yellowstone herd. Bison from captive herds were introduced that year. Between 1915 and 1920, intermingling of the introduced and wild animals began, and after about 1921, they were pretty much one herd. The Yellowstone herd was the foundation of many of the domestically held herds in North America. Culls have been part of buffalo management practices in the park since 1902, in the interests of keeping the herd at what officials consider a sustainable level. To cull the herds, buffalo are hunted, captured, and slaughtered. The culls have increased with herd size, and in the Winters of 1994–97, they increased dramatically, affecting over 1,944 animals—or more slaughters than in the previous 20 years combined. This practice has drawn dramatic opposition from not only Native peoples, but environmentalists and animal rights activists nationally and internationally.[26]

The Yellowstone Herd

In general, these interim plans provided for agency personnel from Montana and the National Park Service to cooperatively shoot bison moving from Yellowstone National Park to Montana in order to achieve the objectives of protecting private property, providing for human safety, and maintaining Montana's brucellosis class-free status.

—Yellowstone Environmental Impact Statement, July 1997[27]

The Winter of 1996–97 chilled Indigenous peoples across the Great Plains to the bone. The harsh winter had already caused a very large natural die-off among the Yellowstone buffalo and forced the surviving buffalo out of the park to lower elevations in search of food. As they crossed the invisible border between Yellowstone National Park and the state of Montana in search of winter foraging ground, they were targeted for slaughter. Some were captured, penned, and sold for meat, while others were shot on both public and private lands. Some 1,100 buffalo were killed by government agencies.[28] The total estimated herd as of the following Spring was just 1,700 animals, down from 3,436 in September 1996.

The fear that the buffalo would infect cattle with brucellosis is said to be the driving force in the Yellowstone buffalo kill. However, there has never been a single documented case of transmission of brucellosis from wild buffalo to cattle, including the 40 years that buffalo and cattle grazed side by side in Wyoming. Plus, the much larger Yellowstone elk herd, which numbers over 200,000 by many estimates, is known to be widely infected with brucellosis, but has not been the subject of a public slaughter (except by the lucrative hunting industry).

Brucella abortus originated from domestic cattle and has infected most of the wild herds. Most domestic herds are brucellosis-free. Buffalo themselves seem to survive with the disease, with only limited long-term impact. First discovered in the early part of the century, the disease in some cases can cause miscarriages. Transmission of the disease can only occur in limited ways, primarily through direct contact with contaminated aborted fetuses, birth membranes, uterine fluids, or vaginal discharges from infected animals. Ingestion of contaminated material is the primary route of infection. According to Margaret Meyer, former professor of veterinary medicine at the University of California at Davis and a leading authority on brucellosis, "a bison would practically have to abort in a cow's face to pass it on."[29]

Plus, according to Yellowstone Environmental Impact Statement data, it is likely that less than 10 percent of the Yellowstone buffalo actually harbor brucellosis, what Intertribal Bison Cooperative executive director Mark Heckert calls a "political disease."[30]

It is this incongruity between science and politics that has driven a good portion of the public debate and the direct action taken by some to oppose the killing of buffalo. The Yellowstone slaughter is ostensibly about buffalo versus cattle, that age-old mythological conflict between Indians and cowboys. Yellowstone itself is a national park that was established for beauty, not viability. Buffalo, on the other hand, are a "serve yourself" sort of critter; they will forage for food, and they will survive. They will roam. Put that survival instinct up against cattle, national politics, and a rigid invisible border, and you get the picture.

The problem is that agency officials have allowed cattle to graze on the park grazing allotment, a tract of land adjoining Yellowstone, as well as other areas outside the park, which are actually administratively designated for wildlife use. Some opponents to the Yellowstone kill are working to have the regulations enforced. Others propose removing the cattle from any possible conflict area, expanding the grazing lands, and if necessary as a last-ditch effort, removing the wild animals in intact family units. By the Fall of 1998, over 65,000 comments had been received by the National Park Service on their environmental impact statement, which proposed to continue with "lethal management practices."[31] The so-called preferred alternative is a sort of potpourri of ideas, heavily dominated by a sense that those who have guns should make public policy. The federal proposal at present includes a very limited acquisition of some lands and continued lethal management with no provisions for live removal of the future herd.

It is not surprising that over four-fifths of Montana's agricultural income from livestock and livestock products comes from cattle and calf sales. Cows are king in Montana, and many of the ranchers don't do poorly, either. The average net worth of a Montana rancher is $800,000. (Put that figure up against the hefty public subsidy figure for most of the public range lands, and the irony becomes apparent.[32]) However, cattle interests directly impacted by the buffalo herd and Yellowstone are few. It is estimated that there are between 1,800 and 2,000 buffalo cow-calf pairs north of the park, and 900 to 1,000 cow-calf pairs in the West Yellowstone area. In contrast, nearby Galltain County has about 27,000 beef cows, and Park County about 3,570 beef cows. Those cows deemed to be possibly affected by wild buffalo constitute less than 10 percent of the two counties' combined beef cattle population, which is less than 0.1 percent of the state's cattle population.[33] This also includes all those cattle grazing on public land adjacent to the park and directly competing with bison on public land.

Basically, all this buffalo killing is in honor of 3,000 or so cows and their babies, who continue to graze on public land, land actually designated first for wildlife and only secondly for livestock.

Healing the Community, Healing the Buffalo Nation

> Those of our ancestors who survived the nineteenth century found
> sanctuary on the reservations. In 1894, the last wild buffalo herd in the
> United States—about 20 head—found sanctuary in Yellowstone
> Park.... Like us, they are the last survivors.
>
> —Caleb Shields, Tribal Chairman of the Assiniboine and Sioux Nations,
> Fort Peck Reservation, Montana[34]

Rosalie Little Thunder's work is about spiritual healing. It is also about
saving buffalo. Rosalie's arrest came at Yellowstone. It was March 5, 1997. A
group of 75 people, including Lakota spiritual leader Arvol Looking Horse, con-
gregated around 147 brucellosis-negative bison in a holding corral. They shared
a pipe and prayers for the buffalo and to release the spirit of the buffalo that
were killed before. During their lunch break, they heard the shots. The Department of Livestock had killed eight buffalo a mile north of them. Rosalie and
several others wanted to go to the site and pray. Government officials warned
them about arrests for trespassing on privately held land, and Rosalie Little
Thunder was arrested, handcuffed, and placed in a patrol vehicle on charges of
trespassing. The scene was a replay for some, particularly Rosalie and Evelyne
Ironcloud of Pine Ridge. "It was that *déjà vu* feeling that you've been here before," Rosalie Little Thunder says. The slaughter was "really devastating to not
only buffalo nation but to the Indian nations as well," explains Evelyne
Ironcloud. "We believe that the way they treat the buffalo is the way that they
treat the Indians."[35] Many Native people view the historic buffalo slaughter as
the time when the buffalo relatives, the older brothers, stood up and took the
killing intended for the younger brothers, the Native peoples. That is why the
Yellowstone slaughter cuts to the quick of the Lakota and other buffalo cultures
of the Great Plains.

Rosalie is a beautiful Lakota grandmother who has been an educator,
longtime political activist, artist, and board member of the Seventh Generation
Fund and the Honor the Earth fund, both national Native foundations. She was
arrested in the Winter of 1997 as she prayed "for the buffalo spirits, that they
would go peacefully" amidst the slaughter at Yellowstone.

She remembered the story her father told her about the Little Thunder
massacre, which occurred in September 1855 in Nebraska. She is speaking
slowly and deliberately, as if deep inside herself. "It was when they first started
the hunts for the Indians. In 1851, the first Fort Laramie treaty session had taken
place. My dad's oral history talked about it. They were camped down by the
North Platte River on the North Bank. They still lived in that area."

Rosalie then refers to the chief at that time, whose name was also Little Thunder. "Then that General Harney came, the one that peak's named after. Little Thunder went out to meet him with the truce flag, and he met him, and he fed him salt pork and hard tack. That's what they had to eat then."

I listen to her and begin to shake, writing as best as I can, as the story unfolds. "There was a grandma there. That grandma had her ten-year-old grandson with her. She said to him, 'Stay here, don't come out yet.' And she laid her shawl over him and hid him in the bushes by the tall grass. They started shooting down the people then. And when she was shot, she threw herself on her shawl on top of that little boy. That way she hid him. That little boy, he was my grandfather." The oral history is passed on, as Rosalie retells the story. "He remembered his grandmother's blood dripping through the shawl onto him. He said he stayed there until there was no sound. He and the surviving members went back to Pine Ridge on foot. Close to 70 people were killed there."

Then comes Rosalie's addition to the oral history. "This was so strange: that's what that whole scene was when they were killing the buffalo. That was what was coming back to me. I had my ten-year-old grandson standing next to me. And they started killing the buffalo, just like that, shooting them down. I covered his face with my shawl, and told him to go move." It was the same story, a hundred years later. "You get the sense that nothing changed from 1855 to 1997. Actually that time span is just a clap of thunder in our history. It's not that long."

Rosalie Little Thunder has a dream. Not only does she want to stop the slaughter of the Yellowstone herd, she wants to see those buffalo back on the land, at Yellowstone, in national grasslands, and with buffalo peoples. By 2003, the Yellowstone herd will likely return to its size prior to the big slaughter of 1996. And Rosalie Little Thunder and others believe that preserving that herd and allowing them the space they need will be the key to the viability of the rest of the buffalo. After all, these are the survivors.

Buffalo Commons

It's often said that change always happens; the question is: Who determines the direction of the change? The fact is that the Great Plains are transforming, and the region's cattle, monoculture, and crop economy is changing, because it does not work.

Since the 1920s, a great span of the heartland has been drastically declining in human population. By 1990, 133 counties, constituting about a quarter of the United States, had reverted to "frontier" status, with fewer than two people per square mile. By 1999, 62 percent of Montana was frontier status. Forty percent of the U.S. land mass is home to only 1 percent of the population. Many of these areas are in significant economic decline. Over one-quarter of loans to farmers in Nebraska and the Dakotas are delinquent.[36] All of this is combined with some additional facts, like the average age of a farmer (elderly), high poverty levels, and other indicators like low levels of construction in the region.

Edward Valandra of Rosebud reservation reported in his 1994 study that Native populations were increasing substantially in many of these same areas.[37] While non-Indians are moving out of the Great Plains region, Indian populations are growing, with the highest birthrate in the country. Between 1985 and 1990, Montana's population dropped 6.1 percent to 799,065, North Dakota's dropped 7.3 percent to 638,800, Nebraska's by 2.4 percent to 1,578,385, Oklahoma's by 3.9 percent to 3,145,585, and South Dakota's by 3.1 percent to 696,004.[38] On the other hand, Native people in those same states have experienced significant population increases; almost one-third in every case. The Sioux population increased by 36 percent to 107,321 between 1980 and 1990, and Blackfoot numbers increased by 73 percent to 37,992 between 1980 and 1990.[39] What the region will look like 20 years from now is an excellent policy question, and one ripe for discussion in the context of the buffalo commons.

Demographically, those figures may be matched with present Native landholdings, and they demonstrate the possible foundation of the buffalo restoration efforts and the buffalo commons. In west central South Dakota, for instance, Lakota landholdings total over 7.5 million acres, almost two and a half times the landholdings of the federal government.[40] That land could be combined with areas like the Badlands (which really does belong to the Lakota in any case) to make larger buffalo ranges. As it turns out, it would actually save the government money to buy out non-Indian interests in the region. In the case of the Badlands reserve, for instance, Daniel Licht argues that the purchases needed would only be 940,000 acres. Even if this land was bought at an above-market price, the cost would only be $210 million, with a high, animal-proof perimeter fence, figured at $2,000 per mile, costing another $4.2 million. In comparison, Licht notes that in 1991 alone, the federal government spent some $87.4 million on 2.1 million acres of conservation (in planted cropland) in South Dakota, and it proposes to spend $800 million more.[41]

In early February 1999, I listened to Frank and Debra Popper, two demographers from Rutgers University, talk to the North Dakota Farm Managers Association meeting in Fargo, North Dakota. Academics from the East looked at the declining population figures and put two words together: *Buffalo commons*. They coined a term and gave name to a vision of a decade ago, one that has in many ways rocked the foundation of American agriculture policy and imagery.

The Poppers stood small in a room teeming with North Dakota ranchers, to whom a decade ago they had recommended packing it in and letting the buffalo return. The Fargo *Forum* had denounced the proposal in an article headlined, "The Nuttiest Ideas Never Seem to Die."[42]

Now, in 1999, the Poppers were invited back by the farmers themselves, who after a few tough winters, a wheat blight that decimated the monocropped fields, and some continuously bad federal policies, look worse for the wear than ever. In 1998, almost 75 percent of North Dakota farmers receiving Farmers' Home Administration loans were in default. There is, by any measure, a crisis that does not seem to subside. And, in 1999, even the most staunch and parochial of farm managers listened with some interest to the Poppers.

Cowboys and Indians One Hundred Years Later

There is, as well, at least one South Dakota rancher who is thinking about all of this—Marvin Kammerer. His 2,000-acre ranch abuts the Ellsworth Airforce Base near Rapid City, South Dakota, and on a good day, you can watch bombers careen overhead as they come in to land. Kammerer's farm was the site of the 1980 Black Hills International Survival Gathering, which drew 10,000 people from around the world to talk about the environment, culture, and sustainability, and to this day, Marvin remains one of the most outspoken ranchers in the region, the pages of the *Rapid City Journal* often filled with his letters or stories about his latest fight for the perpetual underdog. He is a man of immense moral strength in a vast expanse of ecological and, to a great extent, cultural disarray.

His concept, he says, "is that the landed cultures have a hell of a lot more in common than they have differences." Kammerer set up a foundation, a land trust with his 2,000 acres, now called the Kammerer Lakota Foundation, which is aimed at restoring a more collective land ethic to the region. The trustees of the foundation are two Kammerers, two Lakotas, and a fifth individual. "I look on the land as a resource, not a commodity," he explains. "It is a responsibility. It's crazy to me that you have to own something, when it's a gift from the Creator. It's not property, it's sacred.... We are immigrants as far as I am concerned. We are squatters, and we are still squatting."[43] Among the Lakota landholdings, the dreams of those like Marvin Kammerer, and the economics of a dying mythology, there may be, over the long term, the foundation of an actual buffalo commons: that vision of the Ghost Dance being actualized on the land by the people and their relatives who live there.

Pte Oyate: The Buffalo Nation

Birgil Kills Straight is one of the leaders of the Wounded Knee Memorial Ride, which commemorates the fateful journey taken by Chief Big Foot and his small band that tragically ended at Wounded Knee in 1890. Birgil, Jim Garret, Alex White Plume, and others have talked about running a buffalo corridor from Standing Rock, Cheyenne/Eagle Butte, down to Pine Ridge, following Chief Big Foot's historic path. Edward Valandra eyes the same land and proposes approximately 2.2 million acres of land as the foundation of a viable landbase for a buffalo herd. Their vision is the beginning of something big, pretty much as big as the dream has to be in that immense region.

Some 41 tribes are members of the Intertribal Bison Cooperative (ITBC), a nonprofit organization founded in 1993, that works to enhance tribal efforts at buffalo restoration and is also active in opposing the slaughter at Yellowstone. Since its inception, ITBC, with an annual budget of around $1 million, has provided technical assistance to member tribes and public relations and information to the larger society. They were instrumental in negotiating an agreement between the tribal organization and the National Wildlife Federation to support the transfer of live buffalo from Yellowstone to tribes.[44]

On other reservations, whether the Taos Pueblo in northern New Mexico or the Seventh Generation Buffalo Cooperative on the Standing Rock reservation in North Dakota, there are buffalo growing and communities welcoming home their relations. The larger ecological and cultural vision is the long-term extension of these small pieces of work. That is how buffalo are restored to larger regions in order to truly be buffalo.

According to conservation biologists like Reed Noss, much of the land on which the buffalo presently roam is not suited for their long-term viability. "Because biology has been absent from design decisions," Noss writes, "park boundaries do not conform to ecological boundaries, and most parks and reserves are too small to maintain populations of wide-ranging animals over the long term or to perpetuate natural processes."[45] Noss considers that buffalo require reserves on the scale of one to ten million hectares (2,470,000 to 24,700,000 acres). Those must be contiguous acres, with corridors as well as core areas. In core areas, the major populations reside (or roam, in the case of the buffalo.) Corridors, such as rivers, between "primary genetic pools," or herds, allow for some genetic diversity. Around such a reserve should be some sort of buffer zone. According to Noss, an average population of 1,000 individuals must be maintained to assure population viability. Noss's objectives are to maintain native biodiversity in perpetuity (including all species) and "design and manage the system to be responsible to short-term and long-term environmental change and to maintain the evolutionary potential of lineages."[46]

Braids of a Grandmother's Hair

My grandma had a little bag that she always carried around with her. She was 102 years when she died. In that bag were some of her most special things. She would take them out once in a while. She had these two long braids that they took and cut off at her boarding school. That was very traumatic for her for all of her life. That's what she said about the buffalo. If you take their horns it's like cutting off our braids. It's the same thing.

—Fred Dubray, Intertribal Bison Cooperative[47]

Let the buffalo be the buffalo. That is the message most Native people who work with buffalo will give. There is a clear sense among people who raise buffalo that the strength of the buffalo is their nature, and that domesticating them makes them lose their uniqueness. Fred Dubray is a sort of Indian cowboy from Cheyenne River. A seemingly quiet man under a big cowboy hat, he tells me the story of his grandmother's braids, and gets a thoughtful look.

"The way that buffalo relate to the land changes if you domesticate them," Fred continues. "And then you change the land. There is a hierarchy in the herd. Any time you take one animal out for slaughter or for trade that changes. Those horns are what they use to protect their status." (Many ranchers remove the horns from the buffalo for domesticating purposes, although Dubray does not.) Michele Fredericks, his wife, interjects now, anxiously listening to the conversation. She adds, "When they lose a horn, their status is diminished."

One of the things we learn from the buffalo is that it is not about the individual buffalo. It is about the herd. This is a lesson that Dubray feels is critical to the recovery of his community. "We really believe that we need to go on as tribes. We can succeed as individuals, but in that process we lose our [collective] identity [as a tribe]. We are a collective. That is how we are like the buffalo."

In between all of these good ideas and the 150,000-plus buffalo presently being raised largely by individual ranchers, there is a deep-seated philosophical question in raising buffalo themselves. Economic and political pressures, like those from the U.S. Department of Agriculture, have driven many buffalo ranchers to treat buffalo quite a bit like cattle, by dehorning, using feedlots, and interfering in their social structure. That trend alarms many Native people, including Fred Dubray.

"What buffalo means to me is life itself on this continent. And our culture itself," Fred Dubray explains. "When we talk about restoring buffalo itself, we're not just talking about restoring animals to the land, we're talking about restoring social structure, culture, and even our political structure." Dubray continues, "We recognize that the bison is the symbol of our strength and unity and that when we bring our herds back to health, we will also bring our people back to health." That health, Dubray and others would say, is not about being domesticated. Dubray works to actualize this through Pte, the Cheyenne River Nation's corporation that is already growing the buffalo herd. Pte has about 500 bison on 320,000 acres. Their objective is to have 10,000 head in ten years.

Dubray continues,

> Buffalo mean everything to us. And they teach us all kinds of things. I spent a lot of time watching them, and they teach you how to respect yourself better, how they relate to each other and live in other species, and how they respect each other. Those are things that are real to Indian people. [But restoring the buffalo] is not just for Indian people, it is for this country itself. The heart of this country needs to be re-established. They are killing off and destroying the last wild herd, there at Yellowstone. Probably because they're wild. That is something that America needs, too.

The buffalo also heal the land when they return, almost as they fall into stride as prairie-makers. Dubray talks about the transition on Cheyenne River. "The cattle industry has been on our land for approximately 130 years, and they totally ruined our grasses with exotic grasses. Today, we have the buffalo in those pastures [and have] recovered almost 95 percent of the original Native grasses."

"Bringing Back the Way"

As your eyes scan the land at Pine Ridge, there is something that you do see clearly: *indigenous prairie*. Native prairie grasses span much of the uncultivated tribal landholdings on Pine Ridge. The same appears true on Yankton, Cheyenne River, and a number of other northern plains reservations. It is an ironic twist at the end of the twentieth century—the last pitiful vestiges of biodiversity on the Great Plains remain with the last remnants of Indigenous cultural diversity: Native people.

Richard Sherman is a wildlife biologist with the Oglala Parks and Recreation Program on Pine Ridge. He walks through the 17,000-acre pasture —one of the pastures for the Oglala herd. He stops, points out various buffalo delicacies—prairie turnips, sage variety, and mushrooms—that all thrive in the buffalo pasture.

The pasture is a model of Richard's larger vision of Lakota land stewardship, which he describes as "a culturally appropriate system based on the values and philosophy of the Lakota people." Much of this land, except that leased to non-Indian agricultural interests, seems prime for the program. How long does it take to restore a prairie? "It doesn't take too long," Richard explains, "to heal the land once it starts. It's happening right here on our buffalo pasture."[48]

Forty miles away as the magpie flies, Alex and Debbie White Plume's family is, in its practice, striving to "bring back the way." After dealing with 25 years of reservation politics (Indian Reorganization Act governments, FBI oppression, AIM, etc.), the White Plume family just sort of withdrew up a canyon into Alex's grandfather's allotments and began growing things. "The Buffalo Nation, the Horse Nation, the Plant Nation," as Debbie calls them, all share the 1,200-acre landbase with the White Plume's *tiwahe* (close family) and the *tiosapaye* (extended family)—the traditional form of government in Lakota culture. Each nation helps the other nations care for themselves and each other.[49]

Ben Sherman, Richard's brother, gets a sparkle in his eyes when he talks about his Buffalo Gap Rescue Project. Sherman and his colleague Dana Echohawk found a 500-year-old buffalo jump site near Beulah, Wyoming, at which over 20,000 buffalo were believed to have been killed. Ben wants to see not only a buffalo jump interpretive center (something like the Head Smashed In Buffalo Jump interpretive center in Alberta, a World Heritage site), but a live buffalo herd as well. Over the past few years, he has carefully and patiently cultivated a relationship with the Nature Conservancy, which, as it turns out, has some similar interests. The Wyoming chapter of the Nature Conservancy began working with Ben and his project, and through a new office in Rapid City has begun negotiating easements and ownership of acreage. "They've purchased over 2,000 acres of property in the area," Ben explains, encouraged by their commitment. "I'd just like to see buffalo back in the hills again," he says, and smiles.[50]

Faith Spotted Eagle coordinates the Braveheart Project Learning Circle, or *Inhanktunwan Winyan* (Yankton Women), on the Yankton reservation. There, she and a group of women have spent the last four years working directly with over 70 young women to restore the traditional societies, their teachings, and the mentoring that is a result of formal women's societies. In traditional buffalo society, she says, "the primary role that women had was dividing up the buffalo, once the buffalo were killed. There were some women who were buffalo callers," Faith explains. "The third role was to be the ultimate environmentalist, to be able to use everything in the buffalo. Finally, there was the role of mentoring younger women to realize the primacy of our relationship with buffalo. That's the essence of what the braveheart society is about."[51] The healing that Maria Yellow Horse Brave Heart-Jordan discusses as essential to the community is under way, in the holistic approach of bringing back buffalo and buffalo cultures.

Between the hope of the white buffalo calf's arrival and the archaic and lethal management policies of the federal government, there is a change occurring in the buffalo nation. When the white buffalo calf was born, something was remembered, in an oral history from Rosalie Little Thunder, in the cry of a buffalo calf looking for its mother in the snow. This spring, more calves will be born, and some new grass will come into Yellowstone, into the prairies. And that grass will be the promise of the future, that grass will once again call the names of the buffalo, and the buffalo people will remember their relations and rejoice.

> With the teaching of our way of life from the time of being, the First People were the Buffalo people, our ancestors which came from the sacred Black Hills, the heart of everything that is.... I pray for the health and well being of many nations. I humbly ask all nations to respect our way of life, because in our prophecies, if there is no buffalo, then life as we know it will cease to exist.
>
> —Chief Arvol Looking Horse, 19th Generation Keeper of the
> Sacred White Buffalo Calf Pipe[52]

Mahealani Pai, Kona, Hawai'i. Photo © Franco Salmoiraghi

Ua Mau Ke Ea o Ka Aina I Ka Pono
The life of the land is perpetuated by righteousness

—traditional Hawaiian teaching

H a w a i ' i

The Birth of Land
and Its Preservation
by the Hands of the People

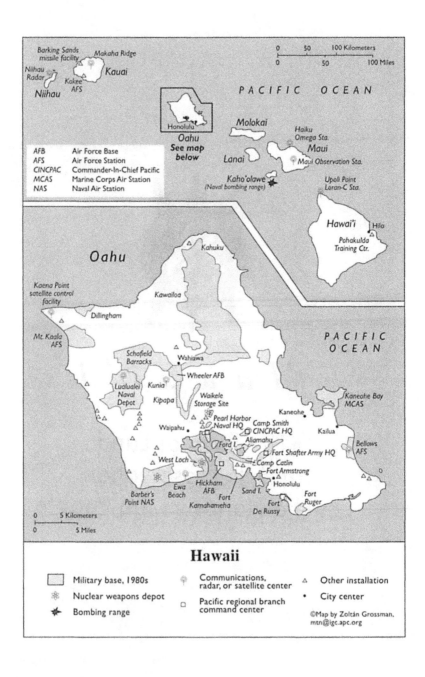

Barking Sands
missile facility   Makaha Ridge
Niihau
Radar   Kokee
          Kauai   AFS
Niihau

PACIFIC OCEAN

0   50   100 Kilometers
0   50   100 Miles

Honolulu
Oahu
**See map
below**

Molokai
              Haiku
              Omega Sta.
Lanai   Maui
              Maui Observation Sta.

Kaho'olawe
(Naval bombing range)

Upoli Point
Loran-C Sta.

AFB	Air Force Base
AFS	Air Force Station
CINCPAC	Commander-In-Chief Pacific
MCAS	Marine Corps Air Station
NAS	Naval Air Station

Hawai'i   Hilo
          Pohakulda
          Training Ctr.

Oahu

Kahuku

Kaena Point
satellite control
facility

Kawailoa

Dillingham

Mt. Kaala
AFS

Schofield
Barracks   Wahiawa

Wheeler AFB

Lualualei   Kunia
Naval   Kipapa   Waikele
Depot   Storage Site

                                Kaneohe

PACIFIC
OCEAN

Kaneohe Bay
MCAS

Waipahu

Pearl Harbor
Naval HQ   Camp Smith
                  CINCPAC HQ   Kailua
                  Aliamahu

Ford I.
West Loch   Fort Shafter Army HQ

                  Camp Catlin
                  Fort Armstrong

Bellows
AFS

Barber's   Ewa
Point NAS   Beach
            Fort
            Kamahameha

Hickham
AFB   Sand I.   Honolulu

                     Fort
                     De Russy

Fort
Ruger

0   5 Kilometers
0   5 Miles

Hawaii

◻ Military base, 1980s

❄ Nuclear weapons depot

✦ Bombing range

⊕ Communications,
  radar, or satellite center

▫ Pacific regional branch
  command center

△ Other installation

• City center

©Map by Zoltán Grossman,
mtn@igc.apc.org

It was in 1996 that my family and I wandered through lava-strewn back roads near the Kona harbor on the big island of Hawai'i, trying to find Mahealani Pai. One of the many homeless families we encountered directed us to the Pai family land. Past the porta-potties and the *heiau* (traditional Hawaiian temple) were some tents, a couple of pole houses on a jetty between fish traps, and a group of 20 or so people being addressed by a man with a flip chart. An environmental justice workshop from the University of Hawai'i was underway. A tall, husky man, a former national surfing champion wearing a long ponytail, t-shirt, and sweat pants, walked toward us, extending a hand: Mahealani Pai.

Every day, Mahealani Pai wades out into the waves and makes his offerings, then turns toward the *heiau*. He is the caretaker of the *heiau* at Honokohau near Kona. The Pai family has cared for the *heiau* and the *Wai 'Opio,* traditional fish traps, which adjoin the temple, for 14 generations.

The livelihood of traditional Hawaiians is based on a complicated and intricate set of relations in a powerful environment of land and sea. The Pai family's traditional fish trap, an ancient method of trapping fish behind a submerged rock wall, leaves the fish secure at low tide. The wave motion always shifts the rocks back to the ocean floor, so such traps must be maintained every day. That responsibility and that wall have existed since 900 BC, according to the Pai family.[1]

"We know this is where *tutu,* them came from, where they lived, and where they are buried," says Mahealani Pai of his family's five acres of land. "We don't own it, but we know that we belong to it."[2] "We don't own the land," echoes his mother, Mabel Pai, "but we take care of it. It's like when the kings of Hawai'i give you land to take care of. We believe God owns the land, not people."[3] The Pai family never owned the fee simple (white man's private property title) to their land. But the title-owner, the Greenwell family, maintained a cooperative understanding with the Pais, along with a dozen other families. "All they asked us was to keep up the place. They understood how special this was to our family, and they knew who the old folks were," says Mahealani.

If only things could stay simple. In the mid-1990s, a development company called Nansay Hawai'i bought the white man's paper title to 450 acres next to the Pai land. They proposed to construct a "destination resort development" with 330 multiple-family residential units, 380 single-family homes, a golf course, and a health club.[4]

This proposed development posed an immediate threat to the Pai family's fish traps, ceremonial worship, and *iwi* (bones), one that would totally inundate a fragile ecosystem and lifestyle with boats, docks, and tourists. The right of Native Hawaiians to practice traditional activities on privately owned land had often been accommodated in the law, so in 1995, the Pais contested the development in court. The court ruled that the state, and by extension, private property owners, are required to preserve and protect Native Hawaiians' rights to practice traditional activities. Or in this case, if Hawaiians are gathering shrimp and fish from ponds sitting on a resort's property, the resort may have to provide them with access and preserve the ponds.

"Nansay's argument," declared the court, "places undue reliance upon Western understandings of property law that are not universally applicable in Hawai'i. Hawaiian custom and usage have always been a part of the laws of this state."[5] The court effectively threw a wrench into the development question at Kona. The Nansay project fizzled out.

There is always, it seems, a problem of aboriginal and traditional land title and the white man's private property. In the tumult of land laws passed in Hawai'i, the end result is always, it seems, the same—the Native people become landless. So it was to be with Mahealani Pai.

In 1988, the Pai family's agreement with the Greenwell family was put in jeopardy by the National Park Service (NPS) when it "bought" all of the Greenwell parcels for a sweet sum of $17 million.

What the NPS proposed to do was quite strange. The NPS intended to create a park, Kaloko-Honokohau National Historical Park, as "a center for the presentation, interpretation, and perpetuation of Hawaiian activities and culture."[6] But to make this cultural presentation, they would need to throw out all of the Native Hawaiians actually living on the land. A conflict between a living culture and an historic culture, as determined by a federal agency, ensued.

A living culture is manifested through a way of life. An historic culture, in this case, was a tool for the NPS. The NPS magnanimously granted a special use permit to the Pai family, but Mahealani rejected the permit, believing it to indicate an acquiescence to federal rights. Then Pai sued the NPS for aboriginal rights to the land. The case, *Pai Ohana v. The United States,* was lost in 1994. Then came a string of eviction threats, seven in all.

The final eviction threat was fulfilled on February 14, 1997, when the NPS, hell-bent on its park of historic Hawaiian culture, evicted the Hawaiians.

As reporter Michael Lloyd writes, "Shortly before 10:00 a.m., and after a number of supporters left voluntarily,...officials arrested Pai and eight other supporters. 'I ku mau mau!' ['We stand together!'] came the chant from the teary-eyed supporters of the Pai Ohana [family], watching from the southern side of the channel at Honokohau Harbor. 'I ku mau mau!' answered Mahealani Pai, standing on the north side, thrusting his shackled hands into the air."[7]

The Birth of Land

There are few places in the world where you can witness the birth of land. Pele, the Volcano Goddess, makes Earth, and the Hawaiians are witness to the creation each day. According to Hawaiian oral history, their islands were born when Papahanaumoku, Mother Earth, mated with Wakea, Father Sky. From this union came the first taro plant, then the first *ali'i nui*, and finally the Hawaiian people, or the *Kanaka Maoli*. From the Earth herself.

Long ago, the first inhabitants of the Hawaiian islands arrived from Tahiti. Over a millennium, the Polynesian people, like their relations spread throughout the Pacific, learned to adapt to island life, the richness of the new land, the wealth of the water, and the limitations necessary for continued generations of survival on fragile and isolated islands.

Hawaiian cultural practice is entirely intertwined with the natural world. Spirits and deities govern each of the elements. The *lokahi* is a symbol of the "greatest of the traditions, values, and practices of our people," explains Hawaiian nationalist Mililani Trask. "There are three points in the triangle—the Creator, *Akua;* the peoples of the earth, *Kanaka Maoli;* and the land, the *'aina*. These three things all have a reciprocal relationship."[8]

The Hawaiians transformed the land dramatically. New species of animals and plants were introduced to the island, and a vibrant economy was founded. The *Kanaka Maoli* combined upland agriculture, *mauka*, and ocean fishing, *makai*, and developed fishponds and intensive garden systems, all cared for by the extended family, or *Ohana*. In the late 16th and early 17th centuries, for instance, they embarked on a tremendous, 50-year development project—they planted a breadfruit forest that spanned the entire big island of Hawai'i. "Because the long-range benefits were obvious to them," writes historian Marion Kelly, "they persisted and achieved their goal."[9] By the end of the 1700s, the islands supported upwards of a million *Kanaka Maoli*.[10]

The *Haole* Arrival

Change creates chaos.

Meandering and pillaging through the Pacific, Captain James Cook and his crew arrived by chance in Kona in 1778. The waves of foreigners that followed Cook brought foreign epidemics, which devastated the native population.

Typhoid fever came in 1804, followed by influenza epidemics, whooping cough, mumps, leprosy, measles, smallpox, diphtheria, cholera, and, finally, the bubonic plague. By the 1820s, only about 200,000 Hawaiians had survived the onslaught. Seventy years later, only 40,000 Hawaiians remained.[11]

Unable to make sense of their ongoing plagues, the Hawaiian traditional belief system was shaken. Community leaders interpreted the constant death as a sign of a loss of favor, as a sign that Hawaiians had committed some wrongdoing that had brought down the wrath of their Creator. European missionaries worked to soothe the pain and anguish of the chaos with Christianity. Following the missionaries were the industrialists, including loggers, sandalwood interests, whalers, cattle ranchers, and later sugar and pineapple growers.

Once colonial interests put their handprint on title laws, there is a tendency for intergenerational land tenure and land-ownership patterns to change in bizarre ways. As the colonial interests began to influence the lawmaking of the Hawaiian monarchy, the patterns of land-ownership changed. Foreign advisors to the monarch argued that adopting European concepts and institutions of private land tenure would preserve the land from foreign control. The impact of European diseases on Hawaiians was used as an argument to buttress the change. "Missionaries…argued that Hawaiians were dying as they were lazy and licentious, and therefore the only means that would stem the death of the people was private ownership of land…[it] was the *pono* [righteous] thing to do."[12]

Amidst the chaos and pressure, the monarchy reluctantly agreed to privatize the land. The land commission, headed by an American missionary, allotted the land. Tasked with dividing the land between the government, the *ali'i nui* (chiefs), and *maka 'ainana* (common people), the commission proved astonishingly efficient at alienating people from their land. Although there were 88,000 Hawaiians in 1848, only 8,200 received land awards, mostly three-acre lots (a far cry from subsistence holdings), or one percent of the land. Thirty-four *ali'i nui* received larger portions, but were required to relinquish some 50 percent of their lands. Of so-called government lands, the vast majority became footholds for foreign control, not unlike the American homesteads of the 1880s. Missionaries were given hefty allotments of 560 acres apiece for their work in Christianizing and providing the foundations for multinational industrialists such as Castle, Cooke, Alexander, and Baldwin, the founding fathers of great agricultural fortunes. Since sugarcane producers had to pay duty taxes in order to import Hawaiian sugar to America, they increased their pressure to annex Hawai'i.[13]

In 1893, with just a fraction of the original population surviving, the *haole* (whites) overthrew the Hawaiian government. Samuel Dole invaded Hawai'i and plotted a coup that toppled the Native constitutional government of Queen Lili'uokalani. "If we had had a million Hawaiians in 1893," writes Lilikalá Kame'eleihiwa, "we would still have our country. *Haole* diseases were, and remain, allies of *haole* imperialism."[14]

In 1898, the United States annexed Hawai'i by congressional resolution, without the consent of or compensation to the *Kanaka Maoli*. The U.S. government claimed over two million acres of Native lands, and the *Kanaka Maoli* lost control over most of their territory. As the Hawaiian saying goes, "As we gazed at their heaven, they stole our land from beneath our feet."

In 1921, the government passed the Hawaiian Homestead Act, which earmarked 200,000 acres of land for Native Hawaiians. (The prime land, now of interest to sugar barons and other newcomers, was excluded from the Act.) No financing for homestead development was provided. In 1946, the United States listed Hawai'i as a non-self-governing territory under its administration, along with American Samoa, Alaska, Guam, Puerto Rico, and the Virgin Islands. This status remained in effect until September 1959, when the United States notified the United Nations Secretary General that Hawai'i had become a state of the Union.[15]

As it turns out, the U.S. did not follow international law in its doling of statehood to Hawai'i. As Mililani Trask notes, "Our peoples were not given independence or Free Association status, nor were we allowed to choose our form of government."[16] In November 1953, the U.N. General Assembly had passed Resolution 742, outlining the terms of removal from the status of non-self-governing territories. These included freedom of choice; ethnic and cultural considerations; and economic, social, and cultural jurisdiction. The U.S. violated these provisions.

In 1959, Hawai'i was admitted as a state of the United States in direct contradiction of international law, which until that year had listed Hawai'i as having a special colonial status of non-self-governing territories. The State Admissions Act made Native Hawaiians "wards" of the newly formed state of Hawai'i. This meant that like children and mentally disabled individuals, the

Kanaka Maoli would have no standing in U.S. federal courts. According to sovereignty activist Dr. Kekuni Blaisdell,

> Under Article 73 of the UN Charter, the United States was ordered to prepare the Territory of Hawai'i for self-government. Instead, we got two choices: become a state or remain a territory. The people didn't know they had a right to demand a third choice: for decolonization and independence.[17]

Whether under federal or state jurisdiction, the two million acres originally earmarked for Native Hawaiians were illegally transferred to private interests.[18] Of the 194,000 acres that the Department of Hawaiian Homelands (DHHL) today estimates that it oversees on behalf of the Native Hawaiians, over 45 percent is leased out to farmers, for a mere $4 per acre per year. Fourteen percent is designated as public land, i.e., state parks or forest reserves. The military claims over 200,000 acres.[19]

As a result, fewer than 6,000 Native Hawaiians ever received land, 22,000 remain on waiting lists for homestead awards, and hundreds of homeless Hawaiians live on beaches throughout the state, under the constant threat of arrest. It is estimated that 30,000 Native Hawaiians have died while still waiting for their land.[20]

Today, 95 percent of Hawai'i's land is owned or controlled by just 82 landholders. The federal and state governments claim over 50 percent of the land.[21] Rent in Hawai'i's largest city, Honolulu, is comparable to Manhattan's. A single family owns the entire island of Ni'ihau. The pineapple interests, such as Del Monte and Dole, until recently controlled much of the island of Lana'i, as well as much of other islands. The U.S. Department of Defense owned the entire island of Kaho'o'lawe until 1990, when then-President George Bush returned it to a public trust.[22]

As a Hawaiian from the Wai'anae coast said, "We can barely pay house rent, and they like build apartments....With inflation now, hard to buy tomatoes, carrots.... You cannot eat 'em, those buildings."[23]

Today, the life expectancy and rates of infant mortality, homelessness, and incarceration of Native Hawaiians are on par with the dismal conditions found in much of Native America.[24] More Native Hawaiians live below the poverty line than any other ethnic group in Hawai'i. Fifty-five percent of the *Kanaka Maoli* do not complete high school, and only seven percent hold college degrees. Although *Kanaka Maoli* make up only 19 percent of the state's population, they comprise 40 percent of the prison population. Dr. Kekuni Blaisdell refers to this as ethnocide and genocide.[25]

The Militarization of the Pacific

The initial militarization of Hawai'i took place after formal annexation in 1893. Four days later, 1,300 Army troops landed near Diamond Head and became the first military stronghold in the region. This initial encroachment has expanded substantially as U.S. military interests in the Pacific were augmented. After World War II and the subsequent annexing of more Hawaiian land, Hawai'i became a central outpost in what is euphemistically known in military circles as "the American Lake"—the Pacific Ocean.[26] The Department of Defense took over many of these lands under martial law the day after Pearl Harbor was bombed in 1941. Today, there are over 100 military installations in Hawai'i staffed by 150,000 military personnel. Their activities comprise the state's second largest source of income, or a whopping 35 percent of the state's direct revenues. For most native Hawaiians, the U.S. military is a clear occupying force.

Since the end of World War II, Hawai'i has been the center of the U.S. military's Pacific Command (PACOM), from which all U.S. forces in the region are directed. It serves as an outpost for Pacific expansionism, along with Guam, the Marshall Islands, Samoa, and the Philippines. The PACOM is the center of U.S. military activities over more than half of the earth, from the west coast of the United States to Africa's east coast, and from the Arctic to Antarctica, covering 70 percent of the world's oceans.[27]

Not surprisingly, the U.S. military until recently controlled some 254,000 acres of land in Hawai'i, or 6.3 percent of the total land, proportionately more than in any other state.[28] This includes holdings on Oahu, which encompass 25 percent of the land and include valuable "submerged lands," i.e., estuaries and bays like Kaneohe Bay.

The vast militarization of Hawai'i has profoundly damaged the land. According to the Environmental Protection Agency, there are more federal hazardous waste sites in Hawai'i—31—than in any other U.S. state. Many of these sites were contaminated by military activities.

The Navy itself acknowledges releasing some 4,843,000 gallons of radioactive liquid waste into Pearl Harbor from its submarines between 1964 and 1973. Similarly, the Navy dumped over 2,000 55-gallon steel drums of solid radioactive waste 55 miles off the Hawaiian shoreline onto the ocean floor.[29]

As journalist Kathy Ferguson writes,

Among the wastes the military disposes of are pesticides, waste oil, asbestos, chromic acids, PCBs, solvents such as TCE, and solid nuclear wastes.... Given the small, fragile ecosystem of Oahu, [there is a] possibility of these wastes...contaminating the Pearl Harbor aquifer, which is the main source of drinking water for Honolulu.[30]

The military's response to these risks is neither exemplary nor even responsible. When it takes action, it is usually the result of prodding by outside groups or mandates by outside agencies. Even then, the military's protectiveness seems directed toward itself rather than the environment. For example, the military defended the release of freon gas (which is destructive to the ozone layer) from rocket launches off Kauai on the basis that the releases took place in the atmosphere, which is outside the state's jurisdiction. The Pentagon's FY '91 budget for environmental cleanup amounted to less than a third of a percent of its overall budget.[31]

As well, there are the direct problems associated with military accidents. In 1944, an accidental detonation of conventional ammunition at Pearl Harbor killed and injured more than 500 people. Subsequent accidental bombings of Maui, Ni'ihau, and fishermen off of Kauai in 1965 and 1969 illustrate some of the carelessness of the military in this environment.[32] Wai'anae, on the island of Oahu, was accidentally shelled by the army four times between 1987 and 1990. There are approximately 3,000 nuclear weapons stored in Oahu, and unexploded bombs have historically littered many valleys and beaches on the islands.

On the mountain above the beach at Makua, on the island of Oahu, the military had a bombing range. Nevertheless, in January 1983, the state bulldozed Hawaiian homes there to make way for a state park. The Hawaiians who were forced out waded through live ammunition, which had washed up on the beach during the 1982 Hurricane Iwa. Twelve families remained as squatters on their own land. "The state constantly rips off our land," explains Mililani Trask, "then it turns around and calls us squatters."[33]

Kaho'o'lawe

Hawai'i's eighth island, Kaho'o'lawe, doesn't appear on many tourist maps of Hawai'i. One of the only ways to get there is to be thrown off a nearby boat. One pre-dawn morning in 1984, I jumped off a boat into the depths of the waters surrounding Kaho'o'lawe. Unfamiliar with ocean swimming, and a somewhat uneasy swimmer at best, I began to swim furiously to shore, eyes scanning for some light. My ears picked up the laughter of the Hawaiian women frolicking in the water, playing in the surf, and allowing the ocean to take them to shore, kissed by the waves, as it were.

Kaho'o'lawe was named after Kanaloa, god of ocean and foundation of the Earth. Kaho'o'lawe is known as "the carrying away," for the ocean currents that merge and flow southward from this island, a major departure point to Tahiti. At one time, the island boasted a monastery, an astronomical university, and widespread traditional cultural practice among its people.

On December 8, 1941, one day after the bombing of Pearl Harbor, the military declared martial law and took possession of the entire island. In 1965, some 500 tons of TNT were detonated on the island, near Hanakanaia Bay, to simulate the effects an atomic blast would have on nearby ships. The 100-foot-wide crater the explosion left extends below sea level and cracked the water table on part of the island, creating a salt-water pond devoid of life.[34] Every two years, Australia, Canada, Japan, and New Zealand practice their military tactics in unison on the island.

Native Hawaiians not only opposed and rejected the militarization of their *'aina,* their land, but they began a process of land recovery that rippled far into other islands and indeed into other military-occupied indigenous communities worldwide.

Beginning in 1976, the Native Hawaiian-led group Protect Kaho'o'lawe Ohana (PKO) initiated a series of occupations of the island, leading to lengthy litigation and arrests. A subsequent federal lawsuit sought to force the military to comply with environmental, religious freedom, and historic preservation laws.

It was in 1977 in the increasing mobilization to protect and recover Kaho'o'lawe that George Helm and Kimo Mitchell, two leaders of PKO, mysteriously disappeared at sea while searching for other Native Hawaiians from the island. They are presumed drowned.

The multitude of strategies, press, litigation, prayers, and sacrifices finally resulted in a 1980 consent decree (an out-of-court settlement) between the PKO and the Navy. The decree, a result of the 1976 civil suit in federal court, mandated that the Navy scale back their operations, begin economic restoration, and clear surface ordnance from 10,000 acres of land on the island. The consent decree also allowed the PKO access to the land for four days a month, ten months of the year.

It was under this "access" for Hawaiian ceremonial purposes that I visited the island. PKO's sophisticated political work, combined with their educational outreach, under which 4,000 people visited the island, helped to transform the island's destiny. In 1981, the entire island was placed on the National Register of Historic Places, acknowledging 600 archeological sites and 2,000 historic features. Ironically, the island was the only National Historic site also used as a bombing range.

On October 22, 1990, President Bush directed the Navy to end its use of Kaho'o'lawe. Two weeks later, a congressional bill placed a moratorium on the bombing.[35]

In 1992, a federal study recommended that the island be returned to the Native Hawaiians, that further military or commercial use be barred, and that the federal government pay for the removal of unexploded bombs. According to the study, it would cost between $110 million and $400 million to clear the island of unexploded bombs and restore it.[36] Two quit-claim deeds, one written in English and the other in Hawaiian, were signed in 1994, formally returning the land to the state of Hawai'i to hold in trust for the Hawaiian Sovereign Nation. Journalist Christopher Merrill described the scene:

> On the hot, overcast afternoon...about 700 people gathered at Palauea Beach on the west coast of Maui for the Conveyance Ceremony. First they stood in silence at the edge of the sea, gazing at Kaho'o'lawe in the distance. They gripped a rope made of sennit, they listened to 100 soundings of the conch and the solemn beat of ceremonial drums. Warriors dressed in Ti leaf cloaks clutching long spears kept watch over a crowd of native people and settlers, tourists and sailors. Waves lapped at the shore, saltwater washed over the feet of the television crews... and Governor John Waihe'e declared this day a reaffirmation to the Hawaiian Nation of our destiny. If this can happen to Kaho'o'lawe, there will be other great ceremonies like it in the future.[37]

Native Hawaiian activists have a vision for the future of this land. It includes a sacred location and healing place for all Hawaiians and a natural marine and land reserve, where the ecosystem can be restored. This land base creates a precedent for the rest of Hawai'i, which they hope eventually to have under the jurisdiction of a re-established Hawaiian nation.[38]

Endangered Ecosystems and Voyeuristic Vacations

Tourists outnumber Hawaiians, six to one. That is to say, there are about 1 million residents of Hawai'i, and in 1990, there were six million tourists. Tourists outnumber Native Hawaiians 30 to one. Tourism income represents almost half of the state's revenue, driving a good deal of the economy—and the ecological destruction. As Shelly Mark, former director of the Hawaiian State Department of Planning and Economic Development, suggests,

> Ownership of the land has shifted to corporations off the islands. Rate of return on investment has become the most important thought. There is a conflict between the life of the land and sea, versus the life of the corporate boardroom. Tourism drives up the living and land costs for locals, but provides only low paying, low quality jobs.[39]

Tourism fuels "development" and subsequent ecological destruction, whether it is modifying shoreline (i.e. Waihe'e State Park) or the industrialism associated with tourist infrastructure. In 1973, for instance, researchers from Save Our Surf, a nonprofit advocacy organization, found that Hawai'i's three largest industrial companies had dumped hydrocarbons, toxic wastes, and cement into Ke'eni lagoon, covering 32.5 acres of land.[40]

After the United States, Japan is the main engine behind tourism development in Hawai'i. More and more hotels on the islands are owned by Japanese companies. The Japanese government, in an effort to reduce international friction over its trade surplus, encourages international travel among its citizens. In 1986, the government set a goal of sending 10 million Japanese abroad, and in 1990 they succeeded.[41]

The majority of the financial benefits of tourism find their way back to the country that invests in tourism, rather than the place that hosts tourists. According to the World Bank, up to 90 percent of each U.S. dollar spent in a host destination will eventually "leak back" to the United States, since U.S.-based international corporations control much of the infrastructure of the tourism industry.[42]

According to University of Hawai'i Professor Haunani-Kay Trask (Mililani's older sister and an outspoken nationalist), tourism is the latest wave of colonialism:

> This is not America, this is a colony. The sugar and pineapple plantations were the first wave of colonialism. The military and finally tourism are the next waves of colonialism. The purpose of a colony is to take its land, to take its resources, and exploit its people. The transformation of the Hawaiian people and their land into servants of tourism

is called commodification. It means turning a cultural attribute or a person into a commodity to make a profit.[43]

The Hawaiians have been so commodified that they can be replaced. Now, for an "authentic" welcome, airlines hire Filipina women to dress in mumuus and greet tourists as they disembark their planes. But according to Haunani-Kay Trask, tourism is not meant to sell *haole* culture:

> It's here because we are the native people of this *'aina*. It is our culture that tourists come to see. It is our land that tourists come to pollute. That is the secret.... Without Hawaiians, without beautiful Hawaiian women dancing...there would be no tourism.... It deforms our culture, so that Hawaiians think that to dance the Hula is to dance for tourists.... Hawaiians grow up thinking that our culture is a *haole* interpretation of culture...and if you smile real nice, some *haole* is going to take you out.[44]

As ecotourism researcher Deborah McLaren elaborates, tourism

> contributes to misperceptions of both hosts and guests. Tourism offers to the consumer both the culture and some of the last intact, pristine environments of Indigenous people as commodities to be purchased. It provides a chance to purchase a non-threatening experience for a limited period, with little chance that consumers will ever have to actually acknowledge the impact of their presence on the host culture, society, and environment.... [It] presents a skewed and magnified version of consumer culture. The fact that a tourist may have a job is never perceived by local youth. Instead, each day, they observe only what tourism presents, leisured consumers with no ties to the community, few responsibilities, discretionary income, and enormous economic power, and vacation lifestyles they would not normally have at home.[45]

The tremendous tourism development in Hawai'i has profoundly damaged the land. More than a third of the 526 plants and 88 birds on the United States' threatened and endangered species' acts are originally from Hawai'i, even though the state's land mass is just 0.2 percent of the total U.S. land mass. Conservationists call Hawai'i the "endangered species capital" of the nation.[46] This ecological havoc likewise threatens Native Hawaiian culture:

> When a fishpond is dredged and filled for resort development and construction jobs, we destroy a generations-old resource as a sacrifice for short-term jobs and luxury developments. When our agricultural areas

are left without water so that golf courses can be kept green and scenic, we lose the opportunity to subsist on our land.[47]

Mililani Trask laments the condition of the land, a land endangered by those who wish to enjoy its beauty:

> It is hard to return to your traditional lifestyle when the species upon which we lived, those that fed us, have gone from the earth, forever, you cannot return. You have to go to the museum to look at the stuffed birds, but you cannot eat them. It is hard to return to our traditional practice when pesticides and herbicides toxify the food base, the land base, the food chain.[48]

Birthing a Nation

> A difficult birth does not make a baby any less beautiful.
>
> —Mililani Trask

As diverse as the Hawaiian landscape—from the snowpacked Mauna Kea to the rainforest of Kauai—is the political terrain of the nationalist struggle. Whether it is the constant occupations of beaches, the rebuilding of small villages, or the thousands-strong demonstrations, there is a very prominent Hawaiian Nation emerging from behind the tourist billboards and developers' cranes.

In January 1993, the 100-year anniversary of the overthrow of Queen Lili'uokalani's government, 17,000 Hawaiians marched to Iliolani Palace in Honolulu to demand access to and control over Hawaiian trust lands and to demand recognition of their sovereignty. A 24-hour religious vigil and years of organizing work had preceded the march.[49] Nine months later, on November 23, 1993, the U.S. government did something it rarely does: apologize. Signed into law by President Bill Clinton as PL 103-150, the Apology Bill "offer[ed] an apology to Native Hawaiians on behalf of the United States for the overthrow of the Kingdom of Hawai'i." The bill acknowledged:

> Hawaiian people lived in a highly organized, self-sufficient, subsistence social system based on communal land tenure with a sophisticated language, culture, and religion.... Whereas, on January 14, 1893, the United States minister assigned to the sovereign and independent kingdom of Hawai'i, conspired with a small group of non-Hawaiian residents...to overthrow the Indigenous and lawful Government of Hawai'i.

> Now, therefore, be it resolved by the Senate and House of Representatives...the Congress apologizes to Native Hawaiians...for the overthrow...and the depreciation of the[ir] rights to self-determination.[50]

The Apology Bill received substantive support, except from Washington State's Republican Senator Slade Gorton, a virulent opponent of Native sovereignty, who grumbled that "the logical consequences of this resolution would be independence."[51]

Mililani Trask is a centerpiece in the movement for Hawaiian sovereignty, as the past head of state for a Native Hawaiian government called *Ka Lahui,* which has registered 22,000 citizens. Her elegant stature is readily apparent. She commands the floor, and takes it when necessary. In that job she was both head of state and a statesperson. Naturally. She is also the only person I have ever met who has a photo of herself, the Pope, and Mother Theresa on her office wall, and is both a devout Buddhist and practitioner of Native Hawaiian religion. As an attorney, she spent years litigating trespass, harvesting, and Hawaiian rights cases (and was frequently paid in chickens and poi).

An incredibly eloquent orator, attorney, and organizer, she has been a beacon in the work to rebuild the Hawaiian nation. She explained the beginning of the process of building *Ka Lahui,*

> Our Queen, she said that all of our people were to pray for the enlightened justice of American wisdom.... In 1987, we decided that after 93 years of praying we should do more.

> We called the Hawaiian leadership of all the islands to come and put back together the fundamental documents and a constitution for Hawaiians. We had no place to hold this meeting. We had a church that invited us to go there, and all the Native leaders went there. We had some tents, as you do in Indian Country. We set up the tents, and we worked. There were 250 of us who came and wrote our own constitution.[52]

Ka Lahui works on several different aspects of the sovereignty struggle —on the internal struggle among native Hawaiians, on their relationship to the United States, and on the *Kanaka Maoli*'s relationship with other nations. Their work on the internal struggle concerns language and cultural restoration, among other things. In relation to the United States, they work on transferring trust assets, revenues, and lands to the Native nation, and getting access to the federal court system. For example, they call for the nationalization of the largest privately held tract in the state, a charitable trust created in the will of the last direct descendant of King Kamehameha I, Bernice Pauahi Bishop. The income from this land is meant to benefit the Kamehameha Schools (private trust fund schools) for Native Hawaiian children. But the trustees consider the $2 billion in assets inadequate to school more than 3,000 of the 55,000 eligible children.[53]

As part of *Ka Lahui*'s international work, Mililani Trask represented Indigenous women at the United Nations Conference on the Status of Women. There, I saw Mililani move deftly from government delegation to non-governmental organization, from adversary to ally, without a flicker. The Hawaiians, Pacific Islanders, and their allies formed the Unrepresented Peoples Organization, of which Mililani Trask serves as Vice Chair. These and other activists are struggling to compose a draft declaration on the rights of Indigenous peoples.

According to Mililani,

> The world is not so large, it is quite small. There are 27 species of birds on the endangered species list which live in Hawai'i and nest in the Arctic National Wildlife Refuge, and if they develop the oil in the refuge, we will not have those birds. The world is quite small.... Because [each act] is a pebble in a pond. Small pebble, large ripple.[54]

Ka Lahui has signed two dozen treaties with other nations, treaties that oppose unfair international trade agreements, support biodiversity, and oppose nuclear testing in the Pacific basin, among other issues of concern. *Ka Lahui*'s work is exemplary and a part of a mosaic of changing dynamics in the entire Pacific Basin—a region of islands inhabited by Polynesian and Melanesian people with a shared history of occupation by distant militaries.

While *Ka Lahui* is the largest of the sovereignty groups, there are others, reflecting the diversity of the island. The Nation of Hawai'i, or *Pu'uhonua*, has 13,000 citizens and a constitution. *Ka Pakakuu*, with 2,500 members, acts as a liaison among a number of different groups, from the anti-nuclear movement to Native Hawaiian gays and lesbians. A fourth organization, the Institute for the Advancement of Hawaiian Affairs, is a think-tank run by Hayden Burgess, a Hawaiian attorney, whose Hawaiian name is Poka Laenui.[55] The work of these activists all express the same sentiment, as echoed in David Malo's poem:

E iho ana a luna,
E pi i ana o lalo.
E hui ana na moku,
E ku ana ka paia.

That which is above shall be brought down,
That which is below shall be lifted up.
The islands shall be united,
The walls shall stand upright.

—David Malo, *Ka Lahui,* Ho okupu[56]

Curating a Temple

After a bitter battle, the NPS succeeded in evicting the Pai family from their land in 1997. Now the NPS has a created park (and nude beach) for the purpose of preserving Hawaiian culture, with no Hawaiians in it. How clever.

In 1998, Mahealani Pai graciously agreed to meet my family at his fishponds, now the centerpiece of Kaloko-Honokohau National Historic Park and nudist beach. We walk past scantily clad sunbathers who bask in the rays, oblivious to the ponds and to Pai. Mahealani winces at their immodesty, but his eyes shimmer as he looks at the fishponds. As my eyes scan Mahealani Pai's fish traps, *heiau,* shrimpponds, and beach, I see the work of generations building and maintaining a relationship to the *'aina.* It is clear that the only ones who can care for an area so well are those who have prayed there for a century.

That opinion is not, however, held in Washington. But in the long term, what Washington decides may not matter. What happens 5,000 miles away is really of only limited consequence to the *'aina* and the *Kanaka Maoli.* As Mililani says,

> The beginning of nationhood, the beginning of sovereignty, and work-
> ing for self determination, has to do with making right your path with
> the Creator and practicing your ceremony and your culture. This is the
> predicate to political work in sovereignty Nation building, and as we
> say in Hawai'i, don't worry about sovereignty and community work
> unless your spirit is right, that is the first thing.[57]

There is something growing in the taro patches, more powerful than can be imagined in Washington. And that is kept, as it has been for generations, in the hearts and memories of the Hawaiians.

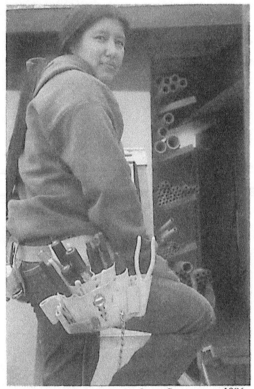

Debby Tewa. Photo by Owen Seumptewa, 1996.

Native
SUN

Determining a Future

opi *potskwaniat* means "Hopi pathway to the future," a phrase aptly applied to the work of the Hopi Foundation and NativeSUN on the Hopi reservation in northeastern Arizona. Each day before climbing onto the Hopi rooftops, Debby Tewa drinks a cup of coffee, first at her small, one-room stone house, and then at the bustling NativeSUN office in the village of Kykotsmovi. There, amidst a wind turbine, composting toilets, solar water pump, and energy-efficient light bulbs, she maps out her plan for the day. Later, on a sun-baked mesa, she straps on her tool belt. She clambers up a ladder onto the flat roof of a 200-year-old stone house, looks out over a hundred miles of desert, and takes a deep breath. Glancing across the village of Hotevilla, she sees the sun glinting off the roof-based solar panels and smiles. She is home, and she is the Hopi Foundation's solar electrician.

Her eyes span the 1.5 million acres of the Hopi reservation, high atop mesas nestled within the borders of the Navajo reservation. Twelve thousand Hopi live in a dozen 1,500-year-old Hopi villages, the oldest continuously in-habited villages on the continent. The contrast between America's newness, escalating speed, and dramatic change and the Hopi's resilience, tenacity, and ability to withdraw from the world is a wonder. By and large, change comes slowly and deliberately to Hopi. And it comes largely through the doings of the Hopi people.

The Hopi Foundation is one of these paths of change. Founded in 1985, the foundation has restored ancient ceremonial houses, offered language and cultural classes, and developed a health program with the tribal government. In an unusual move for the rather isolated Hopi community, the foundation even crossed the borders of Hopi to create a sanctuary for Indigenous refugees from Central America in Tucson, Arizona.

NativeSUN is the foundation's solar project. NativeSUN has installed photovoltaic solar panels atop 300 houses on the Hopi reservation and in nearby Navajo (Diné) ranching communities. Most of those panels were installed by Debby Tewa, a.k.a. Solar Debby, a Coyote Clan resident of Hotevilla.

Many Hopi have resisted electrification by utilities, and one-third do not allow electric power lines in their communities. The Hopi traditionals "don't al-low power lines into the villages, because [then] the utilities will have right of way" onto Hopi land, Tewa explains. Village leaders "think that if we don't pay the bills, [the utilities will] take even more land."[1]

As the Hopi Foundation puts it,

> The force field of electricity emanating from the power lines is considered to be disruptive to the atmosphere, ambience, and balance of the plaza and ceremonial areas, at the same time blocking the aesthetics of the sky and the panoramic vistas of the mesas.[2]

But solar power maintains Hopi self-sufficiency. "When you get your own system," says Tewa, "it's yours. There's no power line, [and] no right of way into the villages."[3] The solar project began as a demonstration in collaboration with the Arizona Energy Commission. It did not take long to turn into a fledgling business. NativeSUN, although reliant on foundation support (such as from the Joyce Mertz Gilmore Fund and others), leverages local capital for infrastructure development. Hopis and other clients can choose from an array of systems: two panels, four panels, eight panels, stationary or rotating. Most of the options are already operational somewhere on the reservation or on display at the NativeSUN office.

A revolving loan program makes the solar systems affordable for the community. At a 12-percent interest rate over five years, most people pay off their systems without too much trouble. Elders are accorded an 8-percent interest rate. The average system costs an average of $5,885 for a four-panel system, which, despite the seemingly high initial investment, quickly balances out over a lifetime of utility bills.

Tewa talks about the change in perspective brought about by solar energy. "With this system, you purchase it, and it's yours. It teaches you to be conservative, because you're getting your power from batteries. You can't just leave your hallway light on for three or four hours. It teaches you to be independent."

"Philosophically and traditionally Hopis tend to want to be self-sufficient," says Owen Seumptewa, a former director of NativeSUN. "They didn't want to be indebted to anyone else. Traditional Hopi philosophy is the belief that you didn't want to borrow money. Of course, we've seen a change in that, borrowing money, 'cause we had to lend money here in order to provide solar electric systems, but again, the end result is to be self-sufficient by providing your own electrical power."[4]

The Hopi Foundation was founded to stave off an impending cultural crisis. Since the advent of colonialism, "non-Hopi influences brought on to the reservation were creating problems," explains Hopi Foundation chair and founder Doran Doltan. "It was basically Hopi trying to find themselves, being torn between the Hopi way of living and the modern way of living, and not being able to reconcile the two."[5] Dalton's words are echoed by Lois Minkler, the associate director of the foundation:

> We've been taught through western models for a long, long time, that the answers come from the outside. When you focus on the deficiencies of people, then the perception is that the people are weak and that they're unable to do things for their own conditions.... Our approach is that the strengths are inherent in communities.[6]

The Energy Crisis

What the Hopi Foundation and community have done is common sense for the rest of us as well. Use less, produce what you can on your own, and be cognizant of the implications of each decision on others.

This is more than a spiritual and cultural decision—it is a necessary economic one as well. Imported fossil fuels are nonrenewable, unreliable, and wreak potent damage on the environment, as has been well documented.[7]

The problem will worsen. The International Energy Agency projects that fossil fuel emissions will exceed 1990 levels by 17 percent in 2000 and 49 percent by 2010.[8] According to the Worldwatch Institute, the rate of climate change triggered by these emissions is projected to exceed natural rates by a factor of ten.[9] Indeed, 1998's storms, hurricanes, floods, and other natural disasters are reckoned to have been the worst on record, incurring $89 billion in property damages—greater than those of the entire decade of the 1980s put together, adjusted for inflation.

As economist Richard Douthwaite concludes,

> No stable, sustainable community can...exist without a secure, sustainable supply of energy at a steady price, and the only way that both security and price stability can be guaranteed is by having energy sources within community boundaries and under community control.[10]

Colonialism and Self-Reliance

Native peoples are the poorest population in North America, yet our lands are home to a wealth of resources. Two-thirds of the country's uranium; one-third of all western low-sulfur coal; and vast hydro-electric, oil, and natural gas resources are all situated on Native land.

Some of the largest corporations in the world have mined these resources and grabbed the value added, generally paying Native communities but a pittance. As journalist and energy policy researcher Marjane Ambler writes,

> Overall, development of energy resources has contributed little to most tribal economies as energy-related employment has been low, and tribes and energy development companies have not reinvested revenues to broaden the tribal economic base. Like many dependent on mineral extraction–based economies, energy tribes have survived boom-and-bust cycles that have prevented long-term economic development.[11]

Yet Native communities across the country must cope with the tremendous messes left behind by resource extraction: huge slag piles, uranium mill tailings, and abandoned uranium mine shafts (over 1,000 on the Navajo reservation alone).

The final insult is that the energy mined from Native lands is often not used for Native communities. In 1975, for instance, the Navajo Nation (which surrounds the Hopi reservation) produced enough energy to meet the needs of the state of New Mexico for 32 years. Yet 85 percent of all Navajo households had no electricity. In 1996, some 18,000 Native households were still unserved by utilities.[12]

As a result of this underdevelopment of infrastructure, many Native communities do not consume many energy resources. This in itself is an opportunity, as Native peoples are less addicted to fossil fuels than the rest of the country. And indeed, the push for alternative energy, self-reliance in energy, and energy efficiency is growing in Native communities. Today, in the era of energy-utility deregulation, many tribes are considering developing their own utilities, pooling their consumers to secure better rates from local utilities, and producing alternative energy.

A 1998 handbook called *Native Power,* produced by the Native American Renewable Energy Education Project at the University of California, Berkeley, was particularly influential, showcasing alternative energy projects on various reservations and in Native peoples' homes, and outlining possible energy-efficiency and self-reliance measures for tribes. [13]

Also in 1998, a coalition of 28 northern plains tribes, the Intertribal Council on Utility Policy (ICOUP), brought a group of traditional elders together with NASA scientists and others to talk about global warming. "Things are not in balance," remarked ICOUP president Patrick Spears.

We are living with the resources. We know that one form of life affects every other form of life. We know there's a spirit in all things, including rocks. And we know that environmental degradation has contributed to climate change. When you step on one strand of a spider web, it all moves.[14]

ICOUP's continuing work has been to inform and pique tribal governments' interest in energy protection, consumption, and infrastructure, and each season the work of these communities grows.

Alternative Energy and the Future

Just as the human body adapts itself to the regular intake of "hard" drugs, its systems coming to depend on them to such an extent that the user goes through a period of acute distress if they are suddenly withdrawn, so the use of "hard" fossil energy alters the economic metabolism and is so highly addictive that in a crisis, a user-community or country will be prepared to export almost any proportion of its annual output to buy its regular fix. Even in normal conditions, a community in an industrialized country can devote a fifth of its external income to buying energy, an expense that not only constitutes a serious drain on its resources, but locks the community into the unpredictable gyrations of the world trading system.

—Richard Douthwaite[15]

Although some fossil fuel giants, such as British Petroleum, Enron, and Royal Dutch Shell Oil have forged their way into alternative energy programs, most of the powerful fossil-fuel and nuclear-energy lobby strenuously opposes the development of renewable energy. Much is at stake. The United States is the single largest energy market in the world. Following Canada, U.S. residents are the second largest per-capita energy consumers in the world.

In general, the U.S. government has been beholden to the fossil-fuel lobbies. Between 1948 and 1992, nuclear power received 65 percent of all federal funds for energy research and development.[16] Although research on how to manage nuclear wastes continues to consume a lion's share of federal funds, between 1996 and 1998, 28 percent of federal research dollars went toward renewable energy, compared with 16.6 percent for nuclear power.

If wind and other alternative energy sources received anywhere near the subsidies that the nuclear and coal industries do, they would become far more feasible and cost-effective. The potential is great. Solar power presently fills about 1 percent of U.S. energy needs, but the solar industry estimates that the sun could provide up to 20 percent of worldwide power needs by 2030.[17] According to the American Wind Energy Association, by the year 2010, wind power could generate 30,000 megawatts a year, or enough electricity to meet the needs of ten million households and offset 1,000 million metric tons of carbon dioxide emissions annually.[18] Wind energy is now the fastest-growing renewable-energy source, with 35 percent more wind generation capacity in 1998 than in 1997. In 1998, 9,600 megawatts of wind power produced enough energy for 3.5 million suburban homes, the third-largest wind-energy capacity in the world.[19]

Community organizing victories have led to a few large wind projects in the country so far. Altamont Pass near San Francisco provides enough power for 700,000 people. A new project called Buffalo Ridge in southern Minnesota, a direct result of anti-nuclear activism, generates enough power for over 35,000 people. In 1998, a 42-megawatt project in Wyoming and a 25-megawatt project in Oregon came on-line, providing enough energy for another 22,000 people.

At the current rate of installation of wind energy programs, the World Energy Council projects that wind power will provide energy for between 60 and 158 million people globally, even at U.S. consumption levels. At the end of 1997, 6,190 megawatts of wind energy capacity were installed on the worldwide market, costing $8.5 billion and employing 40,000 people.[20] Although wind power won't be able to provide all the electricity we need, it is half as expensive to build as a nuclear power plant of similar capacity, produces electricity much more quickly, and costs up to 50 percent less to consume.[21]

Many tribes have great potential for wind energy. Many Native peoples live in the Great Plains, a region that energy analysts call the "Saudi Arabia of wind energy." The Blackfoot reservation alone has class-five wind potential, and less but still significant wind potential exists on Standing Rock, Turtle Mountain, Northern Cheyenne, Crow, Pine Ridge, Rosebud, White Earth, and many other reservations. It will take community initiative and commitment to make the change. Whether it is solar, wind, low-head hydro-electric, or otherwise produced, alternative energy is part of the path to the future.

Back on the mesas of Hopi, Debby Tewa grabs some fancy equipment and heads out down the dirt roads. Tewa has been traveling to small villages in northern California, Minnesota, and Ecuador to explain how the power of the sun can help villages. Back home at Hotevilla, she is happy to look out at the panels glinting in the sun, quite an accomplishment. Her next project is on its way: composting toilets.

This is part of the process of evaluating European technologies, deciding which are of value to Hopis—or to any community—and which aren't. By deliberating before acting, NativeSUN is making an example of working with one's own hands, heart, and determination.

Walt Bresette. Photo courtesy of Speak Out Speakers & Artists.

We are walking upon the faces of those yet to come.

—Iroquois teaching

The
Seventh
Generation

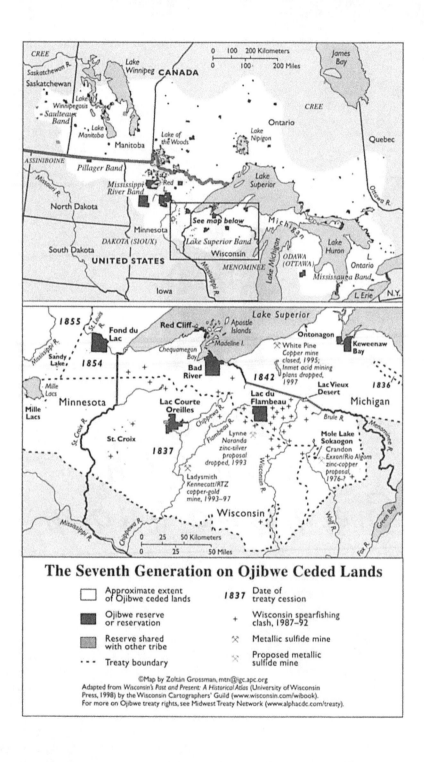

The Seventh Generation on Ojibwe Ceded Lands

	Approximate extent of Ojibwe ceded lands	*1837*	Date of treaty cession
	Ojibwe reserve or reservation	+	Wisconsin spearfishing clash, 1987–92
	Reserve shared with other tribe	⚒	Metallic sulfide mine
- - -	Treaty boundary	⚒	Proposed metallic sulfide mine

©Map by Zoltán Grossman, mtn@igc.apc.org
Adapted from *Wisconsin's Past and Present: A Historical Atlas* (University of Wisconsin Press, 1998) by the Wisconsin Cartographers' Guild (www.wisconsin.com/wibook).
For more on Ojibwe treaty rights, see Midwest Treaty Network (www.alphacdc.com/treaty).

Somewhere between the teachings of western science and those of the Native community there is some agreement on the state of the world. Ecosystems are collapsing, species are going extinct, the polar icecaps are melting, and nuclear bombings and accidents have contaminated the land.

According to Harvard biologist Edward O. Wilson, 50,000 species are lost every year. Three-quarters of the world's species of birds are declining, and one-quarter of all mammalian species are endangered. Tropical rainforests, freshwater lakes, and coral reefs are at immediate risk, and global warming and climate change will accelerate the rate of biological decline dramatically.[1]

The writing is on the wall, in bold letters. There is no easy answer, and even scientists themselves seem to recognize the necessity of finding new strategies and understandings. In an unusual gathering in late 1998, for instance, NASA scientists met with Indigenous elders to discuss global warming and to hear the elders' suggestions on possible solutions. The response the scientists received may have been only part of what they had hoped for. As one observer summarized, the elders pretty much responded, "You did it, you fix it."[2]

In the final analysis, we humans can *say* whatever we would like—rationalize, revise statistical observations, extend deadlines, and make accommodations for a perceived "common good." But "natural law," as Yakama fisherman and former director of the Columbia Intertribal Fishing Commission Ted Strong explains, "is a hard and strict taskmaster."[3] Dump dioxin into the river, and you will inevitably eat or drink it. Assent to acceptable levels of radioactive emissions, and sooner or later, those sensitive cells in the human body will likely respond.

The challenge at the cusp of the millennium is to transform human laws to match natural laws, not vice versa. And to correspondingly transform wasteful production and voracious consumption. America and industrial society must move from a society based on conquest to one steeped in the practice of survival.

In order to do that, we must close the circle. The linear nature of industrial production itself, in which labor and technology turn natural wealth into consumer products and wastes, must be transformed into a cyclical system. In the best scenario, natural resources must be reused or not used at all, and waste production cut to a mere trickle. Those who watch carefully—*onaanaagadawaa-*

bandanaawaa—know that this will require a technological, cultural, and legal transformation.

Many Indigenous teachings consider the present a time of change. Anishinaabeg teachings recognize this time of change for the people of the Seventh Fire as both a reality and an opportunity. According to these prophecies, Anishinaabeg people retrace their steps to find what was left by the trail. There are two separate roads from which to choose, for both the Anishinaabeg and those called the "light-skinned people."

Anishinaabeg elder Eddie Benton Benai, from the Lac Courte Orielles reservation in Wisconsin, is a teacher of the Anishinaabeg Midewiwin society. He discusses the two roads as

> the road to technology and the other road to Spiritualism. They [elders] feel that the road of technology represents a continuation of headlong rush to technological development. This is the road...that has led to modern society, to a damaged and seared earth.... The [other] road represents the slower path that Traditional Native people have traveled and are now seeking again. The Earth is not scorched on this trail. The grass is still growing there.[4]

A similar teaching of the Six Nations Iroquois Confederacy recognizes the importance of future generations. "In each deliberation, we must consider the impact on the seventh generation from now," they say; that is, undertake conservative thinking, and use careful deliberation. Such consideration would have preempted thousands of decisions made by the U.S. government.

Rethinking the Constitution

Walt Bresette, an Anishinaabe man from the Red Cliff reservation in northern Wisconsin, passed to the next world in early 1999. His passing was a huge loss to the Native environmental movement. But his groundbreaking work on re-envisioning the Constitution and Native treaty rights for the benefit of all people and the earth continues. Bresette was part of the Seventh Generation movement, a movement that calls for a radical amendment to the U.S. Constitution.

The preamble to the U.S. Constitution declares its intent to be to "secure the blessings of liberty, to ourselves, and our posterity." In reality, U.S. laws have been transformed by corporate interests to cater to elite interests in society. While the U.S. Constitution makes no mention of corporations, according to anti-corporate analysts Richard Grossman and Frank Adams, "the history of

Constitutional law is, as former Supreme Court Justice Felix Frankfurter said, 'the history of the impact of the modern corporation on the American scene.'" Over the course of two centuries of court decisions, corporate contracts and their rates of return have been redefined as property that should be protected under the Constitution. In this way the "common good" has been redefined as "maximum corporate production and profit."[5]

Appointed judges have handed down decision after decision increasing the privileges of corporations. Corporations have been granted the power of "eminent domain" and the right to inflict "private injury and personal damage" when pursuing "progressive improvements." Most significantly, in 1886, the Supreme Court treated private corporations as "natural person[s]" protected by the Constitution and "sheltered by the Bill of Rights and the Fourteenth Amendment."[6]

Consequently, American public policy and the legal system have largely come to reflect short-term views despite the intergenerational perspective foundational to the U.S. Constitution. At the 1995 United Nations Conference on the Status of Women in Beijing, Corrine Kumar from the Asian Women's Human Rights Campaign spoke of the legal challenges in the national and international arena of this era. "The violence of the times," she explained, "has outstripped the law."[7] We have little understanding of or protection from the combined and cumulative impact of industrialism's complicated chemical soup on our bodies, ecosystems, or future generations. Public policy is lagging far behind our ability to destroy ourselves.

The rights of the people to use and enjoy air, water, and sunlight are essential to life, liberty, and the pursuit of happiness. These basic human rights have been impaired by those who discharge toxic substances into the air, water, and land. Contaminating the commons must be recognized as a fundamental wrong in our system of laws, just as defacing private property is wrong. On that basis, the Seventh Generation Amendment to the Constitution of the United States declares,

> The right of citizens of the U.S. to enjoy and use air, water, sunlight, and other renewable resources determined by the Congress to be common property shall not be impaired, nor shall such use impair their availability for use by the future generations.[8]

Bresette's other work included transforming court decisions on treaty rights into tools to transform northern Wisconsin into a sustainable, protected region. The Supreme Court's 1983 *Voigt* decision affirmed Anishinaabeg hunting, fishing, and gathering rights in ceded land in northern Wisconsin and was initially greeted with widespread outrage by non-Indians (See Chapter Six). Since then, the broader community has come to accept these rights, and Bresette and others want to expand them in ways that would benefit Indians and non-Indians alike. "A close reading of the court ruling suggests that these harvesting rights actually set extremely high environmental standards, certainly the highest in any region of the state," Bresette argued. In other words, the *Voigt* decision can be interpreted to mean not only that Indians have the right to fish and hunt in the ceded territory, but also the right to be able to "eat those fish and deer." That means that the state "should be prohibited from allowing damage to the fish by loose environmental regulation."[9]

We must follow Bresette's example and charge ourselves with curbing the rights of corporations and special interests, transforming the legal institutions of the United States back toward the preservation of the commons, and preserving everyone's rights, not just those of the economically privileged. On a community level, we must support local self-reliance and the recovery of Indigenous systems of knowledge, jurisdiction, practice, and governance.

Native people in our own reservation communities must dialogue about change, the path ahead, the options, and how we will make a better future for our children. As the conveners of the Indigenous Environmental Statement of Principles note,

> Our traditional laws lead us to understand that economic development cannot subsist on a deteriorating resource base. The environment cannot be maintained and protected when "growth" does not account for the cost of environmental and cultural destruction.[10]

The choice between the technological and the spiritual will be based on both collective and individual decisions, both simple and complex. For just as life itself is a complex web of relationships and organisms, so is the fabric of a community and a culture that chooses its future. Either way, according to Indigenous worldviews, there is no easy fix, no technological miracle.

The challenge of transformation requires the diligence and patient work evidenced by many of the people discussed in this book. And from the Everglades to the subarctic, their voices for change are increasing in volume.

There is, in many Indigenous teachings, a great optimism for the potential to make positive change. Change *will* come. As always, it is just a matter of who determines what that change will be.

Notes

Notes to Introduction

1   Pierson Mitchell in *Wana Chinook Tymoo,* a publication of the
     Columbia River Intertribal Fishing Commission, Winter 1999, pp.
     12–13.

2   Bill Yallup Sr. in *Wana Chinook Tymoo.*

3   Interview with Susana Santos, October 1996.

4   Interview with Margaret Saluskin, June 1994.

5   Seventh Generation Fund, "1995 Funding Proposal for Environment
     Program," Arcata, CA. See also Council of Energy Resource Tribes,
     "Inventory of Hazardous Waste Generators and Sites on Selected
     Indian Reservations," Denver, CO, July 1985.

6   Interview with Chris Peters, Seventh Generation Fund, May 4, 1994.

7   Akwesasne Task Force on the Environment, "Superfund Clean Up of
     Akwesasne: Case Study in Environmental Injustice," *International
     Journal of Contemporary Sociology*, October 1997, p. 4.

8   Wabunoquod quoted in Robert H. Keller, "An Economic History of
     Indian Treaties of the Great Lakes Region," *American Indian Journal*,
     1976, p.14.

9   Interview with Loretta Pascal, June 22, 1995.

10   Ted Strong in *Wana Chinook Tymoo.*

11   Ted Strong, Panel Presentation, Lewis and Clark University, October
     22, 1998.

Notes to Ch. 1: Akwesasne

1   This and other quotes from Katsi Cook are from an interview conducted on August 9, 1997, unless otherwise noted.

2   Tim Bristol, "First Environment," *Turtle Quarterly*, Fall 1992, p. 29.

3   "Haudenosaunee Statement to the World," *Akwesasne Notes*, Spring 1979.

4   Ward Churchill, *Struggle for the Land*, Monroe, ME: Common Courage Press, 1993, p. 93.

5   Akwesasne Freedom School literature, 1995.

6   Churchill, p. 98.

7   Janci Whitney Annunziata, "An Indigenous Strategy for Human Sustainability," Haudenosaunee Environmental Taskforce for the U.N. Environmental Program, 1992, p. 21.

8   Annunziata, p. 21.

9   Mary Francis Hoover, "Mohawk Land Under Attack: Akwesasne's Environment," *Turtle Quarterly*, p. 43.

10 Akwesasne Task Force on the Environment, "Superfund Clean Up of Akwesasne: Case Study in Environmental Injustice," *International Journal of Contemporary Sociology*, October 1997.

11 Hoover, p. 20.

12 Theo Colburn, *Our Stolen Future: Are We Threatening Our Fertility, Intelligence, and Survival? A Scientific Detective Story*, New York: Penguin, 1997, pp. 88–89, 151, 189.

13 Hoover, p. 45.

14 Laurie Garrett, "PCBs Linked to Human Breast Cancer: New Study Addresses Environmental Factors," *The Sun*, June 8, 1992, p. 3A.

15 Janet Raloff, "Because We Eat PCBs...," *Science News Online*, September 14, 1996.

16 "Haudenosaunee Statement to the World," *Akwesasne Notes*.

17 Akwesasne Task Force on the Environment, "Superfund Clean Up."

18 Kallen Martin, "Akwesasne Industrial Contamination—Environmental Recovery," *Winds of Change*, Summer 1996.

19 Akwesasne Task Force on the Environment, "Superfund Clean Up," pp. 8, 9.

20 Martin, p. 21.

21 Akwesasne Task Force on the Environment, "Superfund Clean Up," p. 9.

22 Martin, pp. 19–20.

23 Interview with Ken Jock, August 10, 1997.

24 Martin, pp. 19–20.

25 Winona LaDuke, "Katsi Cook, Mohawk Mothers' Milk, and PCBs," *Indigenous Woman*, 1993.

26   See Donald A. Grinde and Bruce E. Johansen, *Ecocide of Native America: Environmental Destruction of Indigenous Lands and People,* Santa Fe, NM: Clear Light Publishers, 1995, pp. 171–203.

27   LaDuke, "Katsi Cook, Mohawk Mothers' Milk, and PCBs."

28   Syni-An Hwang, Edward F. Fitzgerald, Brian Bush, and Katsi Cook, "Exposure to PCBs from Hazardous Waste Among Mohawk Women and Infants at Akwesasne," *Technology: Journal of the Franklin Institute,* Vol. 333A, 1996, pp. 17-23.

29   Interview with Ken Jock, August 9, 1997.

30   Council on Economic Priorities, "Campaign for Cleaner Corporations," Research Report, New York: December 1992.

31   Council on Economic Priorities, pp. 3, 4.

32   Theo Colburn, speech at State of the World Forum, San Francisco, CA, October 3, 1996.

33   Colburn, speech.

34   Mary Esch, "Local Reservation Is Making News on the National Level," *Massena Observer,* December 17, 1987, p. 65.

35   Interview with Jim Ransom, August 2, 1999.

Notes to Ch. 2: Seminoles

1   This and other quotes from Danny Billie are from an interview conducted on September 27, 1997, unless otherwise noted.
2   Thomas E. Lodge, *The Everglades Handbook: Understanding the Ecosystem*, Boca Raton, FL: St. Lucie Press, 1997, p. 142.
3   Dan Georgakas, *The Broken Hoop*, Garden City, NY: Zenith Books, Doubleday and Co., 1973, p. 52.
4   Georgakas, p. 51.
5   Georgakas, p. 52.
6   Catherine Caufield, "Selling a Piece of Your Mother," *Whole Earth*, Fall 1998, p. 61.
7   Caufield, p. 61.
8   World Resources Institute, *1993 Information Please Environmental Almanac*, Boston, MA: Houghton Mifflin, 1993, p. 159.
9   Indian Law Resource Center, "Vanishing Wetlands and Traditional Florida Seminole," Research paper, Helena, MT, 1994, p. 2.
10 Indian Law Resource Center, p. 4.
11 Lodge, p. 181.
12 Lodge, p. xix.
13 *National Real Estate Investor*, 36 (3), March 1994, p. 54.
14 Dennis Jordan, "Mercury Contamination: Another Threat to the Florida Panther," *Endangered Species Technical Bulletin*, 15 (2), pp. 1, 6.
15 Lodge, p. 91.
16 Sally Deneen, "The Panther's Last Stand," *E: The Environmental Magazine*, October 1994, p.18.
17 Catherine Caufield, unpublished manuscript intended for *The New Yorker*, January 30, 1996.
18 Caufield, "Selling a Piece of Your Mother," p. 62.
19 www.semtribe.com.
20 Catherine Caufield, unpublished manuscript, p. 6.
21 www.semtribe.com.
22 Seminole Tribe of Florida, "Tribal Enterprises: Gaming," 1997.
23 Seminole Tribe of Florida, "Tribal Enterprises: Gaming," 1997.
24 Seminole Tribe of Florida, "Billie Swamp Safari," 1997.
25 Jordan Levin, "When Worlds Collide," *South Florida*, June 1994, p. 84.
26 Levin, p. 95.
27 Levin.
28 This and other quotes from Bobby Billie are from an interview conducted on September 27, 1997, unless otherwise noted.
29 Caufield, "Selling a Piece of Your Mother," p. 62.
30 Caufield, unpublished manuscript, p. 2.
31 Interview with Lori Pourier, June 1998.

32   Interview with Martha Billie Davis, September 27, 1997.

33   Dagmare Thorpe, *People of the Seventh Fire*, Ithaca, NY: Akwekon Press, 1997, p. 22.

34   Deneen.

35   "Recovery Proceeds for Everglades Panthers," *National Parks*, Jan-Feb 1995, p. 14.

36   Correspondence with J. Patrick Lannan, July 1, 1999.

37   Correspondence with Lannan.

38   Thorpe, 25.

39   Levin, p. 84.

40   Correspondence with Lannan.

Notes to Ch. 3: Nitassinan

1   These are the names for the land of the people who live there: to the west, it's Eeyou Aski (Cree), to the south, Anishinaabe Aski (Ojibwe).

2   Marie Wadden, *Nitassinan: The Innu Struggle to Reclaim Their Homeland*, Vancouver, British Columbia: Douglas and McIntyre, 1991, p. 28.

3   *On Indian Land*, September 1997, p. 14.

4   Wadden, p. 29.

5   Wadden, pp. vii–ix.

6   Hugh Brody, *The People's Land: Inuit, Whites and the Eastern Arctic*, Vancouver, British Columbia: Douglas and McIntyre, 1991 (1975).

7   Hugh Brody, *Living Arctic: Hunters of the Canadian North*, London: Faber, 1987, p. 13.

8   Jacques Cartier, *Two Navigations to Newe France*, Norwood, N.J.: W. J. Johnson, 1975.

9   Alan Cooke, *The Exploration of Northern Canada, 500 to 1920: A Chronology*, Toronto: Arctic History Press, 1978.

10 Brody, *The People's Land*, p. 31.

11 Translation by Mark Drouin, from a speech at an organizers' conference, Montreal, January 31, 1987.

12 Testimony in court, provided by Mennonite Central Committee, 1989.

13 www.innu.ca.

14 Barbara Harsanyi, "NATO Flights Threat to Innu and Environment," *Between the Issues*, October–December 1989, pp. 18-19.

15 Friends of Nitassinan, "NATO's War on the Innu and the Earth," newsletter, August 1996, p. 4.

16 Ian Bailey, "Newfoundland Minister Rules out Armed Response to End Innu Standoff," *Canadian Press*.

17 Winona LaDuke, "Occupation of Nitassinan," *Indigenous Woman*, 1 (4), 1989, p. 14.

18 Kevin Cox, "Priest Local Hero to Natives," *Toronto Globe and Mail*, February 12, 1990, p. A3.

19 Robert Jobst, "Thunder," *Gauntlet*, November 9, 1989, pp. 12–13.

20 Rick Bauman, "Innu Battle for Their Land," *Ottawa Citizen*, November 18, 1989, p. G3.

21 Wadden, p. 93.

22 Bauman, p. G3.

23 Wadden, p. 95.

24 Wadden, p. 48.

25 R. John Hayes, "Innu Still Shut out of Power Deal," *Windspeaker*, December 1, 1996.

26 Friends of Nitassinan, "Churchill Falls: One of the World's Great Cataracts," newsletter, August 1996, p. 2.

27   Drouin, March 19, 1989.

28   Boyce Richardson, *Strangers Devour the Land*, Post Mills, VT: Chelsea Green Publishing, 1991, p. xi.

29   Andrés Picard, "James Bay: A Power Play," *Toronto Globe and Mail*, April 13-17, 1990.

30   Interview with Jim Huggins, March 11, 1989.

31   Friends of Nitassinan, "Project Two Georges Churchill Dams to Be Announced," *Nitassinan News*, 4 (1), March 1998.

32   Interview with Ian Goodman, January 16, 1998.

33   For instance, Long Island Lighting Company's plants.

34   In the northeast United States, the prices are between 2 and 3 cents per KWH. Goodman, January 16, 1998.

35   Goodman not only believes that it's unlikely that they can bring the power in cheaply, but points out that "It takes seven years to build a dam, if you can sign a contract for a high price in a secure market that will guarantee your risk. They're going to build it on 'spec,' that's the situation now." Interview with Ian Goodman, January 16, 1998.

36   Interview with Ian Goodman, January 16, 1998.

37   Andre Caille, head of Hydro-Quebec, announced the goal of making the utility one of the five major energy companies in North America, on par with Enron and Duke/Energy and other colossals. Tom Holzinger, "Letter from Quebec: Save Our Wild Rivers: HQ Proposes Eight New River Diversions to Feed U.S. Market," *Nitassinan News,* August 1997, p. 3.

38   Interview with Ian Goodman, January 16, 1998.

39   Friends of Nitassinan, *Nitassinan News*, March 1998, p. 3.

40   Friends of Nitassinan, "Victory at Emish: Innu and Inuit Blockade Construction," *Nitassinan News*, November 1997, p. 3.

41   Julia Panourgia Clones, in Lenora Foerstel, ed., *Creating Surplus Populations: The Effects of Military and Corporate Policies on Indigenous Peoples*, Washington, DC: Maisonneuve Press, 1996, p. 227.

42   Moira Welsh, "Chief Finds 'Lack of Hope' in Davis Inlet," *Toronto Star*, February 2, 1993, p. A2.

43   Michael Valpy, "Davis Inlet," *Toronto Globe and Mail*.

44   Sara Little-Crow Russell, "Ghost Dance," *Nitassinan News*, August 1997.

Notes to Ch. 4: Northern Cheyenne

1   Gail Small, "The Search for Environmental Justice in Indian Country," *Amicus Journal*, March 1994.

2   This and other quotes from Gail Small are from an interview conducted on May 29, 1999, unless otherwise noted.

3   George Bird Grinnell, *Pawnee, Blackfoot, and Cheyenne: History and Folklore of the Plains*, New York: Scribner, 1961, p. 381.

4   Dee Brown, *Bury My Heart at Wounded Knee*, New York: Holt, Reinhardt, Hovinston, Inc., 1970, p. 98.

5   Charles J. Kappler, ed., *Kappler's Indian Affairs: Laws and Treaties*, Washington, DC: U.S. Department of the Interior, 1979.

6   Brown, p. 319.

7   Brown, p. 323.

8   Native American Graves Protection and Repatriation Act (NAGPRA) Notification, October 5, 1993, p. 51845.

9   People's Grand Jury Committee, "The AMAX War Against Humanity," Washington, DC, April 22, 1977, p. 16.

10 People's Grand Jury Committee, p. 18.

11 Richard Nafziger, "Transnational Energy Corporations and American Indian Development," in Institute for Native American Development, *American Indian Energy Resources and Development*, University of New Mexico, 1980, pp. 11–13.

12 Nafziger, p. 13.

13 National Academy of Sciences/National Academy of Engineering, Report to the Energy Policy Project of the Ford Foundation, "Rehabilitation Potential of Western Coal Lands," draft document, Washington, DC: Ford Foundation, 1973, p. 42.

14 People's Grand Jury Committee, p. 27.

15 People's Grand Jury Committee, p. 27.

16 American Indian Policy Review Commission, Washington, DC, May 17, 1977, p. 339.

17 American Indian Policy Review Commission, p. 342.

18 Ken Peres, "Keystone to Survival: The Multinational Corporations and the Struggle for Control of the Land," paper for the 1980 Black Mills International Survival Gathering, p. 72.

19 People's Grand Jury Committee, p. 118.

20 National Academy of Sciences, p. 1.

21 National Academy of Sciences, p. 135.

22 Nafziger, p. 42.

23 Nafziger, p. 42.

24 Interview with Mike Lee, December 24, 1997.

25 Gail Small, "The Search for Environmental Justice in Indian Country."

26   Interview with Jeff Barber, August 12, 1998.

27   Simon Ortiz, *From Sand Creek*, New York: Thunders Mouth Press, 1981.

Notes to Ch. 5: Nuclear Waste

1   See Anna Gyorgy and friends, *No Nukes: Everyone's Guide to Nuclear Power*, Boston: South End Press, 1979. See also Ward Churchill and Winona LaDuke, "Native North America: The Poltical Economy of Radioactive Colonialism," in M. Annette Jaimes, ed., *The State of Native America: Genocide, Colonization, and Resistance*, Boston: South End Press, 1992.

2   Grace Thorpe, "Our Homes Are Not Dumps," in Jace Weaver ed., *Defending Mother Earth: Native American Perspectives on Environmental Justice*, Maryknoll, NY: Orbis Books, 1996, p. 55.

3   This and other quotes from Faye Brown are from an interview conducted on January 20, 1998, unless otherwise noted.

4   Peter H. Eichstaedt, *If You Poison Us: Uranium and Native Americans*, Santa Fe, NM: Red Crane Books, 1994, pp. 32–55.

5   Ernest Callenbach, *Bring Back the Buffalo*, Washington, DC: Island Press, 1996, p. 227.

6   Interview with Harvey Wasserman, July 13, 1999.

7   Virginia Sanchez, "Nuclear Risk Management for Native Americans," Western Shoshone Defense Project newspaper, Spring 1997, p. 14.

8   Daniel Berger, "We're All Downwinders," *The Nation*, October 13, 1997, p. 6. See also Peter Eisler, "Study Shows Contaminants Fall Out from Nevada Test Site," *USA Today*, July 25–27, 1997, p. 1.

9   Berger, p. 6.

10 This and other quotes from Virginia Sanchez are from an interview conducted on September 16, 1997, unless otherwise noted.

11 This and other quotes from Jean Belile are from an interview conducted on January 13, 1998, unless otherwise noted.

12 Frederick Hoxie, ed., *Encyclopedia of North American Indians*, Boston: Houghton Mifflin Company, 1996, p. 418.

13 Winona LaDuke, "Whitewashing Native Environmentalism: Reservation-based Organizations and the National Pie," *News from Indian Country*, Mid-Winter, 1993.

14 Interview with Nilak Butler.

15 This and other quotes from Judy De Silva are from an interview conducted on January 14, 1998, unless otherwise noted.

16 This and other quotes from Steve Frobisher are from an interview conducted on January 12, 1998, unless otherwise noted.

17 This and other quotes from Grace Thorpe are from interviews conducted in February 1994, unless otherwise noted.

18 Weaver, p. 52.

19 Interview with Grace Thorpe.

20 Interview with Margene Bullcreek, August 2, 1997.

21   Cherie Parker, "NSP's Skull Valley Duggery," *Twin Cities Reader*, January 6, 1997.

22   "Goshute Defend Money, Nuclear Waste Dump," *News from Indian Country*, November 1997, p. 6A.

23   Weaver, p. 52.

24   Monika Bauerlein, "Prairie Island Revisited," *Native Americas*, Summer 1995, p. 26, 28.

25   Interview with Faye Brown.

26   Prairie Island Coalition Fact Sheet, April 1994.

27   Bauerlein, p. 28–29.

28   Greg Gordon, "Nuclear Waste Site in Nevada OKed," *Minneapolis Star Tribune*, April 16, 1997.

29   Michael Marriote, Testimony to Senate Energy Committee, Nuclear Information and Resource Service, February 5, 1997, p. 11.

30   Simon Ortiz, *It Was That Indian, Woven Stone*, Tucson, AZ: University of Arizona Press, 1992, p. 295.

31   Interview with George Crocker, July 14, 1999.

Notes to Ch. 6: White Earth

1   The Wabanaki, Wampanoag, Abenaki, Potowatami, Menominee, Shawnee, and Odawa people are all descendants of those migrants and speak variations of Algonkin. Almost a third of the continent is named in these Algonkin-derived languages.

2   Robert Shimek, "Indians, White Pine and Wolves: Their Struggle for Survival in Minnesota," unpublished manuscript, p. 2.

3   According to William Folwell, "At the close of 1890, no fewer than 284 mining and quarrying companies had been incorporated under the laws of Minnesota." William Watts Folwell, *A History of Minnesota*, Saint Paul, MN: Minnesota Historical Society, 1930, p. 17.

4   Robert H. Keller, "An Economic History of Indian Treaties of the Great Lakes Region," *American Indian Journal*, 1976, p. 14.

5   Laura McLeod, "Timber Barons in Central Minnesota: 1880s to 1910s," unpublished paper, p. 7.

6   McLeod, p. 8.

7   McLeod, p. 2.

8   *Little Falls Daily Transcript*, May 11, 1893, in McLeod, p. 11.

9   McLeod, p. 9.

10   Buckhard's medal was the last medal of honor awarded in the so-called Indian Campaign, in which some 428 medals were awarded, more than for the Korean and Vietnam Wars combined. Shimek, p. 3.

11   Folwell, pp. 238–44. See also Melissa L. Meyer, *The White Earth Tragedy: Ethnicity and Dispossession at a Minnesota Anishinaabe Reservation, 1889–1920*, Lincoln, NE: University of Nebraska Press, 1994, and Winona LaDuke, *The White Earth Anishinaabeg: From Self-Reliance to Dependency and Back Again*, Antioch University Masters Thesis, 1988.

12   Folwell, pp. 263–64.

13   Meyer, pp. 168–70.

14   Interview with Windigoowub, Fred Weaver, August 10, 1981.

15   Interview with Robert Shimek, March 15, 1998.

16   Eduardo H. Galeano, *Open Veins of Latin America*, New York: Monthly Review Press, 1973, p. 13.

17   Interview with Bill Gagnon, June 1983.

18   Laura McLeod interview with Sunfish Oppegard, August 1997, in White Earth Land Recovery Project harvester study.

19   Folwell, p. 283.

20   LaDuke.

21   Meyer, p. 230.

22   Rudolph C. Rÿser, "Anti-Indian Movement on the Tribal Frontier," Occasional Paper #16-3 of the Center for World Indigenous Studies, Olympia, WA: August 1995, p. 10.

23   Rÿser, p. 15.

24   Rÿser, p. 29.

25   *Milwaukee Journal,* December 7, 1994, cited in Rÿser, p. 29.

26   Rÿser, p. 41.

27   Meyer, p. 230.

28   Meyer, pp. 229–30. See also LaDuke.

29   Meyer, p. 230.

30   See Keller.

31   White Earth Tribal Council, "Report on Service Population and Labor Force 1976-1986," White Earth Tribal Planning Department. See also U.S. Census, 1990.

32   White Earth Tribal Council, "Land Use Needs Assessment," Ponsford, MN: White Earth Land Recovery Project.

33   White Earth Reservation Biology Department, "Fisheries Reports: 1983–1990," Ponsford, MN.

34   Rick Whaley, *Walleye Warriors: An Effective Alliance Against Racism and for the Earth,* Philadelphia, PA: New Society Publishers, 1994, pp. 23, 27.

35   David Melmer, "Ojibwe Upheld: All Indian Country Eyeing Treaty Ruling," *Indian Country Today,* April 5-12, 1999, p. A1.

36   Randy Cruz, audiotape, June 1985.

37   See Suresh Ramabhai, *Towards a Total Revolution: A Documentary of Vinobaji's Toofan Yatra in Bihar,* Thanjavur, S. India: Sarvodaya Prachuralayam, 1968.

38   Laura McLeod interview with Gordy Goodman, August 1996, in White Earth Land Recovery Project harvester study.

39   White Earth Land Recovery Project, "Forestry Proposal," Ponsford, MN: 1994.

40   White Earth Land Recovery Project, "Forestry Proposal."

41   Menominee Tribal Enterprises, "The Menominee Forest Based Sustainable Development Tradition," Menominee Tribe, 1997, p. 2.

42   White Earth Land Recovery Project, "Land Use Needs Assessment."

43   White Earth Land Recovery Project, "Language and Culture Funding Proposal," Ponsford, MN: 1998.

44   Mark Dowie, *Losing Ground: American Environmentalism at the Close of the Twentieth Century,* Cambridge, MA: Massachusetts Institute of Technology Press, 1995, p. 148.

45   Bob Shimek commented to them, "Didn't seem like you guys used your say too much over the past 20 years of clearcutting on the refuge."

46   Dagmare Thorpe, *People of the Seventh Fire,* Ithaca, NY: Akwekon Press, 1996, p. 79.

47   Interview with Ronnie Chilton, March 15, 1998.

48   In 1973, Minnesota courts had decreed that these four annexed townships were off-limits for Indian harvesters without a

state-allocated permit. Since these townships are located within the 1867 treaty area, they are considered by Anishinaabeg to be our land.

49   Interview with Lennie Butcher, June 20, 1997.

Notes to Ch. 7: Buffalo Nations

1   This and other quotes from Birgil Kills Straight are from an interview conducted on November 20, 1997, unless otherwise noted.

2   Interview with Buzz Ironcloud, October 15, 1997.

3   Interview with Shilo Comeau, October 15, 1997.

4   National Wildlife Federation, "Bringing Buffalo Back," July 15, 1999.

5   Jim Robbins, "An Old Rite Is Invoked to Protect Park's Bison," *New York Times*, March 2, 1999.

6   National Park Service website, www.nps.gov/wica/bison.htm.

7   Intertribal Bison Cooperative, *Buffalo Tracks*, Winter/Spring 1997.

8   Valerius Geist, *Buffalo Nation: History and Legend of North American Bison*, Stillwater, MN: Voyageur, 1996, p. 91.

9   Tom McHugh, *Time of the Buffalo*, New York: Knopf, 1972, pp. 210, 249.

10   Richard Irving Dodge, in Jeremy Rifkin, *Beyond Beef: The Rise and Fall of the Cattle Culture*, New York: Plume, 1992, pp. 74–75.

11   Edward Everett Dale, *Cow Country*, Westport, CT: Greenwood Press, 1982.

12   General Accounting Office, American Indian Policy Review Commission, 1977, pp. 310–11.

13   General Accounting Office, p. 311.

14   Interview with Fred Dubray, October 29, 1997.

15   Richard Manning, *Grassland: The History, Biology, Politics, and Promise of the American Prairie*, New York: Penguin Books, 1995.

16   Rifkin, p. 202.

17   Manning, p. 69.

18   A comprehensive study found that only 15 percent of the range land was in good condition, and 85 percent of the grasslands have less than a 50 percent level of vegetation. Rifkin, p. 207.

19   Manning, p. 161.

20   Manning, p. 163.

21   Interview with Mario Gonzales, November 2, 1998.

22   Maria Yellow Horse Brave Heart-Jordan, *The Return of the Sacred Path: Healing Historical Trauma from Unresolved Grief among the Lakota*, Smith College dissertation, 1995.

23   Brave Heart-Jordan.

24   Utng Erickson, in Brave Heart-Jordan.

25   Geist, p. 119.

26   National Park Service, "Draft Environmental Impact Statement for the Interagency Bison Management Plan for State of Montana and Yellowstone National Park," U.S. Department of the Interior, July 1997, p. 148.

27   National Park Service, p. 19.

28   Robbins.

29   Quoted in Ernest Callenbach, *Bring Back the Buffalo,* Washington, DC: Island Press, 1996, p. 137.

30   According to the National Park Service, "The precise relationship between serological tests and presence of *B. abortus* bacteria in bison is not well understood at this time, but the available evidence indicates that roughly one-quarter of the seropositive bison in Yellowstone may actually harbor the bacteria." Further, only 39 percent of randomly tested buffalo were found to be seropositive. National Park Service, p. 113.

31   Robbins.

32   United Nations researcher and wildlife biologist Virginia Ravandal estimates that the bill footed by the American taxpayer is a 91 percent public subsidy on the value of the rangeland/grazing permits, minus the amount paid by these same ranchers.

33   Todd Wilkinson, "No Home on the Range," *High Country News,* February 17, 1997, p. 1.

34   Intertribal Bison Cooperative, *Buffalo Tracks,* Winter/Spring 1997.

35   These and other quotes from Rosalie Little Thunder and Evelyne Ironcloud are from an interview, unless otherwise noted.

36   Callenbach, p. 204.

37   "In five counties (Bennett, Corson, Jackson, Lyman, and Mellette), a thirty-year census population sample (1960-1990) shows a steady Lakota population gain and a continuous non-Lakota population loss such that the Lakota are now a significant population, constituting between 30 and 48 percent of the counties' 1990 population base. Indeed, at the twentieth century's end, four of the five counties (Bennett, Corson, Jackson, and Mellette) are projected to have a Lakota majority population, while in Lyman County, the Lakota population will remain a significant non-majority population." Edward Charles Valandra, *Titonwan Lakota Bison Reservation Initiative,* University of Colorado Masters Thesis, 1994, p. 34.

38   Edith R. Hornor, ed., *Almanac of the Fifty States,* Palo Alto, CA: Information Publications, 1998.

39   "Characteristics of American Indians by Tribe and Language," U.S. Census, July 1994.

40   Valandra.

41   Daniel Licht, *Ecology and Economics of the Great Plains*, Lincoln, NE: University of Nebraska Press, 1997.

42   Rick Springer, "An Idea Endures," *Fargo Forum,* January 31, 1999.

43   Interview with Marvin Kammerer, June 27, 1998.

44   This proposal is not currently active, however.

45   Reed Noss, "The Wildlands Project Land Conservation Strategy," *Wild Earth*, Special Issue, 1992, p. 11.

46   Noss, p. 15.

47   This and other quotes from Fred Dubray are from interviews conducted in October 1997.

48   Interview with Richard Sherman, June 24, 1998.

49   Interview with Alex and Debbie White Plume, June 24, 1998.

50   Interview with Ben Sherman, July 20, 1998.

51   Interview with Faith Spotted Eagle, June 30, 1998.

52   Statement by Chief Arvol Looking Horse, spiritual gathering, Rapid City, SD, April 4, 1997.

Notes to Ch. 8: Hawai'i

1   Michael Lloyd, "Paradise Lost: Pai Ohana's Struggle for Their Ancient Homeland," *Kuleana, Magazine of Noholike,* Spring 1997, p. 61.

2   This and other quotes from Mahealani Pai are from an interview conducted on January 13, unless otherwise noted.

3   Lloyd, p. 6.

4   Interview with Mahealani Pai.

5   Janice Otaguro, "Who Owns Your Land? Ask Mahealani Pai: He's the Islander of the Year," *Honolulu Magazine,* January 1996, p. 32.

6   Interview with Mahealani Pai.

7   Lloyd, pp. 5–8.

8   Dagmare Thorpe, ed. *People of the Seventh Fire,* Ithaca, NY: Akwekon Press, 1996. P. 197

9   Marion Kelly, "The Kona Story: 16th- and 17th-Century Hawaiian Enhancement of the Environment," in Ulla Hasager and Jonathan Friedman, eds., *Hawai'i Return to Nationhood,* Copenhagen, Denmark: International Working Group on Indigenous Affairs, 1994, p. 141.

10   Haunani-Kay Trask, "Native Hawaiian Nationalism in Hawai'i," in *Hawai'i Return to Nationhood,* p. 16.

11   David E. Stannard, *American Holocaust: The Conquest of the New World,* Oxford: Oxford University Press, 1992, p. 268.

12   Lilikalá Kame'eleihiwa, "The Role of American Missionaries in the 1893 Overthrow of the Hawaiian Government: Historical Events, 1820–1893," in *Hawai'i Return to Nationhood,* pp. 114–115.

13   Kame'eleihiwa, pp. 114–115.

14   Lilikalá Kame'eleihiwa, "The Concepts of Sovereignty and Religious Sanction in Correct Political Behavior," in *Hawai'i Return to Nationhood,* p. 40

15   Mililani Trask, "Hawai'i and the U.N," in *Ka Lahui Hawai'i-Ho'okupua,* Hilo, HI: Masterplan, 1995, pp. 14–15.

16   Mililani Trask, pp. 14–15.

17   Mindy Pennybacker, "Should the Aloha State Say Goodbye, Natives Wonder," *The Nation,* August 12, 1996, pp. 21-25.

18   Ka Lahui, *Breaches of the Hawaiian Homelands Trust,* Hilo, HI: 1992.

19   Winona LaDuke, "Occupied Hawai'i," *Open Road,* Winter 1984, pp. 8–9.

20   Haunani-Kay Trask, p. 74.

21   John Kelly, "Tourism in Hawai'i," in *Hawai'i Return to Nationhood,* p. 181.

22   LaDuke. See also Christopher Merrill, "A Little Justice in Hawai'i: Kaho'o'lawe Lives," *The Nation,* September 5, 1994.

23   LaDuke.

24   Lilikalá Kame'eleihiwa, "The Hawaiian Sovereignty Movement," *Dark Night Field Notes*, Winter-Spring 95, p. 27.

25   Pennybacker, pp. 21–24.

26   Jim Albertini, Nelson Foster, Wally Inlis, and Gil Roeder, "The Dark Side of Paradise: Hawai'i in a Nuclear World," Honolulu, HI: Catholic Action of Hawai'i/Peace Education Project, September 1980, p. 1.

27   Albertini et al., p. 3.

28   Noa Emmet Aluli and Darianna Pomaika'i McGregor, "The Healing of Kaho'olawe," in *Hawai'i Return to Nationhood*, p. 200.

29   John Edwards, "Washington's Pacific Thrust," *Far Eastern Economic Review*, June 13, 1980, p. 40, cited in Albertini et al., p. 18.

30   Kathy Ferguson, Phyllis Turnbull, and Mehmed Ali, "Rethinking the Military in Hawai'i," in *Hawai'i Return to Nationhood*, pp. 183–196.

31   Ferguson, et al., p. 187.

32   Albertini et al., p. 188.

33   Interview with Mililani Trask.

34   Merrill, pp. 23–25.

35   Aluli and McGregor, pp. 200–203.

36   Aluli and McGregor, p. 203.

37   Merrill, pp. 23–25.

38   Aluli and McGregor, p. 207.

39   Interview with Shelly Mark, 1984.

40   Kelly, in *Hawai'i Return to Nationhood*, p. 181.

41   David Nicholson-Lord, "The Politics of Travel," *The Nation*, October 6, 1997.

42   Deborah McLaren, "Indigenous Peoples and Global Tourism Development," Washington, DC. Unpublished manuscript, March 1996, p. 3.

43   Interview with Haunani-Kay Trask, February 10, 1984.

44   Interview with Haunani-Kay Trask.

45   McLaren, p. 4.

46   Elizabeth Royte, "On the Brink: Hawai'i's Vanishing Species," *National Geographic*, September 1995, p. 14.

47   LaDuke.

48   Interview with Mililani Trask.

49   Lilikalá Kame'eleihiwa, "The Hawaiian Sovereignty Movement," p. 27.

50   Noholike Kuleana, "Special Report," Spring 1997.

51   Kuleana, "Special Report."

52   Thorpe, p. 198.

53   Pennybacker, pp. 21–24.

54   Interview with Mililani Trask, September 1995.

55   Pennybacker, pp. 21–24.

56   Ka Lahui, p. 11.

57   Mililani Trask, "The Mothers of the Nations," keynote speech,
      Indigenous Women's Network conference, White Earth, MN,
      September 14, 1995. Published in *Indigenous Woman*, 2 (2), Winter
      1995.

Notes to Ch. 9: NativeSUN

1   Winona LaDuke, "Strapping on a Tool Belt and a Hardhat," *Winds of Change*, Spring 1995, p. 21.

2   Hopi Foundation Annual Report, 1995 and 1997.

3   This and other quotes from Debby Tewa are from an interview conducted on April 19, 1998, unless otherwise noted.

4   Peggy Berryhill, "Hopi Potskwaniat: Hopi Pathway to the Future," *Native Americas*, Spring 1998, p. 36.

5   Berryhill, p. 32.

6   Berryhill, p. 34.

7   See Lester R. Brown, Christopher Flavin, and Hilary French, *State of the World 1997: A Worldwatch Institute Report on Progress Toward a Sustainable Society*, New York: W.W. Norton and Co., 1997.

8   Brown et al., p. 12.

9   Brown et al., p. 10.

10   Richard Douthwaite, *Short Circuit: Strengthening Local Economies for Security in an Unstable World*, Dublin, Ireland: Lilliput Press, 1996, p. 181.

11   Marjane Ambler, in David Howarth, John Busch, and Tom Starrs, *American Indian Tribes and Electric Industry Restructuring: Issues and Opportunities*, Berkeley, CA: University of California, 1997, p. 3.

12   Howarth et al., p. 4.

13   John Busch, John Elliott, Trisha Frank, Vivian Gratton, Tom Starrs, and Jim Williams, *Native Power: A Handbook on Renewable Energy and Energy Efficiency for Native American Communities*, Berkeley, CA: University of California, January 1998.

14   Deborah Dubrule, "A Chilling Tale: Natives Offer Insights on Global Warming," *American Indian Report*, November 1998, p. 23.

15   Douthwaite, p. 179.

16   Ernest Callenbach, *Bring Back the Buffalo*, Washington, DC: Island Press, 1996, p. 227.

17   Correspondence with Harvey Wasserman, January 8, 1999.

18   American Wind Energy Association, "Clean Energy for Our Environment and Economy," Washington, DC, undated.

19   Correspondence with Harvey Wasserman.

20   Harvey Wasserman, "Inherit the Wind: Will Clean Energy Pass Us By?" *The Nation*, June 16, 1997, p. 11.

21   Interview with Harvey Wasserman, February 6, 1999.

Notes to Ch. 10: The Seventh Generation

1   Lester R. Brown, Christopher Flavin, and Hilary French, *State of the World 1997: A Worldwatch Institute Report on Progress Toward a Sustainable Society*, New York: W.W. Norton and Co., 1997, p. 13.

2   Interview with Bob Gough, November 15, 1999.

3   Ted Strong, Panel Presentation, Lewis and Clark University, October 23, 1998.

4   Eddie Benton Benai, "Seven Fires," cited in Terrance Nelson, ed., *Okiijida: The Warrior Society*, Okiijida, Letellier, Manitoba, Canada: ROGCO, 1998, p. 4.

5   Richard Grossman and Frank Adams, in Jerry Mander and Edward Goldsmith, eds., *The Case Against the Global Economy, and For a Turn Toward the Local*, San Francisco: Sierra Club Books, 1996, p. 376.

6   Grossman and Adams, p. 384.

7   Corrine Kumar, United Nations Conference on the Status of Women, Beijing, China, September 7, 1995.

8   Walt Bresette et al., "Seventh Generation Amendment," Anishinaabe Niijii flyer, Bayfield, WI, March 1996.

9   Interview with Walt Bresette, July 9, 1997.

10 "Indigenous Environmental Statement of Principles," Albuquerque, NM, Native Law Institute, 1995, p. 28.

Index

About the Author

Winona LaDuke became involved with Native American environmental issues after meeting Jimmy Durham, a well-known Cherokee activist, while she was attending Harvard University. At the age of 18, she spoke in front of the United Nations regarding Native American rights and has remained one of the most prominent voices for American Indian economic and environmental concerns. She is an Anishinaabekwe (Ojibwe) enrolled member of the Mississippi Band Anishinaabeg, who lives and works on the White Earth Reservations. LaDuke is the Executive Director of the White Earth Land Recovery Project and Honor the Earth, where she works on a national level to advocate, raise public support, and create funding for frontline native environmental groups. In 1994, Winona was named by *TIME* magazine as one of America's fifty most promising leaders under forty years of age. In both 1996 and 2000 she was Ralph Nader's running mate in his Presidential campaigns, appearing on the Green Party ticket. A graduate of Harvard and Antioch Universities, LaDuke has written extensively on Native American and environmental issues. She is a former board member of Greenpeace USA and serves as co-chair of the Indigenous Women's Network, a North American and Pacific indigenous women's organization. She is the author of six books, including *The Militarization of Indian Country* (2011); *Recovering the Sacred: the Power of Naming and Claiming* (2005), and a novel, *Last Standing Woman* (1997, Voyager Press).

About Honor the Earth

The environmental issues discussed in this book represent struggles at the heart of Native America. Developing support for these and other Native environmental issues is the mission of Honor the Earth, a continental foundation and advocacy organization founded by the author, Winona LaDuke, who serves as the organization's Program Director.

Honor the Earth provides both funding and public support to grassroots Native environmental initiatives. Sponsored by three national Native groups—the Indigenous Environmental Network, Indigenous Women's Network and the Seventh Generation Fund—Honor the Earth represents a unified effort in Native America to increase financial and political resources available to communities on the front lines of environmental protection.

Since its founding in 1993, Honor the Earth has raised and distributed half a million dollars to 85 Native groups. At the same time, the organization has significantly increased visibility for Native environmental issues and developed a broad base of support through strategic organizing campaigns, high-impact media work and music events.

Honor the Earth's Programs center around Environmental Justice (the defense of homelands) and Indigenous Knowledge (pro-active initiatives aimed at cultural and ecological restoration). Honor the Earth has also developed two Strategic Initiatives: the Nuclear Waste and Native Lands Initiative, which focuses on the historic injustice of energy policy while promoting a safe energy future and the Indigenous Buffalo Commons Initiative, which works to protect and restore buffalo on the Great Plains. These Initiatives represent focused efforts to raise consciousness, create dialogue and impact public policy long-term around these issues.

Please join us in creating a sustainable future for the coming generations.

Honor the Earth
A Project of the Tides Center
PO Box 75423
St. Paul, MN 55175
1-800-EARTH-07

About Haymarket Books

Haymarket Books is a nonprofit, progressive book distributor and publisher, a project of the Center for Economic Research and Social Change. We believe that activists need to take ideas, history, and politics into the many struggles for social justice today. Learning the lessons of past victories, as well as defeats, can arm a new generation of fighters for a better world. As Karl Marx said, "The philosophers have merely interpreted the world; the point, however, is to change it."

We take inspiration and courage from our namesakes, the Haymarket Martyrs, who gave their lives fighting for a better world. Their 1886 struggle for the eight-hour day reminds workers around the world that ordinary people can organize and struggle for their own liberation.

For more information and to shop our complete catalog of titles, visit us online at www.haymarketbooks.org.

Also Available from Haymarket Books

Brazil's Dance with the Devil: The World Cup, the Olympics, and the Struggle for Democracy
Updated Olympics Edition; Dave Zirin

Ecology and Socialism: Solutions to Capitalist Ecological Crisis
Chris Williams

Ecosocialism: A Radical Alternative to Capitalist Catastrophe
Michael Löwy

Floodlines: Community and Resistance from Katrina to the Jena Six
Jordan Flaherty, preface by Tracie Washington, foreword by Amy Goodman

Kivalina: A Climate Change Story
Christine Shearer

Marx and Nature: A Red and Green Perspective
Paul Burkett, foreword by John Bellamy Foster

Myths of Male Dominance: Collected Articles on Women Cross-Culturally
Eleanor Burke Leacock

Recovering the Sacred: The Power of Naming and Claiming
Winona LaDuke

Too Many People?: Population, Immigration, and the Environmental Crisis
Ian Angus and Simon Butler, forewords by Betsy Hartmann and Joel Kovel

CPSIA information can be obtained
at www.ICGtesting.com
Printed in the USA
LVHW051053311020
670209LV00004B/4